ASPERGER'S CHILDREN

ASPERGER'S CHILDREN
Psychodynamics, Aetiology, Diagnosis, and Treatment

Robin Holloway

KARNAC

First published in 2016 by
Karnac Books Ltd
118 Finchley Road
London NW3 5HT

British Library Cataloguing in Publication Data

A C.I.P. for this book is available from the British Library

ISBN-13: 978-1-78220-359-9

Typeset by V Publishing Solutions Pvt Ltd., Chennai, India

Printed in Great Britain

www.karnacbooks.com

This book is dedicated to three groups who made their own sacrifices in order to allow it to grow. These groups include my Asperger's patients who tolerated my fumbling attempts to understand them, all my helpful colleagues who tolerated my fumbling attempts to explain my ideas, and my family; my very social twin boys who tolerated my absences from their beer-drinking celebrations and my beautiful and long-suffering wife Lynda who tolerated my absences from her side.

CONTENTS

PART III: THE DIAGNOSIS OF ASPERGER'S CHILDREN

PART IV: TREATMENT APPROACHES TO
ASPERGER'S CHILDREN

ACKNOWLEDGEMENTS

I confess to a sense of being split within myself in my attitude and my feelings toward this book. One part of me has the experience of a protracted and very personal struggle around understanding Asperger's children. This struggle was accompanied by the expenditure of much emotional and intellectual sweat, seasoned with the leaven of anguish, along with the sacrifice of time I could have spent with family. This effort in turn leads to a sense of possessiveness of this work and of personal ownership of many of the ideas herein. Part of this sense of personal possessiveness also derives from many hours spent with Asperger's children, striving to understand what they were communicating, and trying to construct bridges and ways of being helpful to them. This book is the distillation of many deeply personal therapeutic relationships with these children.

However, there is another and stronger part of me that experiences the writing of this book as the work of a huge committee including many people, with my contribution being only a part of the whole enterprise. Indeed, without the contributions of many others, this book could certainly never have been written. I imagine a huge table stretching off into the haze around which is seated a large committee. My imaginary committee is comprised of both the living and the dead, all working in concert to push knowledge a fraction further ahead. Most of the members of this large committee have names. Some can never be given names, including all the patients who have struggled along with me and who have increased my knowledge as we struggled together, "co-constructing" this knowledge, as the current idiom would put it.

Even though some of the nametags of those seated at this table are too distant to be read, and some committee members have no name-tags at all, I can make out quite a few of them. I now read a few of the nametags I can see in front of the committee members, and I try to say something about the deeply appreciated contributions some of them have made to the co-construction of this book. Though no longer with us in the flesh, Melanie Klein, Wilfred Bion, Donald Meltzer, and Frances Tustin have strong presences at my imagined table. So does my first teacher of child psychoanalysis, Otto Weininger. Over there speaking together I can see Thomas Ogden and James Grotstein. The more people I see at the table, the more my indebtedness grows. I am very grateful to Judith Mitrani and Anne Alvarez for their encouragement. And there's Paulina Kernberg, who many years ago gave the fledgling supervisors of what was then called the Toronto Child Psychoanalytic Program their first instruction in the art of supervision.

There have been so many conferences, meetings and organisations whose representatives I see around the table. I laboured for twenty years in the Child and Family Services Department of Credit Valley Hospital. Louis Peltz, Marino Battigelli, Cindy Cyr, and especially Marta Bruchkowsky challenged my thinking and pushed me to con-sider new ideas. In 2008, I had the privilege of giving a case presenta-tion on Dan (whom you will meet in Chapter Six) to the International Psychoanalytical Association Third International Inter-Regional Con-ference on Clinical Infant, Child, and Adolescent Psychoanalysis in Our Changing World. I had the wonderful opportunity to discuss my patient Dan with many of my international colleagues. My own ana-lyst, Ian Graham, attended and made a number of helpful comments. I am especially grateful to Nilde Jacob Parada Franch who responded to my presentation of Dan. I want to explicitly acknowledge her con-tribution in discussing my paper, which was the concept of "projec-tive identification into distant objects". I found this concept extremely useful, though I have slightly re-named it here—calling it "projective identification into remote objects", because I felt this was a slightly bet-ter fit with Asperger's, but also likely in response to that aspect of my split self which asserts personal possessiveness of what is in this book, and in an attempt to "own" this concept. In both informal and more formal conversations, a number of participants in this conference commented supportively and helpfully on my presentation. Their contributions are woven into the present paper either implicitly or with specific acknowledgment. Two of my colleagues from CAPCT (the Canadian Association of Psychoanalytic Child Therapists) helped me whip my presentation on Dan into presentable shape, and the echoes of their helpful suggestions still reverberate in Chapter Six dealing with Dan. They are Biddie Tuters and Sally Doulis. I am also grateful to Biddie Tuters for her encouragement (and her nudging) in my presenting a paper on autism to the Toronto Psychoanalytic Society, some aspects of which have found their way here.

Another profoundly helpful experience was to attend in 2014 the seventh International Conference on the Work of Frances Tustin, entitled "Spilling, falling, dissolving: Engaging anxieties of the emerging self". This conference was the impetus behind much of Chapter Ten in this book—"The anxieties and defences of asperger's children." The presentations at this conference and the opportunity to speak with many international colleagues were exceedingly helpful and motivating. Many of the participants in this conference are seated around my imaginary table. I will not try to read all their nametags. I point to only a few, including Didier Houzel, Judith Mitrani, Lawrence Brown, (who presented a wonderful paper dealing with an Asperger's child) and Ann Smolen (who presented another wonderful paper on Asperger's). There were many others.

A number of my colleagues from CAPCT (the Canadian Association of Psychoanalytic Child Therapists) who are also teachers and supervisors in our training institute CICAPP (Canadian Institute for Child and Adolescent Psychoanalytic Psychotherapy) donated their time and energy to reviewing and commenting on drafts of many parts of this book. In particular I thank Dannette Graham and Robyn Weddepohl. I have also collaborated with Robyn in trying to find the best possible structure for treating Asperger's adolescents. The results of this ongoing and mutually supportive collaboration appear in Chapter Sixteen—"Treatment of asperger's children—The Toronto experiment".

Prominently seated around the table are my colleagues at our treatment centre in Toronto called The Willow Centre. My colleagues allowed me to present much of this book at our weekly clinical rounds over a number of weeks. They were strongly supportive of the present work, and provided numerous detailed and helpful suggestions. My deepest thanks go to these colleagues, including Rex Collins and Carol-Jane Parker. Also members of the large committee which made this book possible are my numerous Asperger's patients who have over the years been able to tolerate my fumbling attempts to understand them and to be helpful to them.

I cannot forget the person seated just to my right at the table. She is my dear wife Lynda Holloway. Lynda has tolerated much, put up with much, and during the writing of this book has sometimes seen me all too little as I retreated to my "hidey hole" in the basement.

There are numerous other members of the committee whom I have not mentioned specifically. I am grateful for the opportunity to have been part of this huge committee and to have benefitted so much from the support, understanding, and thoughtfulness of so many committee members. The part of me that asserts personal possessiveness of this book begins to blush, hang its head, and fade away. The keyboarding was indeed all mine. The writing was truly the product of a large committee. I thank every one of you seated around my imaginary table. You have certainly all enriched my life. I hope that in this "co-constructed" effort, we will together contribute something to the enrichment of the lives of those with Asperger's.

Finally, I would like to express my gratitude to the staff of Karnac who have been so supportive of me during the process of publication, and in particular express my gratitude to Publishing Assistant Cecily Blench who has always been very patient and very responsive.

ABOUT THE AUTHOR

Dr. Robin Holloway provides psychoanalytic psychotherapy to children and adolescents. He is a graduate of CICAPP (the Canadian Institute for Child and Adolescent Psychoanalytic Psychotherapy) where he is a supervisor and a teacher. He worked in a public hospital and participated in weekly diagnostic intake meetings for children with autism spectrum disorders. He is now in private practice at the Willow Centre in Toronto, where he has continued to treat high-functioning autistic children and those with Asperger's Disorder. Previous publications include an article dealing with high-functioning autism.

CHAPTER ONE

Introduction

I now provide an outline of the contents of this book, how it has been organised, and sketch in some of the main conclusions I have formed. The aim is to give the reader a "pre-conception" or a road map of where things are going, to make reading and digestion of the content a bit easier.

There are four main parts which comprise this book, these four parts being: Part I: The psychodynamics of Asperger's children; Part II: Theorising about the aetiology of Asperger's; Part III: The diagnosis of Asperger's children, and Part IV: Treatment approaches to Asperger's children.

Part I: The psychodynamics of Asperger's children is the "clinical heart" of this book. This part contains ten chapters. Chapters Two through to Eight all begin with the heading "Some clinical dialogues with Asperger's patients". These seven chapters recount clinical dialogues with eight different Asperger's patients whom I had the privilege to treat over the years. These patients are arranged in order of increasing age, beginning with Peter and Joe (Chapter Two) who were both nine years old when I saw them, and concluding with Anthony (Chapter Eight) who was thirty-one years old. By accident, they also repeat the approximate order in which I met these children. Each chapter contains one or more selected fragments of clinical dialogue which I had with each of my patients. They were recorded shortly after the sessions in which they occurred, and are accurate in their gist even if not accurate word for word. The selection of these dialogues was made in order to illustrate the conclusions I describe in Chapter Nine ("The psychodynamics of Asperger's children"). What I conclude is that Asperger's children regularly (and likely invariably) employ two main defensive operations: splitting of the self into victim and bully aspects, and projective identification into remote objects. These two processes are described in detail in Chapter Nine, and are hopefully persuasively illustrated in the clinical dialogues reported in Chapters Two through Eight. In Chapter Nine, I also discuss the possible role trauma may play in the production of Asperger's disorder in children.

The longest of the "clinical dialogues" occurs in Chapter Three, which relates parts of conversations I had with twelve-year-old Matt. This is the longest of the "clinical dialogues" chapters, and has a slightly different structure from all the others. All the other "clinical dialogues" are derived from single sessions. The clinical dialogue with Matt in Chapter Three is presented as a single dialogue, but is a compendium of selected dialogues from a number of sessions which occurred over a period of months. Matt was an extremely articulate preadolescent who was able to describe in intricate detail the ongoing and shifting relationships between the two aspects of his split self, which he referred to as the "antelope" aspect (referring to the victim part of the split) and the "tiger" aspect (which was the bully part of the split). My hope is that assembling these various selections into one continuous dialogue will give the reader a more complete and accurate conception of how the parts of the split in Matt's self interacted with each other.

Chapter Ten, entitled "The anxieties and defences of Asperger's children," is designed to be a continuation of and further elaboration on the content of Chapter Nine. As to the anxieties experienced by Asperger's children, I suggest there are two main kinds, which I refer to as "existential anxieties" and "relational anxieties". The former kind of anxieties, the "existential anxieties", involve what I call "separateness anxiety", meaning the perception of being separated from another experienced as part of the self, and thus as amounting to a rupture of adhesive identification. The "relational anxieties" involve separation anxiety, understood in the traditional psychoanalytic fashion.

The defences of Asperger's children are described as operating on three levels. The first level involves the "cornerstone defences" of Asperger's children as outlined in Chapter Nine, that is, splitting of the self into bully and victim aspects, and projective identification into remote objects. The second level involves a series of defences which are typical for Asperger's children, but are not "mandatory" in the way the cornerstone defences seem to be. The third level consists of defences typically understood as employed by autistic children. These are the "autosensuous defences" which include the use of autistic objects and autistic shapes.

The final chapter of Part I is Chapter Eleven, entitled "Defences in Asperger's children continued—Should we call it splitting or dissociation?" This chapter is conceived of as a direct continuation of Chapter Ten with specific reference to the defences used by Asperger's children. The issue is to distinguish splitting from dissociation. The problem is that splitting is a kind of dissociation and dissociation is a kind of splitting, creating a potential difficulty in adequately distinguishing between the two. At a fundamental level, both splitting and dissociation involve separating two aspects which actually belong together, and keeping these two aspects in a continuing state of separation. Without entering too deeply into theoretical issues around distinguishing these two types of defences, I try to examine how splitting/dissociative defences are used by Asperger's children in order to suggest whether splitting or dissociation is the most likely process being used in cases of Asperger's.

Turning to Part II: Theorising about the aetiology of Asperger's— this part includes two chapters. These are Chapter Twelve: Towards an understanding of the aetiology of Asperger's disorder, and Chapter Thirteen: The sensory vulnerability of Asperger's children. As the title of this part suggests, it is the most theoretical part of the four parts. The attempt is to reconstruct what might happen in the mother–infant dyad when the infant is born with the potential for Asperger's. I suggest that in general, the mother of the Asperger's infant attempts strenuously to make an emotional connection with him and to understand him. At times she is able to do so. I suggest this results in the infantile perception of "the connected mother", which is accompanied by a sense of "the protected self". At other times, she cannot do so. Then the result is an infantile perception of "the disconnected mother", in tandem with a sense of "the overwhelmed and vulnerable self". In Winnicott's language, there is variability in the adequacy of maternal holding. In Bion's language, there is variability in the mother's reverie and alpha-function, and thus variability in the adequacy of the infant's experience of containment.

Chapter Thirteen examines the issue of sensory vulnerability in the infant, and how this kind of vulnerability might contribute to difficulties in the mother–infant dyad.

Part III: The diagnosis of Asperger's children includes one chapter, Chapter Fourteen: The differential diagnosis of Asperger's children. I explain my differentiation of three types of Asperger's a bit more fully just below, because these types are mentioned in the earlier chapters involving "clinical dialogues" with Asperger's children (chapters Two–Eight). It will thus be helpful to the reader to have some preview of what I am referring to.

Chapter Fourteen approaches the diagnosis of Asperger's from the outside, based on external descriptive features, and from the inside, based on internal psychodynamic processes. I review strong criticisms of the diagnosis of Asperger's disorder as it was set out in DSM-IV, concluding that this diagnosis was doomed because it was utterly inadequate from the start. I also criticise the inadequate, unhelpful, and totally lame manner in which the diagnosis of "autism spectrum disorder" (ASD) is handled in the DSM-5, where every aspect of autism is lumped together into one undifferentiated gelatinous glob, Asperger's is ignored, and the clinician who actually treats these children is not helped at all. However, there is also a constructive aspect as well as a critical one. I suggest in detail how the diagnosis of Asperger's (from the outside and based on external descriptive features) could have been salvaged instead of being jettisoned because the DSM-IV attempt at diagnosis was so completely inadequate.

I then consider diagnosis from the *inside* as based on internal psychodynamic processes. This is what *should* have happened in the *Psychodynamic Diagnostic Manual* (2006), but for unfathomable reasons did not. Instead, there was in the PDM an ignominious regression into purely biological psychiatry, which ignored years of psychoanalytic investigation. The reasons for such a demoralising and humiliating capitulation on the part of a manual which is typically extremely helpful is utterly incomprehensible. One can only hope that the next iteration, the PDM-2, will rectify this embarrassing lapse.

I attempt some degree of rectification (in a manner that will hopefully benefit clinicians who actually *treat* children who are "on the spectrum") by outlining three types of Asperger's that may require different treatment approaches, and then trying to suggest in a preliminary way how the three types may be handled differently in treatment.

The three types of Asperger's children that I have so far been able to discern are: the inhibited/avoidant type who are object-shunning, the inhibited but object-seeking and needy type, and the uninhibited and aggressive type who are object-rejecting. In this context, "object" refers to external objects and not to internal objects. Note that these categories are rough and broad in nature, and will not capture the details of many individuals with Asperger's. They are meant only to provide some kind of initial orientation that is helpful to the clinician. This categorisation is based mainly on *which aspect of the split self tends to predominate in the child*. For the inhibited/avoidant type who are object-shunning, it is the victim aspect of the split self that predominates. The focal anxiety tends to be what I call "existential" in nature, that is, the child questions whether they even exist for others in any significant way. For the inhibited but object-seeking and needy type, there is an oscillation which is sometimes very rapid between victim and bully aspects of the split self. Anxieties also tend to involve both existential and relational kinds, so that their questions tend to involve *both* whether they really exist for others, and if they do, whether others can value them. Finally, for the uninhibited and aggressive type who are object-rejecting, it is the bully aspect of the split self which usually predominates. Their focal anxieties tend to be relational, but with a strong paranoid-schizoid colouration, so that they wonder why others are out to hurt, denigrate or belittle them. Details of the three types are outlined in Chapter Fourteen. This initial orientation should help the reader understand the references to the three types in some of the earlier chapters.

Finally, Part IV: Treatment approaches to Asperger's children, embraces two chapters, Chapter Fifteen: Thoughts about the treatment of Asperger's children, and Chapter Sixteen: Treatment of Asperger's children—The Toronto experiment. Chapter Fifteen begins with a review of some of the treatment suggestions in the non-psychoanalytic literature. I then outline two psychoanalytic views. One view outlines the range of psychotherapy and the different types of psychotherapy available to the clinician. This derives from the work of Paulina Kernberg and her colleagues. The other is Anne Alvarez's (2012) description of three levels of psychotherapeutic intervention. I try to suggest how the work of Kernberg can be integrated with that of Alvarez by suggesting how Anne's levels of psychotherapeutic intervention can be mapped onto Paulina's types of psychotherapy. I then attempt to apply this to the treatment of Asperger's children, using my treatment experiences with three Asperger's children to suggest what might be the most useful kind of treatment approach to these children.

Chapter Sixteen: Treatment of Asperger's children—The Toronto experiment is a continuation of Chapter Fifteen, focussing on a specific case, the case of a young adolescent I call Jack and his family. In Chapter Sixteen, I outline how I have attempted to realise in practice the ideal treatment approach outlined in Chapter Fourteen. This involves a collaborative effort involving three psychoanalytically trained therapists. I try to describe the benefits that seem to derive from this approach, and I also try to employ candour and self-revelation (not without risking a degree of embarrassment) in outlining difficulties ("bumps in the road") that this experiment has involved.

This present chapter is intended to be no more than an initial road map and orientation to the rest of the book. It will hopefully provide the reader with an idea of the whole forest we are about to enter. If it does so, it may then make focussing on some of the individual trees easier and more informative. We are shortly to meet Peter and Joe (Chapter Two) and begin the "clinical dialogues" of chapters Two to Eight. I can only hope this road map is useful, and that your trip through the forest proves to be worthwhile.

PART I

THE PSYCHODYNAMICS OF ASPERGER'S CHILDREN

Some clinical dialogues with Asperger's patients—Peter and Joe, age nine

Ve begin our reflections on Asperger's disorder by considering some dialogues between a number of Asperger's patients, ranging in age from nine to thirty-one years, and myself as their therapist. All of these patients are males, reflecting the predominance of males with Asperger's. I present my patients in order of age from youngest to oldest. We begin with Peter and Joe in this chapter, both of whom were nine years of age when I saw them. I saw Matt (Chapter Three) for a number of years, but the dialogue I present is primarily from when he was twelve years of age. Thomas (Chapter Four) was also twelve years of age when I saw him briefly. The remaining four patients whose dialogues I present were also seen over a number of years. Thanos (Chapter Five) was fourteen years of age at the time of the dialogue I will present, and is still in treatment. Dan (Chapter Six) was seventeen years old, Alan (Chapter Seven) was nineteen years old (and still in treatment), and Anthony (Chapter Eight) was thirty-one years of age.

I attempt to tell you enough about each patient so that you can develop an initial sense of the person before you hear our dialogues. These dialogues were transcribed immediately after the session with the patient and are likely to vary only in minor details from what actually passed between us (As Bion points out, however, even a transcript or a videotape tells only a small part of the story, leaving out the emotional ferment, thoughts and fantasies, conscious as well as unconscious, that pass through the minds of both participants). The clinical dialogues I have chosen are hardly random selections of material. I chose only specific fragments of the dialogues we had together. I chose these particular fragments of interactions in the hope of illustrating a specific underlying theme. The main theme I wanted to illustrate was the main defences being used by these children.

The diagnosis of Asperger's disorder applied to these patients was as certain as it could be. Each person was diagnosed by *at least two* mental health professionals, minimally one of these being a psychiatrist and the other myself. Some were diagnosed in a public hospital outpatient mental health setting by a team of three or four professionals, one of whom was myself. The other patients were referred to my private practice having already received a diagnosis of Asperger's disorder from a psychiatrist. After independently assessing each child, I concurred with the psychiatric diagnosis.

The first two patients were both nine years of age when I met with them, both for a relatively brief period of time. At a time when the diagnosis of Asperger's was only starting to become known in North America (in the later 1980s), Peter was the first patient who prompted me to think about Asperger's as involving numerous dichotomies in how these children experience the world and themselves, and splits in the self. Both Peter and Joe must be into their thirties by now. Peter's therapy was halted because his parents had to move away when his father's job forced him to relocate. It was extremely frustrating both for Peter and for me to have his therapy interrupted.

Peter

When I first met him, Peter's parents were concerned about his social interactions at school. When he was with his friends at home, his mother told me that his friends "love his imagination." She added: "He shares his toys. His friends really like to play with him. And verbally he is very strong; his reading is also very strong."

But, she continued, at school Peter can have temper tantrums. His teacher describes him as being "belligerent". There were also what his parents called "obsessional behaviours", which included lining up his pencils and lining up toy cars. He was also "obsessed" with a computer game called "Civilization", which he will play for hours on end. Peter tells me: "I've been bad at school. I've not been good." He makes nonstop noises in the classroom, screaming, roaring like a lion, rambling on in nonsense sentences and according to the teacher, "buzzing around the room". As a result, he attracts bullies. His mother told me: "We are concerned about his social interactions. He seems to be a magnet for bullies. He finds it hard to get along in a group situation".

I felt very sympathetic towards Peter. This is not an unusual feeling for me to have with most Asperger's children. Peter especially pulled for my feelings of sadness and sympathy when he talked to me about his lack of friends. What follows are small parts of my first two sessions of psychoanalytic play psychotherapy with Peter. In session one, he talked to me in a pseudo-adult manner about his interest in the computer game "Civilization".

PETER: You know, you can never trust anyone in that game.
ROBIN: No?
PETER: Even if you find an ally, then, uh, the ally is going to betray you. Or else you're going to betray your ally to get stuff for yourself.
ROBIN: So when you play it …
PETER: When I played it last time, there was a mayor of one town who was fleeing in terror.
ROBIN: It reminds me a bit of what you said about feeling "terrorised" by bullies at school.
PETER: Yeah. Right. But sometimes I terrorise other kids.
ROBIN: (Extremely surprised at this and thinking I misheard him; remembering how sad I felt when he told me about being bullied). Sometimes … *you* …
PETER: Sometimes I terrorise other kids.

Session two occurred shortly before Valentine's Day. Peter asked me to help him make what he called a "love box" for his mother, which I did. This "love box" turned out to be a small but elaborately decorated cardboard box with hearts drawn on the outside and a heart drawn on the inside as well. We pick up the conversation as he is working on his "love box".

ROBIN: So your mother spoke to you about your anger at school?
PETER: Yeah. She spoke to me firmly.
ROBIN: Firmly, eh? So this made you feel … how?
PETER: Angry.
ROBIN: And what happened to your anger at your mother?
PETER: (Drawing a heart on his love box) Will you help me with this? (I wondered if he was referring to his anger as well as to the love box). Uh, they go inside the love box, the angry feelings. But I keep them there. No angry feelings can come out of the love box, only feelings of love.
ROBIN: So the angry feelings … what happens to them?
PETER: There's only love inside and only love comes through the outside.
ROBIN: Maybe you could also feel that there should be *only love* between people, including with your mum, the kids at school and between you and me?
PETER: Uh, maybe, until …
ROBIN: Until?
PETER: (Avoiding my question) Will you help me draw another heart?

Joe

The next dialogues are between Joe, nine years of age, and me. His parents brought Joe to me because of their worries about his social problems at school. They told me that in spite of testing which indicated Joe was intellectually gifted in his verbal skills, he does not understand how to play with other children his age. As a result, he avoids social contact with his peers. Other potential indications of Asperger's included a flat tone of voice, considerably less eye contact than one would expect, an odd gait and poor motor coordination. I enjoyed play therapy with Joe because of his powerful imagination and his willingness to express his fantasies in his play.

Joe had a number of preoccupations. These included card games popular with children of his age. He also frequently blocked sink drains and vents in the bathroom in order, he told me, to "keep the monsters out". He wakes repeatedly at night and says that he "sees illusions", which he finally told me was a ghost. He told me he was terrified of the dark and has bad dreams. In response to my invitation, he described one of these dreams as follows: "I dreamt the world blew up. I was the only one left in it. There was a big cliff."

Joe told me that he still likes to spin around, saying: "If I could just live on a spinning world, I would be happy." He described his own social interactions at school in the following way: "I usually hang out with the little kids but they don't like me—they usually want to fight. When I hang out with the bigger kids, they think I'm a dork."

Joe began treatment in a state of anxious desperation for change, especially in his social interactions. His initial transference was an ide-alising one, so that he very much wanted to come to our sessions and complained when he had to miss any. It felt to me as if I was experienced as a source of goodness from whom he wanted to get as much as he could. He asked me in a pleading way to have one of my toys or my seashells to take home with him. I experienced him as likeable, vulnerable, and needy, provoking a countertransference of wanting to meet his needs and be comforting to him. My countertransference included a wish to rescue him from his predicament, and I made a note to myself at the time to examine my rescue fantasies further. It seemed to me that I was experiencing what Racker (1974, p. 134) suggested was a concordant countertransference in response to Joe's projective identi-fications, coming from a "concordant identification", meaning (Ogden, 1982, p. 72) "the therapist's identification with the patient's experience of self in the internal object relationship that is being played out in the transference."

Joe began psychoanalytic play psychotherapy and was able to play in a very intense and highly imaginative manner. Typical themes included scenes of sustained combat between evil figures and good ones. You will hear the dialogues Joe and I had while we were playing together in a number of sessions, starting with his first session. In session one, Joe was playing with a toy snake which he used to knock over and attack a number of toy human figures around it.

ROBIN: So the snake is …?
JOE: He's hurting everybody who's trying to hurt me. (Joe brings into his play a toy dinosaur with spikes along its back). This is "Spiky". (He brings the two animals close together).
ROBIN: They're getting along together?
JOE: Snake senses Spiky is a friend. (I wonder about the transference here). But the other dinosaurs (pointing to five other dinosaur figures) he, uh, he senses they are enemies. (Snake and Spiky now confront the largest dinosaur). They are hypnotising him—hypnotising him to *destroy* him!

In session six, Joe has brought a toy figure of a boy with him to our session. In his play, the boy is quickly surrounded by a number of threatening animals.

> JOE: (Intensely) There's going to be a *stampede*—they're going to try to *stampede* him!
>
> ROBIN: Oh, oh!
>
> JOE: (One by one the boy figure approaches the animals and knocks them over). See? He has magic powers. He can defeat them *all*!
>
> ROBIN: Wow! Yeah. It sure would be nice if we had magic powers.
>
> JOE: (Making his boy figure jump over the defeated animals). Yeah. (Sadly and apparently changing the subject) I have trouble going to sleep at night.
>
> ROBIN: What makes that happen?
>
> JOE: I hear creaks and cracks.
>
> ROBIN: And they keep you awake?
>
> JOE: Well, I get super-scared of invisible people and I'm scared they could get me.
>
> ROBIN: Well, I can understand what makes it hard to sleep then.

In session thirty-four, Joe uses Play-Doh to make a figure which first becomes a snake, and which he then turns into a human figure. Joe attacks this figure with the Play-Doh implements. It gets hurt, stabbed and finally cut apart.

> ROBIN: Wow, he's really getting it, eh?
>
> JOE: He's weak so he gets it.
>
> ROBIN: Weak?
>
> JOE: Yeah. Like my own weak part.
>
> ROBIN: So what about that part?
>
> JOE: Everyone would like to get rid of their weak part.
>
> ROBIN: Well, it sure looks like you would. You really don't like that part of you?
>
> JOE: No, not at all.

Several features of these dialogues stand out. Splitting in the self becomes fairly visible. We get to see Peter's split between bully and victimised/bullied aspects as well as what Joe feels to be "my own weak part". Peter also separates being terrorised and terrorising others.

Also in view are issues of trust along with relational anxieties which seem to be organised mainly at a paranoid-schizoid level. Peter is clear that "you can never trust anyone in that game", with betrayal never far away. He had comparable difficulties trusting his peers. Peter avoids and denies feelings of anger, perhaps splitting them off, and wishes for there to be only feelings of love. Joe plays out being literally surrounded by enemies, some of whom are invisible, and invokes manic omnipotence in defeating all his enemies. But his omnipotent defence breaks down very quickly.

CHAPTER THREE

Some clinical dialogues with Asperger's patients—Matt, age twelve

I had the privilege of meeting with Matt between the times he was twelve years old and fourteen years old. What you are going to hear about our interactions comes mostly from when he was twelve years of age, but extending into his thirteenth year. When he was referred to me for treatment, Matt presented as a cutely appealing pre-adolescent. His suffering as he described it to me pulled mightily on my heartstrings. He was in considerable psychic torment when we first met, mostly because of his inability to make friends. I liked Matt and strongly sympathised with his plight. Wishes to rescue him from his loneliness and grief were mobilised in me, and made me less wary of therapeutic ambition than I usually would have been.

Matt was referred to me with a psychiatric diagnosis of Asperger's disorder, a diagnosis I came to agree with after our initial assessment sessions and continued to agree with after I came to know him better in our therapy sessions. Matt's appearance was like a young fictional character called Harry Potter. His impact on me was that of a hybrid between Harry Potter and a naïve and vulnerable elf. Matt wore large, round wire-rimmed glasses in the Harry Potter style, and these seemed to magnify the sad liquidity of his large blue eyes. He was quite small for his age of twelve years and he had not yet begun the preadolescent spurt in growth (and his parents had noticed no evidence of pubescent hormonal changes either). He told me sadly that he was one of the smallest boys in his class. Strands of his thick blond hair often projected awkwardly from under his glasses as he would speak to me in a worried and high-pitched voice, his high tone indicating the anxious constriction of his neck muscles.

Matt was definitely cute—vulnerably and puckishly cute. Matt himself recognised this cute aspect of his appearance. He was ambivalent about it. He felt it was positive and likely protective to be cute, but also that it was demeaning for him because it made others treat him as more juvenile than he felt himself to be. He also at times retreated into his cuteness in a regressive way. He made it clear that he would prefer to be young, small, and cute rather than face in any way issues around the adolescent sexual feelings that he had barely begun to experience.

During our very first meeting, Matt burst into tears as he was describing how he could not make any friends in his school and how all the other kids treated him with derision. He had been placed in a class for gifted children, but this did little to shore up his self-esteem. From his point of view, it made things worse because the other kids often referred to him as "a giftie". I found his small and sprite-like, elfin appearance quite touching, but could easily see how his peers at school might joke about it. His sadness at feeling unable to make friends or develop any positive relationships with his peers evoked in me a strong sense of sadness and feelings of paternal protectiveness. My countertransference pull was a sense of great sympathy for him and sadness, which became tinged with feeling regretfully disappointed in myself when his transference became more negative. Matt's transference began in a positive manner, so that he was able to pour out his anguish and relate to me as a sort of father-confessor. Later, more negative aspects developed so that I became disappointing for him because of my perceived inability to help him in the "practical" ways he yearned for.

In the course of his therapy, Matt repeatedly thematised numerous dichotomous situations, meaning situations in which he could play out only one role at a time out of two opposing possibilities. These opposing possibilities all seemed to reflect the nature of the split in his self. For example, Matt spoke of feeling he was an "observer" of his own life rather than really being a "participant" in his life. Another dichotomy he thematised was that of "immigrant" vs. "resident", with Matt expressing the feeling he was an immigrant in his own life, someone who was an outsider and a stranger to most others. This was opposed to being a "resident" in his own existence and feeling comfortably at home in the process of his own life. There were additional dichotomous oppositions based on television and newspaper cartoons, which we came to feel strongly reflected his own self perceptions. These included "beast *vs.* brainiac", with him being all brain and with the beast escaping only in temper tantrums at school. He also referred to the cartoon characters "Calvin and Hobbes", with him in the role of the child Calvin, who is always bested or overcome by his tiger teddy bear and fantasised companion Hobbes. Another dichotomy was that of "prisoner" *vs.* "guard".

However, the dichotomy which was most sustained in Matt's treatment was that of "antelope vs. tiger". It arose repeatedly during his treatment. This dichotomy derived entirely from Matt's own understandings of himself. He always saw himself as having both antelope and tiger aspects. These aspects were often in considerable tension with each other or working against each other, so this split became quite painful for him.

I now present an edited but accurate version of Matt's "antelope *vs.* tiger" dialogues with me. You will hear as a continuous dialogue a number of excerpts which actually took place months apart. I do it this way in the hope it will help you develop a full appreciation of Matt's explanation of the "antelope *vs.* tiger" split. I hope this way of presenting Matt's interactions will function as a sort of "time lapse video" which accurately represents growth by the compression of time.

MATT: (Pointing out of my office window to a plastic bag tangled in the bare winter branches of a nearby tree) See, it's still there. The wind and snow are still hurting it. It's alone. It looks trapped.

ROBIN: And perhaps (uncertain whether this is too direct for Matt) … perhaps there's someone else who could feel lonely, trapped, and hurt?

MATT: (Looking surprised) Yeah, I know, it's … you mean me. (Pausing) I did. I felt hurt at school yesterday. It ruined my day.

ROBIN: Can you tell me about the hurt?

MATT: (Sighs) I didn't do my work in French and I quit, uh, I gave up on the math test. It was too hard for me.

ROBIN: And you were feeling?

MATT: Like a nature programme I saw on TV and it had a tiger and an antelope in it. And I, I can have fits, tantrums at school and all hell can break loose when my tiger gets out of its cage.

ROBIN: And then?

MATT: I do a self-detention.

ROBIN: (Surprised by this) Self-detention? That's when …

MATT: I take myself down to the office and I say I deserve a detention.

ROBIN: As a punishment, a self-punishment?

MATT: Yeah. For the tiger getting out. And the antelope part … (pauses).

ROBIN: (Encouragingly) The antelope part …?

MATT: The antelope part is sad and it's feeling hurt. It's worried about the tiger part.

ROBIN: And maybe afraid?

MATT: Afraid. Yeah. It wants the tiger back in its cage.

ROBIN: So the antelope part is afraid all the time?

MATT: No. No. Like in the TV programme, the antelope can jump around and do neat things. I want to, uh, the antelope can show off and it's, ah, skilled—so it wants the other kids to see how good it is.

ROBIN: Do they?

MATT: Huh?

ROBIN: Do the other kids see how good you are, how skilled the antelope part is?

MATT: (His expression darkening into sadness) No, mostly no. They don't notice.

ROBIN: And then the antelope feels sad?

MATT: Maybe. But it feeds the tiger. The tiger feeds on it.

ROBIN: The tiger feeds on …?

MATT: The tiger feeds on when I feel hurt, and, uh, sad, and when they tease me; that feeds the tiger, the tiger's angry.

ROBIN: So the antelope is …

MATT: The tiger can take bites out of the antelope for, uh, for when it's sad. The tiger doesn't like it.

ROBIN: And the antelope, what is … how is it reacting then to the tiger?

MATT: Afraid, and that the tiger is bad.

ROBIN: And then it takes tiger to the office for a self-detention?

MATT: Yeah, it keeps tiger under control.

ROBIN: But maybe antelope could sort of, well, kind of admire tiger secretly? Admire tiger's strength. And could maybe even approve of tiger a bit, when it had tantrums and scared or preyed on the other students?

MATT: Admire? I guess sometimes. But still afraid of tiger. But sometimes antelope needs tiger.

ROBIN: For example, when?

MATT: When things feel, uh, safe, then tiger isn't needed—only when things feel unsafe.

ROBIN: And when could that be?

MATT: (Hesitating) Well, uh, antelope is skittish. He can easily feel frightened, so, he, well he feels unsafe really quickly.

ROBIN: So tiger gets called to come out really quickly too?

MATT: (Suddenly seeming to change the subject) I have a PC at home, I told you, and did you know a Mac and a PC can't communicate?

ROBIN: (Wondering whether this is a reference to the transference and a hint I am pushing him too much). Yeah, I think I knew that. But maybe that could be like antelope and tiger as well? They're sort of like Mac and PC because they can't communicate?

MATT: Oh. Yeah. Could be. So then …?

ROBIN: Well, maybe antelope doesn't ever make tiger feel safe because antelope is so—what did you say?—skittish. And tiger, even though he's strong, can never really calm down antelope?

MATT: Well, in the antelope and tiger programme on TV, there were other animals that can protect themselves in different ways. There was a fish, what's the name—an archerfish, and it squirts water to knock down its prey. There was a bizarre lizard that can squirt caustic blood from its eyes.

ROBIN: Wow!

MATT: Yeah. Different ways to protect themselves.

ROBIN: I wonder because kids also, they have ways to protect themselves, like making a circle of friends to keep protected from bullies. But you …

MATT: I …

ROBIN: Well, it sounds like tiger sort of attacks yourself before anyone else can, a kind of protection antelope invites, but tiger can also blast anger straight out and this can get you into trouble.

MATT: Yeah; I tormented this girl at school, and …

ROBIN: (Astonished) Tormented?

MATT: Well, I vomited the day before so I told her that her hair smelled like old, dried vomit. I enjoyed that.

ROBIN: Tiger had a good time?

MATT: Yeah. But sometimes tiger makes me feel attacked, like I'm my own worst enemy.

ROBIN: As in the tiger part attacking the antelope part?

MATT: Uh (pausing to consider this) but maybe more like a tiger chasing his own tail—like I saw in a Calvin and Hobbes cartoon. I, uh, I punish myself even before the adults do it.

ROBIN: Like at least you have some control when you punish yourself before someone else can do it?

MATT: Yeah, I think, like that. Tiger maybe comes out when things really hurt, but it's antelope the rest of the time, most of the time. Tiger, uh, goes in, goes back quickly too, and then there's antelope.

ROBIN: What would I see if I watched antelope come out?

MATT: Me, crying. I'm sorry, feeling sorry, afraid.

ROBIN: Sounds confusing.

MATT: Yeah, really.

ROBIN: Maybe confusing to others because they don't know what to expect from you, like which part is coming out?

MATT: I guess so, but for me too.

ROBIN: For you?

MATT: Confusing—I'm not sure which part is going to come out so I'm not sure what others are going to do either. I feel like an alien and like structural collapse.

ROBIN: (Surprised at this wording) Structural collapse?

MATT: (Looking down and seeming embarrassed) I had a hissy fit at school.

ROBIN: (Surprised by his choice of words) A hissy fit? Can you tell me about it?

MATT: It was unfair. We had a supply teacher (meaning a substitute teacher when the regular teacher is absent). I was doing my work and all the other kids were drawing on the blackboard—the supply teacher let them. Then it was my turn, but there was no chalk. So I went out and got a piece, but when I came back … (pauses and seems distressed).

ROBIN: It was really tough for you.

MATT: Yeah, uh, what … I came back and there was no room to draw on, so I got a chair and found an empty spot. And I was just going to start and the teacher said no more drawing time. So unfair. Then Becky …

ROBIN: Sorry, *Becky*?

MATT: A girl in my class. She … (he stops talking)

ROBIN: It felt so bad. You don't have to tell me if …

MATT: No, it's okay. She drew a big, dumb-looking person on the board and then she whispered to me, "It's you, Matt." That was a whiplash moment.

ROBIN: (Struck by his creative wording) Whiplash, wow! I can see why it was, Matt. She was mocking you?

MATT: I … I was there; I blanked out (dissociation?) and then all hell breaks loose; it wasn't too pretty.

ROBIN: You went into tiger mode?

MATT: Yeah. I threw the chalk at Becky—the chalk I never got to use. And then I threw my glasses at the board and I stomped on them and I smashed them; someone loyal got them for me, and …

ROBIN: Holy cow!

MATT: … and I pulled the desk on top of me and I went in a ball and I was crying, and they … a crowd of kids made a circle around me.

ROBIN: How terrible!

MATT: And then all my ideas converged together on how bad I am.

ROBIN: So it was antelope mode now?

MATT: Yeah. Antelope thought I was a lunkhead and it told me I was to blame and I should be punished.

ROBIN: Matt, I think I now get what you told me before about structural collapse.

MATT: Yeah.

The split in Matt's self or ego stands out with abundant clarity. At one point, when Matt "blanks out," there seems to be a strong suggestion of defensive dissociation. However, Matt's vivid and detailed awareness of both aspects of his split self, as well as details of how they interact, suggests a split in the self as opposed to dissociated self-states.

I understand Matt as being a good example of the "inhibited but object-seeking and needy" type of Asperger's, as described fully in Chapter Fourteen, "Differential diagnosis". Matt displays a strong desire and a striving to establish interpersonal relationships, along with a high degree of frustration and painful desperation when his relationships do not work out.

Matt ended his therapy abruptly. The reason he gave was that I didn't help him make friends. A few months before this termination, Matt unexpectedly brought me a beautifully printed and organised summary, entitled "Reasons for feeling unsatisfied". He described these as reasons for being unsatisfied with *himself*, but my feeling was that they were also reasons for feeling unsatisfied with *me* and with the progress of the treatment.

Some of the reasons Matt gave for feeling unsatisfied which he presented to me in his carefully bulleted list were: "not a good brother to my sister; feeling disorganised; feeling bored when there's a lot to do; feeling like not a good student; stress; feel unloved (more like being hated); not doing chores or what mom asked me to do; being hard on myself; unfinished projects of my own; fear of high school in September."

Matt taught me that he might have felt more "satisfied" if there had been intervention of a supportive nature to help him in school, and social skills training to help him make friends (and not feel "hated").

Some of the things I learned from Matt are put into practice in "The Toronto experiment" outlined in Chapter Sixteen. Matt's feelings of being unsatisfied along with my own feelings of not being satisfied with how I handled his treatment are among the main motivations for beginning this experiment as described in Chapter Sixteen.

CHAPTER FOUR

Some clinical dialogues with Asperger's patients—Thomas, age twelve

Thomas was twelve years of age when I briefly saw him. I tried very hard to be useful for Thomas, but my experience was that he wouldn't open the door for me even a crack. Thomas provoked in me a fairly powerful countertransference reaction which included both sadness at not being able to help him, as well as retaliatory anger. It was a frustrating experience to be blocked in every attempt I made to connect with his feeling states, and when my efforts were repeatedly rejected in his denigrating manner.

Thomas's mum brought him to me in desperation because he had been tossed out of several schools, and was constantly getting into trouble with other kids and with the staff of his current school because of his behavioural outbursts. Mum was spending most of her time either appealing for help from, or else officially complaining about the school principal and staff, as a result of what she felt was their unfair and damaging treatment of Thomas.

In retrospect, I evaluate Thomas, along with Anthony who is the subject of Chapter Eight, as two excellent examples of the uninhibited and aggressive type of Asperger's. I also refer to them as the "object-rejecting" group in terms of their external object relations (see Chapter Fourteen for the details). They are the children in which

Asperger "noted sadistic behaviour and frequent acts of malice, about which they showed delight" (Rhode & Klauber, 2004, p. 30). The understanding I arrived at is that for these children, the bully part of their split self is likely to be predominant. Asperger's children who qualify as belonging to the category "uninhibited/aggressive" prefer being "an active bully rather than a passive victim" (Rhode & Klauber, 2004, p. 65) and may demonstrate "the classic picture of bullying, locating the discomfort, fear and hatred in another" (ibid, p. 66). In a comment applicable to Thomas, Rhode and Klauber (2004, p. 23) note that these children may need "help in managing their aggressive impulses".

My attempt to treat Thomas failed because he dug in his heels and refused to come to my office. He continually insisted he was a "normal boy" and didn't need treatment; treatment was stupid in his eyes (and likely experienced as a denigration and a narcissistic injury). The frame of treatment was repeatedly ruptured, feeling to me more like a dysfunctional sieve than a frame, largely because of the mutual semi-symbiotic relationship between Thomas and his mother. Often, Thomas would refuse to enter my office, so his mother would come instead, and shut the door, whereupon Thomas would barge in and insist the time was his, not his mother's. Often, the session would become a sort of filial therapy involving both Thomas and his mother.

Thomas was a tall, handsome, sturdy, burly youth for his age of twelve years. His physical strength and stature made matters worse for him. He could do significant damage to his peers if he got into a fight at school, and his mother, a slight woman, complained she could no longer control him or make him do things—she even expressed some fear (likely mixed with unconscious admiration of him) that he could hurt her if he got out of control.

Thomas's transference to me was unremittingly negative. For him, I was just another adult who would denigrate him and blame him for his difficult behaviour. The very fact he was dragged in to see me implied for him that I felt he was abnormal and deviant. My countertransference was marked by a sense of desperation to be of some value or usefulness in his eyes, and by saddened frustration, disappointment, and counter-hostility around the fact that I was never permitted to be effective for him. I felt stymied and frustrated no matter what I did.

The dialogue I present took place about a month before his treatment finally came to grief. When I went into the waiting room to get him, both Thomas and his mother were in identical poses and had identical expressions, so that I immediately felt that something was severely wrong. Both wore jagged scowls on their faces, with their legs crossed and their heads propped on an arm and a closed fist. My first impression was that they had the weight of the world on their shoulders. Mother explained that she had bought Thomas some apple juice, which he had thrown around all over the street on the way to my office. I wondered whether this could be an expression of his current feelings, which he felt unable to hold in and which had spilled out all over.

A typical exchange between Thomas and his mother ensued. Thomas at first absolutely refused to come into my office. Finally, his mother scowled and said she wanted to speak to me alone, heading towards my door. Then Thomas pushed his way past his mother and into my office, insisting on being there and saying "it's my time". I thought: "here we go again", and felt totally incompetent to deal with the situation.

Thomas and his mother both remained in my office for the rest of the session, though the dialogue was only between Thomas and me. His mother sat on my couch, while Thomas lay down on it with his head nestled in his mother's lap. This struck me not as Oedipal but as symbiotic in nature. Thomas began by ranting at me, calling me a bastard and expressing his extreme anger at having to see me. We start to hear the dialogue between Thomas and me when his theme becomes a dichotomy in his self-experience, one surprisingly similar to the one expressed by Matt, with similar implications for splitting of the self. For Thomas, the split in his self indicated by the dichotomy in his experience was that between pussycat *vs.* tiger.

THOMAS: (Scowling at me) I want to be a normal boy—I *am* a normal boy! I don't need *you*!

ROBIN: Okay, but everyone ...

THOMAS: And how do I explain? How do I tell the teacher and especially the other kids why I had to miss school? Tell them I had an appointment with a *psychologist*? Oh, sure!

ROBIN: (Attempting to be helpful in a "practical" manner). Well, what *could* you tell them? Maybe ...

THOMAS: I wouldn't have to tell them *anything* if I didn't come here.

ROBIN: But do you remember in our last meeting we talked about two parts of you, a tiger part and a pussycat part?

THOMAS: Sure I do, but I don't *want* to remember.

ROBIN: (Relieved at not being totally shut down by Thomas) Okay, but it seems like the tiger part, the angry part, is really out now.

THOMAS: So what?

ROBIN: Well, you remember we talked about the pussycat part as like the, more like the "normal boy" you talked about? And …

THOMAS: I remember; I'm not stupid.

ROBIN: Actually, I think you're smart. So you remember we talked about the pussycat part as, ah, as wanting normal human interaction and even needing it?

THOMAS: I told you I remembered.

ROBIN: Okay. Well, maybe it's the pussycat part that wants to cuddle and snuggle up with your mother like you are now.

THOMAS: (Grunts ambiguously)

ROBIN: Well, the pussycat part wasn't doing so well, was having a tough time when you came in today.

THOMAS: *You* gave me a tough time!

ROBIN: Well, maybe that's what brings out the tiger part—I mean to protect, to protect the pussycat part. You expect me to be unhelpful and a nasty bastard, so …

THOMAS: Yeah and that's why I don't want to come here.

ROBIN: (Now feeling frustrated and incompetent) Well, maybe that's the reason tiger comes out so quickly; he wants to protect the pussycat part that's afraid I'm going to be nasty. You maybe feel your mum is going to be nasty and blaming too.

THOMAS: (Somewhat less angrily and in a more modulated tone) Well, so what?

ROBIN: The "so what" is that if the tiger part comes out quickly, maybe that's all they get to see and then they don't see the pussycat part at all—I mean other people.

THOMAS: (Now calmly) Again, so what?

ROBIN: Well, all you get from others is how they react to only a part of you, like you're only existing as half a person, as the tiger part. They treat you like an angry and aggressive kid and may never get to see—*you*; and you never get to feel how they would treat the normal boy/pussycat part of you. So you live as half a person.

THOMAS: They don't *want*—they don't like all of me. They only care when I get angry and then they laugh (his mother now stroking his hair).

ROBIN: Yeah, they only pay attention when the tiger part is out, so …

THOMAS: Yeah, the angry tiger.

ROBIN: … so maybe it feels like I will only pay attention to you when tiger's right out there. And maybe tiger does grab all our attention, your mum's and mine. And then maybe pussycat—he's sensitive—starts feeling left out, ignored, even resentful.

THOMAS: (Reluctantly) Maybe.

ROBIN: So then it feels like I'm not treating you like a normal boy; the tiger part gets all my attention and, uh, well it maybe feels like I don't care for all of you.

THOMAS: You *don't* treat me like a normal boy!

ROBIN: Well, that's certainly what you experience coming from me.

Hearing this dialogue likely provides some suggestions about why in the end his treatment could not proceed. Thomas dug in his heels. He made such a battle about coming to see me and "not being treated like a normal boy" that his mother said she didn't have the energy to bring him and was afraid of what might happen while she was with him on public transportation (she was afraid to drive with him in the car). His mother turned her energies to lobbying the school board to treat Thomas less harshly and more like the intellectually bright child he was.

Thomas gave me the impression of trying to maintain a sort of emotional equilibrium for himself by keeping everyone else off-balance and in a state of uncertainty and disequilibrium—including his teachers, his parents, and me in the countertransference.

His rapid alternation between the pussycat and tiger aspects of himself enabled him to experience some degree of morally self-righteous control over his environment, while keeping those he experienced as his potential persecutors uncertain, off-balance, and therefore unable to deal with him in a consensual and effective way. If his two alternating aspects were so calming and adaptive for him, in the way he unconsciously experienced them, it is no wonder that he didn't want me to interfere with or to modify the interaction between these two aspects.

In how Thomas describes his own experience, the split in his self between the pussycat and the tiger aspects is quite clear. I think another aspect is the powerful and toxic projective identification Thomas used in trying to control his own anxiety about himself. His repeated mantra is: "You don't treat me like a normal boy". My sense was that Thomas harboured very powerful unconscious feelings about not being a "normal boy". His own experiences of chronically repeated rejections by peers and perhaps by school staff as well (the latter being reinforced by his mother) must have constantly provoked these feelings. His way of dealing with such perceptions was to say, in effect, that the peers and the teachers who reject me are the abnormal ones, not me. When his mother forced him to see me in treatment, this provoked his feeling of being treated as not a normal boy, so that it was beyond his endurance. He used projective identification to put the accusation "you are not a normal boy" into me. He then had much more control over the perception of being not normal and the feelings which accompanied this. He could blame me for treating him in this nasty manner, a "bastard" in his words, and he could reject me instead of himself feeling rejected. He could also exercise a powerful degree of control over the situation by refusing to come into my office and making continued treatment impossible for his mother.

The treatment did not last long enough for me to ever begin to take up the theme of how he himself could sometimes have feelings of not being normal. Most Asperger's children use projective identification, but they use projective identification *into remote objects* and tend to scrupulously avoid projective identifications into the therapist until the treatment is well advanced. Thomas did not follow the usual pattern. He used powerful projective identifications into the therapist from our very first meeting onward.

CHAPTER FIVE

Some clinical dialogues with Asperger's patients—Thanos, age fourteen

Thanos was, at the time of the dialogue I present, a fourteen-year-old of Macedonian heritage. He is a good example of what I refer to (see Chapter Fourteen) as the "inhibited/object-seeking and needy" type of Asperger's adolescent. I met with Thanos between the ages of twelve years and eighteen years of age, the latter being his age at the time of writing, when he had started university and was still in weekly psychotherapy with me. Along with Thanos, Matt (Chapter Three), and Alan (Chapter Seven) would be good candidates for the inhibited but object-seeking type of Asperger's adolescent. These adolescents strongly yearn and strive for interpersonal relationships, often with a high degree of frustrated and painful desperation.

Thanos is a tall, robust, and handsome youth. In the session previous to the session which you will hear part of, Thanos had surprised me by marching into my office and loudly announcing to me: "My mother wants me to talk about my compulsive masturbation!" Thanos's parents had recently separated. The concern his mother expressed to me was that Thanos was merciless in how he teased and denigrated his younger sister. The session you will hear was my last session with Thanos before he departed on a long summer vacation to his native Macedonia. Over the years, his relationship with his younger sister has improved dramatically, so that he is now protective of her and worried about her mental state. After mighty struggles with the course of studies he should best pursue at university, he was able to obtain high grades and enter a course of studies he felt was sensible, rather than pursue studies in his beloved subject of history. After years of beating our way through thickets of intellectualisation, Thanos has been able to tell me how important it is to deal with his feelings.

The dialectical interplay of transference and countertransference between us was mostly quite positive in nature. Thanos treated me as an intellectual sounding board with which he could endlessly discuss detailed and obscure aspects of history and of the computer games which fascinated him. I felt very sympathetic to him in his efforts to make friends, and delighted in his long intellectual monologues in which I was often able to use aspects of the world history he described to begin to talk about his personal and family history. Thanos would talk to me about historical interactions between different countries in the context of European and Middle Eastern geography. I would respond by talking about interactions between different aspects of him in the context of what we called his "internal geography". This is what occurred in the part of the session you will soon overhear.

Thanos had when he was fourteen become preoccupied with an interactive online computer game called "eRepublik". He would talk to me nonstop for entire sessions about events in this game. Part of the game was that participants could compete for positions in different online governments. Thanos had become part of the online Greek government, and he was eventually named the Minister of War for Greece! Spurred on by different political "scenarios" provided by the game's administrators, the different countries involved formed alliances, competed economically and strategically, and went to war with each other. The players would then have to adapt the policies of their different governments to the ongoing outcomes of events as determined by the administrators of the game.

Thanos was quite proud of his participation in the game. It certainly seemed to afford him many narcissistic gratifications which other fourteen-year-olds would be more likely to obtain from their interactions with peers. Thanos told me, for example, that the game was for adults. But even though he was only fourteen, his historical knowledge and his language abilities had convinced the other players he was twenty-four. We start to hear the dialogue between Thanos and me after a lengthy monologue by Thanos in which he has described all the minute details of the interactions on the eRepublik game over the past week. He had given suggestions to or had participated in the deliberations of a number of online governments, including those of Turkey, Greece, Bulgaria, and Macedonia. He described in detail his contributions to each of these governments, how he felt about their functioning, and how he felt about the actual countries in real life. We begin to overhear at a point where I become much more active in commenting on what Thanos is telling me, and his sustained monologue turns into more of a dialogue.

THANOS: And because I'm not an adult, I'm only fourteen, I don't get the respect I need, nowhere. But I can get it online. Only because they think I'm an adult. Online, they respect what I say and the suggestions I give.

ROBIN: I feel badly because everyone needs respect. I hope you feel you get respect here?

THANOS: You take me seriously.

ROBIN: Okay, well, now I'll take you seriously about what you've been telling me about the eRepublik game. You've told me about your interactions with the online Turkish government, the …

THANOS: My contributions.

ROBIN: Right—your contributions to the Turkish government, the Greek government, the Bulgarian government, and the Macedonian government. So by now you know what I usually do—I talk about your internal geography, your internal aspects. So now …

THANOS: Now you're going to do it again?

ROBIN: You got it. It sounds to me like there are three or four internal … aspects to you, like a Turkish part, a Greek part, a Bulgarian part, maybe even a Macedonian part.

THANOS: (Sounding uncertain but curious) Go on.

ROBIN: Well, uh, the Turkish part. It sounds to me like this could be, I mean based on what you've told me, the … ah … more angry, aggressive, even more uncivilised part.

THANOS: Well, yeah—most people look down on the Turks as uncivilised, or they used to.

ROBIN: And this seems to be the aspect that can feel powerful, that starts the fights with your sister Leila, that lets you feel sort of powerful and in control.

THANOS: And what about the other parts?

ROBIN: Well, the Greek part sounds to me like sort of how you want to see yourself. It's the, well, bright, intellectual, civilised, even superior part of yourself.

THANOS: Well, the Greeks were pretty superior in history.

ROBIN: Maybe not so much during the Ottoman Empire, but let's focus on you. The Greek part seems to feel superior, intellectually superior and successful. It seems to look down on the other parts as being more, uh, primitive, stupid and controlled by their feelings. And maybe even there is arrogance—you remember we talked about how the other kids might experience you as arrogant?

THANOS: Sure.

ROBIN: Well, maybe this Greek part sort of looks down on your other parts because it feels intellectually above them?

THANOS: Interesting. But what about the other parts?

ROBIN: I'm not quite so sure about them—the Bulgarian part seems to be the victim part, especially compared to the Turkish part which seems to be more of a, uh, dictator or bully part. The Bulgarian part seems to contain the victim part of you we've talked about, so that this is the part that feels overpowered, misunderstood, disrespected, abused, and fearful—like we've talked about.

THANOS: Let's not get too much into that part!

ROBIN: No, but maybe you'd let me make one more link. I wonder if it's the Bulgarian part that needs to calm and soothe itself with the compulsive masturbation we talked about last time. I'm not sure, but maybe it sort of, uh, tries to debase the other parts by pulling them into the masturbatory activities—so if they take part, Bulgaria can say they are just as, uh, low as it is.

THANOS: And Macedonia, the Macedonian part?

ROBIN: Okay, I'll take the hint and drop Bulgaria. Macedonia I'm least sure about. Your heritage is Macedonian. But in eRepublik, you want to be Greek and definitely not Macedonian, like you just told me. So maybe how strongly you want to feel Greek in the game, not Macedonian, has something to do with your parents, and not wanting to be like them, I mean in the way they fight.

THANOS: Uh, you're right about that. They fight and then they have make-up sex. (I'm surprised at his ability to make this observation). I don't want to be like that. But let's suppose you're right about all these different parts. Sounds kind of right, but then I'll give you a big "so what?"

ROBIN: Yeah, well what stands out for me we've already partly talked about. It's the way each of the three or however many parts seem to want to be the strongest part and to get control of your personality, huh? Like each of the parts we've talked about, at least three of them, seems to put down the other parts.

THANOS: Well, it feels maybe a bit like that.

ROBIN: And even more, like in the eRepublik game, there seem to be alliances between the different parts; battles, attempted takeovers, sabotage, propaganda, the whole thing.

THANOS: I'm not sure I get that yet.

ROBIN: Well, I'm not sure either. But alliances—maybe the Turkish and Bulgarian parts get together to pull down the superior Greek part? And sabotage, maybe the Bulgarian part tries to weaken or degrade the others by pulling them into masturbation? And propaganda—the Greek part strutting about how intellectual and superior it is?

THANOS: I'm not sure.

ROBIN: Well, neither am I. But now it's out there for us to wonder about.

Thanos continues in his therapy at present. We continue to deal with dichotomies, but different ones from those we have just overheard. As Thanos got closer to applying for higher education, he was torn in a different way. Should he apply to study history, which is his true interest and his heart's desire, but which he feels offers little hope for a financially secure future? Or should he instead try to benefit from his high marks in science and apply for medicine, which is not really close to his heart but which offers a financially secure future and an ability to support a family? In the end, he chose neither of these alternatives, but a third one which involves both science and aspects of the humanities. His struggles about what he wants to study continue.

There is a glimpse in this dialogue of how Thanos is very willing to talk about himself, provided what we talk about is "interesting" to him and steers clear of more emotional aspects (talking about Bulgaria and the sexual feelings that this implies). His tendency to use defensive intellectualisation is pretty clear. Splitting of the self also stands out fairly clearly, with Greece representing the victim and Turkey representing the bully. The most interesting aspect, however, is that his splitting of the self involves not a simple duality, but three or possibly four different self-states. A similar situation comes into view when we consider Alan in Chapter Seven.

Some clinical dialogues with Asperger's patients—Dan, age seventeen

I met with Dan from the time he was sixteen years of age until his untimely and tragic death from a rare disorder at twenty years of age. He died after his first very successful year at university, during the summer break. I had been keeping in touch with him through regular weekly "Skype" sessions as he navigated through his freshman year at a university setting which provided excellent support for young people who are "on the spectrum" of autism. In spite of being a likely example of the "inhibited/avoidant" type of Asperger's, Dan had been able to make friendships during his freshman year. Adolescents manifesting this type of Asperger's tend to be behaviourally shy, reticent, inhibited, and phobic or avoidant of interpersonal relationships. There is sometimes *secondary* and autistic-like interpersonal avoidance. In terms of their external object relations, these are the "object-shunning" adolescents. In spite of his phobic approach to peers, Dan was still able to make friendships during his first university year.

Dan was short and thin. He had short, dull reddish hair which tended to stick out in places. In appearance, he was elfin. His facial features were rather small and compact. At age seventeen, his school uniform hung limply on his small frame. He looked, in fact, much like I imagine Peter Pan would look—as if a strong gust of wind could sweep him flying off into the air. Dan lacked flow in his physical movements. He walked in a saccadic, jerky, sometimes almost birdlike manner. As he entered my office, he would typically look down at the floor. Sometimes, though, he would catch my eyes and peer at me intently, as if trying to fathom what I really meant deep down by what I said. Much of the time, his expression was one of anxiously perplexed confusion or consternation. Sometimes, the brief flicker of an elfin grin would flit across his face. Rarely, he could erupt into a beautiful smile like a flower blossoming. At other times, he appeared overwhelmed and dejected. Dan's transference seemed to be mostly one characterised by hopeful if uncertain trustfulness. My countertransference was mainly to him as a victim who deserved sympathy and support, combined with a strong desire to enliven him, which I sometimes had to keep in check.

At one point, it seemed like I would have to stop seeing Dan. Here are some excerpts from the two letters Dan wrote to me at that time. Dan wrote the letters at the end of my employment at a public hospital, when I had to convert to private practice at a fair distance from where I had worked in the publicly funded system. His parents were so committed to his treatment that they were willing to pay for it and to transport Dan to my new office location.

> **Dan's First Letter**: "The more I read about how it used to be and the farther back I go, the more it hits me that I might have been needed or useful there [in the past]. That in turn makes me feel there is no need for me in the time that I exist. ... It makes me question if humanity is even worth saving from their own destructive behaviours, their pride and ignorance to the very fact of life. ... I feel the pain this planet has and will continue to deal with, and it makes me want to end my life or destroy the evildoers who are responsible. ..." [Signed] The Dan none has or will ever know.

> **Dan's Second Letter**: "I am thankful for the time which we have spent every Thursday for the last year. The time that we have communicated was an opportunity that I will remember and value, for I doubt that a connection or the chance to socialise will ever be so fun, useful, and full of meaning. We both have probably learned something, and that is good, for what is life but a process of learning? ... Thank you for being there to hear my inner story

when everyone else failed to read it." [Signed] Your patient and friend; Dan.

I was first of all struck by the fact that Dan wrote two letters. My feeling was that, judging from their tone and content, it was as if two people had written the letters. I got the sense that the first letter was mainly from Captain Hook, and the second letter mainly from Peter Pan.

Dan shared with me a number of dichotomies that for him seemed to characterise his experience, and to reflect the split in his self as well. Among these dichotomies were Captain Jean-Luc Picard of the *Star Trek* television series *vs.* the alien "Q", King Kong *vs.* civilisation, Attila the Hun *vs.* Rome, drunken students *vs.* the police, and Martin Luther King *vs.* Malcolm X. In what you are about to hear, the dichotomy that Dan brings up is that of warrior *vs.* priest.

DAN: (Dan begins in his usual slow and hesitant way). I … uh, I saw a show … it was … about imposters.

ROBIN: Imposters? Sounds like it was interesting for you?

DAN: I … was thinking that … imposters … people who become imposters … are making up for something.

ROBIN: Making up for something?

DAN: Yeah, uh … like something they missed in their life.

ROBIN: Missed what, for example?

DAN: I'm not sure, but … (long pause).

ROBIN: Maybe I shouldn't have interrupted?

DAN: No, it's okay, but sometimes I feel like an imposter.

ROBIN: Would it be too obvious if I asked you about your imposter part; your imposter feeling?

DAN: Uh, it seems to me that I … people … everyone has sort of a warrior part and, uh, a priest part to them.

ROBIN: Are you talking about, like, destructive and good aspects?

DAN: Not … exactly. Maybe. That's part of it.

ROBIN: Okay, and you were saying you have these aspects, uh, parts?

DAN: Yeah. Yeah. But … but usually I don't show either aspect. I hold them both in and …

ROBIN: (Trying to encourage Dan) … and?

DAN: And I act neutral; I try to show myself in a neutral way. I could maybe be, uh, great and I could maybe be, it's like you said, uh, destructive. But …

ROBIN: (Again trying to encourage) … but?

DAN: I'm afraid … afraid of both … afraid to be great and afraid … like what could happen if I let out the warrior, like you say, destructive aspect?

ROBIN: Anything come to mind about these aspects?

DAN: Well, the warrior, we talked about it … it was back in grade six. And we had a clique and this kid, grade five kid, wanted to join, uh, for protection.

ROBIN: Yeah, I remember.

DAN: So we gave him an initiation and, uh, told him to do … impossible or hard stuff, and he didn't do well in his initiation.

ROBIN: Yeah.

DAN: So I got chosen to faze him out, and I did, I really frightened him.

ROBIN: I seem to remember you humiliated him?

DAN: Both. He left the school. So I found out … I know what the warrior … the warrior fascist aspect can do.

ROBIN: We haven't talked about the priest part yet, but I start to see how difficult your dilemma must feel to you. (My colleague Dannette Graham has helpfully pointed out how I changed the topic with Dan here. Instead of asking more about how he frightened the kid, and his possible guilt about this, or asking more about what his "warrior fascist aspect" can actually do, I instead bring up the priest aspect. I think this is resistance by me as therapist, and that I wanted to maintain a picture of him as *victim* and not such a strong one as bully).

DAN: Well that's why I put on, why I show myself as neutral. It makes me feel like I'm an imposter. I'm afraid to let out either the priest part or the warrior part. So … so I neutralise them.

ROBIN: Neutralise, yeah. But have you wondered about letting out the warrior—or the priest for that matter—bit by bit instead of all at once? Like a lawyer can battle with voice and words but not fists.

DAN: There's pressures—grade twelve—and I'm supposed to be making decisions for the rest of my life, and it means I'm supposed to decide about myself, priest, warrior—it's too, uh, fast.

ROBIN: You help me understand. But does the warrior part get stirred up by insult and injury—you've felt enough of that. And you were telling me earlier about your visit to Sick Kids [The Hospital for Sick Children in Toronto], uh, yesterday, wasn't it?

DAN: Yeah.

ROBIN: And you told me they asked you tons of questions and didn't listen to you. Could that have stirred up your warrior part?

DAN: (Pondering) Maybe ... probably.

ROBIN: So ...

DAN: But the kids in my class, they ... they let out the warrior too much. I don't like it; don't like them. They're too defiant.

ROBIN: They defy the priestly authority of their teachers?

DAN: (Smiling) Yeah. I want to do the work. They want to get out of it, defy it.

ROBIN: We're almost out of time. I'll just mention a connection, possible connection for us to wonder about. A couple of months ago, we talked about a Star Trek episode—do you remember?

DAN: Oh, yeah.

ROBIN: The episode where Captain Jean-Luc Picard is put on trial by the omnipotent, uh, super-powerful alien Q? And he has to defend the human race from charges of destructive arrogance?

DAN: Yes.

ROBIN: So is it like Captain Picard is the priest who defends and sympathises with the difficulties of humanity and Q is sort of the warrior/prosecutor who attacks all the shortcomings of human beings—I mean is there a parallel between the Star Trek situation we talked about before and what we talked about today?

DAN: I hadn't thought about it.

ROBIN: But you're thinking about it now?

DAN: (Pondering) I guess ... uh, that does seem right.

ROBIN: Okay, maybe this is more for us to talk about next time.

Dan is extremely articulate in how he is able to talk about the irritating split in his self which forces him to take on a neutral attitude and as a result feel like an imposter. What also stands out quite clearly is the mental anguish Dan experiences in trying to understand and to balance these different aspects of the self. In fact, neither the bully part nor the victim part, neither the warrior nor the priest, feel comfortably authentic to Dan. He struggles with how to express either one, and in the end, as he experiences it, he is forced to suppress both of them and to become an imposter, in effect a nobody.

Some clinical dialogues with Asperger's patients—Alan, age nineteen

Alan was nineteen years old when the therapeutic dialogue presented below took place. Alan continues in treatment at present, and continues to struggle with the splits in his self. He has been in treatment, with some relatively brief gaps, since he was seventeen years of age. As I mentioned in Chapter Five when presenting Thanos and his dialogue with me, Alan, Thanos, and Matt (Chapter Three) would all likely be good candidates for the inhibited but object-seeking type of Asperger's adolescent. Recall that these adolescents strongly yearn and strive for interpersonal relationships, often with a high degree of frustrated and painful desperation (My best guess is that the inhibited/object-seeking type of Asperger's may be the most frequent way in which it presents itself). Alan's struggles have focused on establishing relationships with peers, especially female peers, and escaping from what he feels is the trap of his parental home. His younger sister has gone on to university, leaving Alan with a sense of being stalled in the backwater of his parental home and going nowhere.

Alan does not have a strong sense of identity, in the sense Erik Erikson (1968) has given to this phrase in reference to adolescent development. Erikson's "identity diffusion" would be a good fit for Alan. Alan finds it difficult to identify with either parent. He denigrates both, seeing his mother as concerned about him, but in an anxious and ineffectual way. His view of her is that she is weak, inconsistent, and unable to take a stand or to set appropriate limits, including limits for herself (she can't stop smoking) and for Alan. His father he views as an angry, morose, aloof man who tries to support Alan on occasion, but who seems to be preoccupied with his own possible traumatic experiences from the troubled part of Europe from which his parents came to Canada. His primary experience of his father is outbursts of rage which are not predictable.

Alan's typical way of expressing himself can be intense, but also highly intellectualised in a very detailed and complicated manner. His associative monologues are rich and detailed, but for me very difficult to sort out. The visual analogue I experience when I listen to him is looking at an extremely verdant and wildly tangled stretch of jungle, with twisting vines everywhere, teeming with animals, animal sounds, and riotous colours. It is a magnificent display, but how can I find an entrance into such dense and tangled growth? Which vine can I grab onto to make a start?

His initial transference to me was one of hopeful but limited engagement—limited because he wanted to talk only in conceptual/ theoretical/intellectual ways. Over the course of several years, Alan has become more able to confront and speak about his feelings, but always with the possibility of him slipping away from feelings and becoming lost to my sight in the tangled intellectual vines of his discourse. The countertransference he induces in me is a mixture of pleasure at the intellectual exchanges I can have with this extremely bright young man, along with a degree of disappointed frustration in my attempts to connect with him on the basis of his emotions. This has eased more recently as Alan becomes able to speak of feeling states for increasingly longer stretches of his discourse.

One aspect of Alan that I treasure is his frankness and his ability to correct or supplement what I say, so that I can feel on track with his own thinking, and more recently, feeling. You will hear our first dialogue at a point where he corrects me in a typical way, and also describes a split in his own self-experience. This dialogue between us is a relatively infrequent aspect of our therapeutic relationship. Much of the time, Alan speaks at length in a free associative manner familiar to most psychoanalytic dyads. Our dialogues almost always occur, as does what follows, after I have listened to Alan for some time, and I finally intervene.

ROBIN: So … from what you've been saying so far, it sounds like there are sort of two aspects to your experience? A sort of demanding part that wants a childhood; wants a dad who is not so critical of you, and, uh, sort of an inner father-conscience that wants you to comply?

ALAN: No, it's different from that. The two aspects—I experience them as having different ages, a kid part and, uh, I can't describe it, but more like a veteran.

ROBIN: So "kid Alan" and "veteran Alan". When you …

ALAN: Yeah. That's right. And they're years apart, a very young teen and an old man, or at least an older teen.

ROBIN: So the kid part feels …?

ALAN: It's full of energy and vitality. But the veteran; he's tired, cynical, no energy.

ROBIN: And the kid Alan part, he's angry at your dad for all the yelling that …

ALAN: You keep talking about my dad. But it's more my mother. I got nothing from her. There's a great emptiness there, a blank space. I was playing computer games, yesterday, near the end of school study week. So she sees this and all she says is, "Alan it's almost the end of study week". I was furious. The kid part wanted to fight with her and went up to her to yell at her. But the, uh, veteran sort of guided the kid and it ended up I spoke to her but didn't fight.

ROBIN: I think I get it. Kid Alan felt misunderstood, like you were just taking a break but her comment, her intrusion, made you, made the kid feel criticised, denigrated?

ALAN: Yeah, the kid was pretty angry and the veteran tried to guide it.

ROBIN: I don't know but I get the feeling the kid can feel sort of entitled, like it was *owed* a decent childhood by your parents, especially your mother. Maybe kid even feels he's going to stick it out in the parental home until the decent childhood gets delivered?

ALAN: I'm not sure; sounds like it could be right.

ROBIN: Well, maybe it's partly correct. We'll see what more comes to mind and try to get it fully correct. But the veteran part, it has sort of a paternal relationship with the kid, like has fears about it, and wants to give support, understanding, help and like you said, guidance?

ALAN: (In a complaining tone of voice) Exactly! That's what I was
         trying to tell you. Guiding and helping.

ROBIN: Okay, good, you're helping me understand your experience of
         how these two aspects, uh, interact with each other. And the
         kid part, from what you've told me before, he may be all over,
         uh, all over the place sexually?

ALAN: Well, when I masturbate, I have dominant fantasies and sub-
         missive ones, mostly submissive, but the veteran is dominant
         in my personality.

The split in the self between his kid part and his veteran part is quite
clear from this piece of dialogue, this being my motivation for selecting
it. Things are not as simple or straightforward as suggested in this dialogue from relatively early in his treatment, however. In Chapter Nine,
"Psychodynamics", I present a piece of dialogue from later on in Alan's
treatment relationship with me, indicating further "sub-splitting" in the
kid *vs.* veteran split.

At this point, I want to present another piece of dialogue from very
recently in Alan's treatment. This has to do with his identification as
being a "sub", who wants to be submissive in his sexual activity. Alan
is now almost twenty-two years of age, and has not yet engaged in
any actual sexual activity with a partner. Nevertheless, his identification as being a "sub" seems to find a very close match to the sexual
feelings and fantasies expressed by Anthony in the next chapter. My
initial sense of things, deriving from my relationship with both Alan
and Anthony, is that the split they experience in their sexuality between
being dominant and being submissive is the "sexual echo" of the main
split in their personality between the victim aspect and the bully aspect.
I don't think it's as simple as bully being equivalent to sexual dominance and victim as equivalent to sexual submissiveness. As I have
endeavoured to show, there are likely to be shifts in which part of the
split is most readily observable in the adolescent's personality functioning. As Alan explicitly states in the piece of dialogue above, "when I
masturbate, I have dominant fantasies and submissive ones". How the
bully *vs.* victim split may find expression in the sexual fantasies and
functioning of adolescent and adult Asperger's sufferers may be useful
to understand.

Although Alan had frequently mentioned feelings around him being
predominantly submissive in his sexuality, there seemed to have been
no room to really explore this theme at any length. In the very recent

dialogue presented below, Alan spontaneously took this theme up and then enabled us to struggle with it at some length.

ALAN: That makes me want to talk more about being a "sub", uh, sexually submissive, like we talked about before. But we also talked about BDSM [bondage, discipline, and sadomasochism], and I don't really think I fit into that category.

ROBIN: Okay. Let's hear what's on your mind.

ALAN: Well, it has to do with how I use pornography. Something I find exciting is the sort of incest stuff you can find, like the mother/son stuff, but for me it's not the incest, I don't find the incest part exciting. It's more, like, about control. Okay so there was a girl in one of my classes who seemed to like me a lot. She flirted with me a lot. She came on to me like, kind of helpless and looking up to me for protection. It turned me right off. Some of the other kids in my class said she was interested, and yeah, she was good-looking, and so when I shrugged about it, they wondered, they knew she was interested in me and they wondered, asked me, why I didn't pursue her. She wasn't my type.

ROBIN: Not your type?

ALAN: I don't want to have control, like give protection or tell her what to do; I don't want to be the director about how things are going to go. Like, even with vanilla sexuality …

ROBIN: Sorry; *vanilla*?

ALAN: Yeah, like with two completely normal people, bland and vanilla, and they both find submissiveness and dominance as being difficult and awkward, I mean both partners have some degree of submissiveness and some degree of dominance, so they have to struggle, they have to work it out—like who would do what in what situation and who would have control, call the shots, be the director. It's so much easier, and more exciting, for one to be dominant and the other to be submissive.

ROBIN: Okay if I suggest something now?

ALAN: Yeah, please.

ROBIN: Well, I wonder if you experience submissiveness kind of like it's equivalent to getting something, I mean getting care and attention, and from someone who cares enough to take you in hand, so to speak, to tell you how things should go and take from you the unwanted and, uh, the burdensome responsibility of directing and orchestrating the sexual interaction.

ALAN: Uh, I think you, uh, may be on the right track—can you maybe say a little more?

ROBIN: Well, I'm thinking this is where your mother in the incest, the pseudo-incest stuff could come in. Like your experience was that your mother could never be dominant with you in the form of actively providing what you need and actively bringing it to you, that is, without her anxiety messing it all up. And someone taking control sort of feels like it sort of compensates for what you felt was missing from how your mother was.

ALAN: Well, like I said, I really want the other person to take control.

ROBIN: Could it be that "control" here means for you kind of a guarantee that, like a mother should be, your needs are going to be taken into account, responded to; you are going to be relieved of the responsibility of taking control and the other person is going to care enough to take over and bring what you need right to you.

ALAN: Uh, I feel you're at least getting closer to what it is I experience.

ROBIN: It makes me think about dealing with tension.

ALAN: Tell me about what you mean.

ROBIN: Ejaculation is a release of tension. For you to be excited and then experience the release of tension you need to be submissive and to feel in the submissive position and that releases the burden and the tension for you, of saying how things should go, and the tension of needing to be a sort of manager or director of the sexual encounter. It's almost the mother–child thing, like I said, where it's not incest but the mother has to take control of helping the child manage and deal with his tension.

ALAN: Yeah, well, okay, that sounds like it's just about right.

This dialogue provides a brief but suggestive glance into the intertwined relationships that may exist for many Asperger's people among their experiences of a deficit in the reverie and containing capacity of the mother early in their lives, the split in their selves between the bully and victim aspects, and what precipitates out as a result in their sexual lives, fantasies, and identifications during adolescence in terms of their experiences of submissiveness and dominance as important aspects of their sexuality. More information is provided about this theme as we come to grips with the experiences of Anthony in the next chapter, and some of the details he provides about his experiences as a "sub" in the world of BDSM (bondage, discipline, and sadomasochism).

Some clinical dialogues with Asperger's patients—Anthony, age thirty-one

I was only able to meet with Anthony between the times he was thirty-one years old and when he was thirty-three. The dialogue given below stems from earlier in the treatment when he was thirty-one. Along with Thomas in Chapter Four, and also Jack who does not make his appearance until Chapter Sixteen, Anthony is a good representative of what I call the uninhibited/aggressive type of Asperger's, which includes people who are "object-rejecting" in the conduct of their external object relations. Anthony was a hulking, physically imposing, tall, and muscular young man who still lived with his parents. His robust, imposing, and hulking physique made his interest in the cartoon figure called the "Hulk" seem highly appropriate for him. He had fantasies about the Hulk, and about Bob Banner, who is the Hulk's nerdy and reclusive alter ego. It was certainly not difficult to see Anthony as functioning in the same split kind of way as the cartoon figure, with an imposing and even intimidating exterior, but with a rather nerdy and somewhat inhibited and reclusive underlying personality. It took Anthony and me a while to feel at ease with each other in the transference/countertransference that developed. The treatment felt to me like a sort of hide-and-seek ballet, in which we sometimes came closer and then were distanced from each other in a repetitive clinical *pas de deux*.

Anthony had dropped out of political science studies at university, and spent his time working out at the gym and attending meetings of what he initially referred to as "people similar to me". It took us well over a year of psychotherapy for him to fully explain to me that he and the people who were "similar" to him all belonged to a group of people who participated in "BDSM". In response to my puzzled look when he first used this term, he explained to me that this referred to "bondage, discipline, and sadomasochism". He went on to patiently explain to me his world of "doms" (those who assume a dominant role in sexual relationships) and "subs" (those who take the subordinate or masochistic role). He further explained that he is a "sub" who wants to find a woman who is a "dom" with whom he can have a satisfying and long-term relationship; but that he experiences despair about how likely it is he will succeed in this quest.

When he first began to discuss his sexuality with me, Anthony was extremely hesitant and cautious. It required some time before he was able to be less cautious in how he spoke to me. He spoke of feeling humiliation, indicating that there were times he had problems with impotence when he was with a woman. As he built up a degree of confidence that I would not denigrate his sexual preferences and that I would be, in his words, "supportive" of his sexual orientation, he said he did not mind seeing men's bodies and that he might be bisexual, but with a preference for women.

Both the sadistic and masochistic aspects of his sexual functioning were described quite clearly. Even though he would give detailed descriptions of both aspects mixed together in what he said, they seemed to be strongly separated from each other in his mind no matter how closely they were linked in terms of his external (and internal) object relations. The sadistic aspects tended to take the form of intense self-righteous anger and fantasies of revenge which on occasion threatened to spill over into physical violence.

One example of this was the intense hurt, anger, and revengefulness he described to me when he was referred to as a "do-me sub" by another member of his BDSM group. He spoke about the punishment of and the infliction of erotic pain on the sub or masochist as being one of the most difficult issues in the world of BDSM. He explained to me that he had personal and moral limits as to what he would and wouldn't tolerate from a "dom" in his role as her "sub". He reported that during a BDSM group discussion, a woman had publicly challenged him on these limits, saying that a "sub" such as him shouldn't have such hard and fast limits. She called him a "do-me sub". This, he explained to me in a careful and detailed fashion, meant a subordinate who wanted his dominant partner to "do him" sexually without being willing to reciprocate in the satisfaction of his "dom" partner's sadistic wishes. He was extremely angry at being called a "do-me sub", and described in a very sadistic way how he would like to take revenge on the woman who had called him this. In addition, present at the group discussion was another young man whom he described as having a "dom" and sadistic orientation and who sided with the woman whom he felt had humiliated him. Anthony told me he had come close to engaging in a fistfight with this other young man.

Anthony's transference might best be described as him hopefully wary of me, and full of uncertainty. His way of relating to me was mostly characterised by caution and tentativeness, though this was mitigated by his sense of restrained hopefulness. My countertransference had elements of strong curiosity but also a degree of wariness as well, because I felt I needed to handle him with kid gloves. This came both from my sense of his own vulnerability and how much he felt hurt by others as a child, and also from a sense that there were parts of him which were more ominous and hostile. At times, he made me feel quite uncomfortable about the possibility of him engaging in some sort of physical violence outside of his sessions, describing situations in which he came close to fistfights. I was also well aware of his height and robustness when he entered my office. The transference/countertransference matrix developed into a dialectical dance between us involving both curiosity and cautiousness. In Racker's (1974, p. 136) terminology, this seemed to be a concordant countertransference.

Anthony had been subjected to ridicule and ostracism in high school. He described one incident in which he brought a knife to school hidden in his pants, vowing to himself to kill the first person who ridiculed him. Fortunately, he did not hurt anyone or even display his knife. There were numerous other incidents, such as the "near fistfight" in his BDSM meeting mentioned above, and a time in a locker room when two kids were talking in a highly disparaging manner about another student who was "nerdy" like Anthony. Anthony bumped into one of these students in what could have been a prelude to a fight. He always seemed to be on the edge of some kind of physical violence. Had Anthony ever crossed the line and ended up in jail, Hans Asperger might well have not been very surprised to meet him there.

There were many dichotomous representations in what Anthony described to me over the years, all of these in some way representing the split in his self. Among these dichotomies were the cartoon figure called "the Hulk" *vs*. Bob Banner (the Hulk's nerdy and reclusive alter ego), Obama *vs*. Bush/McCain, Israel *vs*. Palestine and sadism *vs*. masochism (or what amounted to the same thing, "dom" vs. "sub"). In the session you are about to overhear, Anthony begins by speaking of his recent experiences at a BDSM meeting.

ANTHONY: Have you heard of—do you know what a "munch" is?

ROBIN: A "munch"? No, I don't think so.

ANTHONY: It's when a group of kinks, uh, people with kinky sexual tastes, BDSM people like me, get together for lunch and there's a speech, one of them makes a speech.

ROBIN: Okay.

ANTHONY: Well, I went to one last week and I made a speech. I hate making speeches, scares me to hell, but I made a speech.

ROBIN: You'll tell me about it?

ANTHONY: Of course—I talked about assumptions, some incorrect assumptions I'd made ... with a woman, and so things went poorly between us. (I wondered about the transference implications of things going poorly).

ROBIN: As in sexually poorly?

ANTHONY: Yes. But the woman was at the munch where I spoke. So I went up to her, uh, up to her at the end after the speech, and ... I said I hoped she wasn't offended by my using our relationship to talk about. And she said she wasn't, but uh, she'd prefer not to talk about it right there. But then I, I got the idea, noticed, she was talking too loud and there were other people who could hear. And one of the people was that jerk Arnie—I told you about him—he was standing near and it turned out she was with him. His bio [biography] says he's a sub, but I've heard some stories about him being sadistic, like how he confronted his boss at work. Anyway, Arnie came up to her and I left, and I tried to put on a poker face when he walked by—I hate him.

ROBIN: So there was no confrontation between you? (asked hopefully).

ANTHONY: There was a verbal one later, no physical one, though I almost wish there had been. Huh, I don't know if I could beat anyone in a real fight. I took taekwondo and I won my sparring matches, but in a real fight, I don't know about a real fight. I tried to stay away from Arnie (said with apparent shame) and I don't know if he could hurt me in a fight. He threatened to put me in the hospital.

ROBIN: You're pretty big?

ANTHONY: Arnie isn't a small person. And (pushing back his sleeve to show his forearm and upper arm) my arm isn't as thick or well-developed as in a lot of people.

ROBIN: (Sensing a wish for admiration and possibly a sexual undercurrent) You seem pretty strong?

ANTHONY: I'm thinking about a dream I have a lot. Someone is taunting me and getting into a fight with me. I hit this other person as hard as I can but it has no effect on them, so I feel like I'm as weak as a baby.

ROBIN: (Wondering about the transference implications of the dream—does he experience me as taunting him and himself as unable to have any effect on me?) So you know what I do; I ask you what comes to mind about the dream.

ANTHONY: Uh, it's like something that actually happened to me in high school, now that I think about it. There was a guy, forget his name, and he was taunting me beyond, beyond my bloody endurance. So finally I just grabbed him and I punched him as hard as I could in the face. He sure looked surprised but it didn't seem to hurt him. So I hit him twice more and the same thing happened. Then, the teacher finally noticed and sent both of us to the principal's office. We both got suspended for a day.

ROBIN: And that was it?

ANTHONY: When I got back to school after the suspension day, the other students taunted me.

ROBIN: They treated you like you were a bully?

ANTHONY: Yeah, but I got the feeling they were taunting me because I was weak, ineffectual, like I really didn't hurt the other kid at all.

ROBIN: It's almost time to finish, so I'll try to pull together some threads from the dream and from what happened between you and Arnie. My experience is that everyone is likely to have both sadistic and masochistic aspects, but in most people these usually work together pretty smoothly so the person can respond as the situation requires. But for you, maybe for Arnie too, it's like the sadistic and masochistic parts are more separate and isolated, almost like they were different or even antagonistic aspects of yourself. I wonder if it's like you've been in a fight all your life, an internal fight, so that your sadistic and masochistic parts battle for supremacy inside you. Based on what you've told me today and over the months, your sadistic part attacks the masochistic part as hard as it can, like in the dream, but the masochistic part takes all that your sadism can give it and shows itself to be strong and unhurtable, maybe even taunting your sadistic aspect in some way. It also sounded like you activated the sadistic component in Arnie and maybe Arnie activated the masochistic part of you. But we'll come back to this.

ANTHONY: That's a lot. Maybe you're right but I hope the part about Arnie isn't because I don't want to be submissive to him.

Although I have suggested that Anthony belongs to the uninhibited/ aggressive type of Asperger's, the label is a general one and certainly does not capture all aspects of the functioning of the person, Anthony included. There are certainly some quite inhibited aspects to his everyday functioning, but the general flavour he communicated was that he was always teetering on the edge of some kind of aggressive action, whether this was verbal in nature or approaching outright physical violence.

As with Alan, from the previous chapter, the "dom" and "sub" aspects of his sexuality seem to be the "erotic echoes" of a fundamental split in the self between victim and bully. In his fantasies, projective identification into remote objects was also clearly in evidence, including his interest in the Hulk, with Bob banner as a split off aspect of the self of the Hulk, Israel *vs*. Palestine with both being seen in the light of victim and bully, and Obama *vs*. Bush with Bush certainly taking on the role of bully in his mind. Based on the very limited evidence which I have been able to collect over the years, I do get the strong impression that when the Asperger's child reaches adolescence, the split in the self between victim and bully is often likely to find some kind of expression in the sexual functioning and fantasies of the Asperger's adolescent. These fantasies may present themselves as a bully and victim in the sexual form of "dom" and "sub".

CHAPTER NINE

The psychodynamics of Asperger's children

In my experience, every child, adolescent, and adult whom I have treated for a sufficient length of time (say, for at least six months) and who has clearly been diagnosed with Asperger's (meaning by at least two qualified professionals) has demonstrated a combination of *splitting of the self* and *projective identification into remote objects* as central features of their ongoing psychodynamics. As Grotstein (1981, p. 131) points out so clearly, splitting and projective identification work hand-in-hand. With Asperger's patients, I would say these two ways of functioning work hand in glove. Grotstein's statement is that "Splitting and projective identification work hand in hand. Generally speaking, projective identification works as an adjunct to splitting by assigning a split-off percept or self to a container for postponement or for eradication". This is highly apposite in reference to Asperger's persons.

I describe each of these psychodynamic features, splitting of the self and projective identification into remote objects, in more detail below. But first, there is an important question to be fielded. Am I claiming that the two features, splitting of the self and projective identification into remote objects, are a *sine qua non* of Asperger's? Am I claiming that these two features are *pathognomonic* of Asperger's? We might also rephrase these two questions using the simpler language of *necessary and sufficient conditions*. The first question then becomes whether or not the two features, splitting of the self and projective identification into remote objects, are together a *necessary condition* for the diagnosis of Asperger's. The second question is whether or not they are together a *sufficient condition* for the diagnosis. The first question I would answer with a hesitant affirmative, simply because I have not yet encountered an Asperger's patient who, given sufficient time in psychotherapy, has failed to clearly show both of these features. Together they may comprise a necessary condition for diagnosing Asperger's. As to these features being pathognomonic of Asperger's and therefore by themselves a sufficient condition to make a diagnosis of Asperger's, I am less certain. Because these two features are not "observation statements" which can be consensually verified on the basis of observation and interviewing, they certainly would not qualify for inclusion in a diagnostic manual such as the DSM. Whether this combination of two features is *exclusive* to Asperger's and could therefore be used as a basis for diagnosis by an informed psychoanalytic therapist, I am not certain. Later, I suggest in more detail how they might be used in the diagnosis and the understanding of Asperger's. Splitting of the self and projective identification each occurs in a number of psychological disorders. Whether the combination of the two (when the projective identification is into "remote objects" as will shortly be described)—whether this combination is *unique* to Asperger's, I am not sure. I strongly suspect that it is. Further contributions from the therapeutic community may clarify this.

Splitting

In Asperger's children, the splitting of the self is registered in the numerous dichotomies which regularly and inevitably populate their way of communicating, and which appear in their behaviour and emotional life as well. I have experienced no Asperger's patient yet in which the split of bully *vs.* bullied has not been central. Ways in which Asperger's children have described this central split in the self include tormentor *vs.* tormented, abuser and abused, sadist and masochist, victimiser and victim, attacker and attacked, dominator and dominated (or submissive one), rejecting *vs.* accepting, enraged one *vs.* ashamed one, and powerful *vs.* weak. There are many other dichotomies. In describing Asperger's children, it might be helpful to use the generic description of "*bully* vs. *victim*" to describe their split self.

Splits in the self are regularly accompanied by splits in internal objects. These splits in the self are projected into the outside world of external (and remote) objects. The two most common ways these splits are projected and expressed are by perceptions of "fair *vs*. unfair" and "just *vs*. unjust". There are many other ways of projecting the split self. The Asperger's patient frequently describes his own typical and idiosyncratic ways of experiencing the split self and the split internal objects as they are projected into the external world. Recall some of Anthony's ways of experiencing these splits—dominant *vs*. subordinate, Israel *vs*. Palestine, and Obama *vs*. Bush/McCain. Matt was prolific in his ways of experiencing his split, including observer (of life) *vs*. participant (in life), immigrant *vs*. resident (in reference to his sense of his own life), beast *vs*. Brainiac, Calvin *vs*. Hobbes, and his most frequent way of experiencing his own split self, the split of antelope *vs*. tiger.

Alan experienced the split in his self in the form of a kid part and a veteran part, and to a lesser extent, like Anthony, as dominant *vs*. submissive.

Multiple splitting in Asperger's

At this point, a caveat is needed which will temporarily take us away from the main line of our discussion. A dichotomy between two different aspects of the self in Asperger's people is likely to be *schematically* correct, though the situation may not always be so straightforward or so simple. The idea of a bifurcation or a binary split in the self between a bully aspect and a victim aspect is likely applicable to all Asperger's children and is likely accurate as far as it goes. However, what the therapist actually encounters in psychotherapy can be more complex than just a binary split. The splitting processes which come into view are sometimes more complicated than a single split between a bully aspect and a victim aspect. Stated directly, there sometimes seem to be multiple splits in the self at work in Asperger's children.

Consider two patients. These two patients are Thanos and Alan. Their therapies still continue, and the multiple splits they report are still in the process of being understood. Recall that with Thanos (Chapter Five), we heard about a central aspect of his split which conforms to the picture of a fundamental split between a bully aspect (the Turkish part of the split) and a victim aspect (the Greek part of the split). This picture was complicated by other splits which were uncovered, including both a Bulgarian and a Macedonian aspect. The nature of the full process of multiple splits in the self of Thanos awaits clarification in his therapy.

Recently, a more complex picture of the splitting processes used by Alan (Chapter Seven) has also arisen in his therapy. Recall from the part of the therapy which you heard in the dialogue that was presented that the basic binary split he reported conformed well to the schematic model I suggest here. There was a split between the "veteran" aspect (representing the bully part) and the "kid" aspect (representing the victim part). More recently, however, and developing from the interplay of transference and countertransference and co-constructed between both participants, came a more complicated picture of a splitting of the self. This involved a "trichotomy" or tripartite aspects of the self. The picture Alan and I co-constructed involved the "veteran" aspect, but with a further split in the "kid" aspect including what Alan referred to as the "dead kid" aspect along with a "living kid" aspect having the potential for growth. The "dead kid" aspect seemed to be that part of his childhood which he missed when he, in his own words, "grew up too fast". The sense we developed together was that of cumulative trauma resulting from an anxious and uncertain mother unable to contain his emotions or his projective identifications. This combined with the impact of an angry and critical father, whom he experienced as intrusive, and who was likely traumatised and damaged by his own military experiences. The "dead kid" part encapsulates his own sense of deadness and is likely the locus of his depressed feelings as well. The "veteran" aspect was for Alan clearly a *military* veteran, the part of him that had gone "through the wars" and had suffered traumatic emotional neglect and intrusions when he was growing up, instead of him being allowed to go through the normal stages of growth that a kid should experience. As we understood it together, it was as if this "veteran" aspect suffers from post-traumatic stress as a result of cumulative emotional traumas and has as a consequence closed Alan down emotionally and frozen his feelings. Together, the deadness of the dead kid aspect and the emotional coldness of the veteran aspect produced the depressing sense of internal deadness and coldness which is so central and so disruptive for Alan.

The veteran aspect seems, from the perspective of the most recent developments in Alan's ongoing therapy, to be the main and the strongest part of his self-structure. He described his feeling that this part of him is not capable of love, at least not yet. The veteran aspect is the cold, emotionally deadened aspect which cannot tolerate the risks and dangers involved in being able to love and the risks of being open to the feelings of others. This part experiences the risk of loving and the risk of being open to experiencing the emotions of others as also opening the entire self to the risk of hurtful emotional re-traumatisation.

The veteran aspect is experienced by Alan as highly protective. This aspect is vigilant and energetic in its desire to protect the "living kid with potential for growth" aspect, segregate it away from the other parts of his self and deeply (as well as protectively) split it off within his person-ality. In fact, the "veteran" aspect seems to have some kind of alliance with the "dead kid" aspect, resulting in their interaction increasing the persecutory anxieties of both aspects and in making Alan's overall per-sonality functioning feel so dead and cold to him. The "veteran" aspect seems to have good intentions toward the "living kid" aspect and to even be overprotective toward this aspect in a sort of parental fashion. The urgent message "veteran" gives to "living kid" is along the lines of: "get down, take cover, hide away, protect yourself—never ever risk the dangers of emotional warmth and love". In overprotecting the "living kid" aspect to the degree that it does, the "veteran" aspect also deeply splits off the living kid aspect (or facilitates such a split) and sequesters and quarantines "living kid", preventing warm contact with others and blocking the potential for love. Perhaps "living kid" has in fact survived the traumas Alan has experienced and has retained some potential for growth and love *precisely by* being deeply split off and thus insulated both from reality and from the other aspects of the self, especially the cynically despairing deadness of the "dead kid" aspect.

Whether the split between "dead kid" and "living kid" is a subsidiary or a sub-split and is subordinate to the "main split" between "veteran" and "kid" and therefore involves some kind of hierarchical ordering of splittings within the self, or whether instead the split between "dead kid" and "living kid" is on the same level of organisation as the split between "veteran" and "kid"—these issues still remain to be clarified as Alan's therapy unfolds.

To summarise the two points I wanted to make in undertaking this digression: dichotomies are strongly characteristic of the functioning of the self in Asperger's—but the situation can also become considerably more complicated than just dichotomies. It is likely accurate to sug-gest a fundamental and binary split in the self with Asperger's people, a split between bully and victim aspects. But the situation can be more complex than just this fundamental binary split. Second, I point to Frances Tustin's idea of the traumatic origins of autism in children (at least, those children whom she describes as not being brain-damaged). The therapy of Alan suggests possible traumatic aspects in his background. This opens the possibility of some kind of trauma, including cumulative trauma, in the background of some and possibly of many or even all Asperger's sufferers.

Trauma as part of Asperger's

The discussion of trauma involves a second digression before returning to the main theme. There is a tension throughout psychoanalytic writings as to whether autism (in particular) should be considered as psychogenic, and as specifically traumatic in origin, or whether it is instead fundamentally a neurological disorder with psychological consequences. A similar tension is also present between proponents of a psychogenic/traumatic origin for Asperger's and those who view it in a neurological light. In her paper entitled "On psychogenic autism", Tustin (1993, p. 35) gives a very specific point of view, stating that autism "is a reaction that is specific to the pain of a particular trauma", this trauma occurring when the infant "has been overly close to the suckling mother" (ibid, p. 36) and then "the pathological closeness between the infant and the suckling mother has been disrupted by sudden and unexpected awareness of their separateness from each other" (Tustin, 1993, p. 36).

Grotstein (1997) though in many ways highly sympathetic to Tustin, is also highly dubious about a traumatic origin for autism. He quotes Tustin's central claim—that autism is essentially a form of infantile post-traumatic stress disorder, resulting from the shock of a premature and "traumatic awareness in infancy of bodily separateness from the mothering person" (Grotstein, 1997, p. 259). His conclusion is that "autism is a developmental disorder of the central nervous system" (ibid, p. 279), and that Tustin's theory of psychogenic autism "is more and more problematic" and her idea of the traumatic origin of autism "is equally if not even more problematic". He goes on to write that autism is "a nontraumatic disorder of development", and "a predominantly neurological disorder" (ibid, p. 282). However, he still remains optimistic that "psychoanalytically informed psychotherapy" can be "of substantial value" (ibid, p. 280) in the treatment of autism. He does not specify how he sees it as being of value.

Cecchi (1990, p. 403) provides a detailed case history of a little girl "who developed an autistic syndrome as a reaction to a traumatic situation", thus giving some evidence for trauma in the aetiology of autism. Mitrani (2010) uses research on mirror neurons in an attempt to lessen the gap between neuroscientific understanding and psychoanalytic understanding (the latter based on Tustin's ideas) of autism. Mitrani suggests (2010, p. 255) an interaction between neurobiology and mother-infant relationships involving "hypersensitive children" with a "precocious capacity" to perceive the mother's insecurities and who try to take over her functions of holding and containment, but who as a result suffer from an impoverished environment with detrimental impacts on their neural development. In other words, biologically based endowments can, within certain mother-infant dyads, eventuate in traumatic situations which impede neural development. I suggest the possibility of a similar kind of situation with Asperger's children.

Most psychoanalytic writers are quite clear about the neurological underpinnings of Asperger's. Pozzi (2003, p. 1336) comments that Asperger's children may be "easily distressed and highly sensitive to stimuli" as was her patient, and may as a result experience "a lack of adequate containment". Shuttleworth (1999, p. 239) is very clear about "the innate origins of Asperger's syndrome", including "a less than optimal neurological endowment" (ibid, p. 241). There is perhaps "damage, very early in foetal development, to the neurological structures that deliver the experience of primary intersubjectivity" (ibid, p. 262). Allured (2006, p. 398) agrees, noting that "innate neurobiological deficits are life-long".

Perhaps keeping an open mind about the possibility of traumatic aspects in the early development of (at least some) Asperger's children would be beneficial. This is certainly not to suggest there are no neurological differences or difficulties for Asperger's children—there most decidedly are neurological problems. The appropriate note can perhaps be struck by referring to the paper by Cecchi (1990) mentioned previously and at the same time noting some comments by Allured (2006). Cecchi (1990, p. 403), as noted previously, describes a little girl who developed an "autistic syndrome" in response to a horrific and overwhelming trauma. Allured (2006, p. 403) urges us for treatment purposes to respect "the differentiation between autism and environmentally reactive autistic-like depressions" but then goes on to make the comment that in many cases, "these two aetiologies overlap, as the autism spectrum child repeatedly has traumatic interactions with others". I want to sound a note that harmonises with this. Might it be that the neurological difficulties of the Asperger's infant repeatedly interfere with and interrupt the infant–mother relationship, disrupting "the experience of primary intersubjectivity" as Shuttleworth noted, and further that this repeated disruption of the infant's experience of primary intersubjectivity regularly adds up to a cumulative trauma? In other words, are neurological deficits and trauma interwoven and inseparable for the Asperger's infant? I cannot answer this question. I can suggest that the question is worthy of our consideration.

Ideas about cumulative trauma proposed by Khan (1963, 1964) seem to fit quite well with what may happen in the development of Asperger's children. His ideas also seem to fit very well with the concept of container/contained and maternal reverie developed by Bion. Khan argues that cumulative trauma "is the result of the breaches in the mother's role as a protective shield over the whole course of the child's development, from infancy to adolescence" (Khan, 1963, p. 290), such that breaches in the mother's role as a protective shield "are not traumatic singly", but instead they occur over the course of time "and through the developmental process cumulate silently and invisibly" (ibid). Such breaches in the mother's role as a protective shield for the child are not traumatic at the time they occur or in the context in which they happen, but they "achieve the value of trauma only cumulatively and in retrospect". Khan also notes (1963, p. 295) that instances of the mother's role as a protective shield breaking down may occur when some kind of constitutional sensitivity imposes "an impossible task on the mother". This kind of cumulative trauma is said to operate and to build up silently throughout childhood and right up to adolescence. Khan notes (1964, p. 273) that for cumulative trauma to occur, failures on the part of the mother in her function as a protective shield must be "significantly frequent and have the rhythm of a pattern" so that the pathogenic reactions of the infant to these failures begins a process which both "interferes with the mother's adaptation to the infant" and with the child's ego development. Instead of building up a coherent ego structure, "multiple dissociations take place intrapsychically." Khan's ideas about cumulative trauma are highly suggestive when applied to the development of Asperger's children. Although he uses the notion of the mother being "a protective shield", his ideas can also be integrated with those of Bion about container and contained.

There are a number of additional therapists whose writings present a strong case for the presence of trauma in the aetiology of autistic children, and by extension in that of Asperger's children as well. These authors include Fargione (2013), Reid (1999), and Spoladore (2013). Reid in particular argues strongly and persuasively for a diagnostic entity she calls APTDD (autistic post-traumatic developmental disorder). As a result of her evidence, I have included autistic post-traumatic developmental disorder in the tentative nosology of autism spectrum disorders presented in Chapter Fourteen "The differential diagnosis of Asperger's children".

Fargione (2013, p. 178) refers to her patient Martin. She describes him as having "primitive states of mind filled with fears of separateness", along with precocious intellectual development. She feels his precociousness likely contributed to the development of autism. She concludes that his "precocious intellectual development may have made him aware of separateness before he was emotionally ready for such awareness." Her position seems quite compatible with that of Tustin, suggesting as it does that his precocious awareness of separateness was traumatic for him to the extent that autism was the result.

Spoladore discusses "how traumatic events in the first two years of life may cause a child to withdraw from social relationships" (Spoladore, 2013, p. 22) and to develop autism. She underlines (ibid, p. 23) that these are "children who were not born autistic but developed autistic symptoms after a precipitating traumatic event in the first two years of life", and emphasises that "some sort of trauma is central to the autistic withdrawal". Biological predispositions find a place in her thinking. Referring to Reid (1999b), she notes (Spoladore, 2013, p. 24) that "children with APTDD [autistic post-traumatic developmental disorder] may have an innate predisposition to trauma due to extreme sensitivity and intolerance of frustration". She adds that "what may be felt as mildly unpleasant for some babies, can be perceived as overwhelming and traumatising to others" (ibid, p. 24). As a result, she concludes that "what seems to be a genetic impairment may in reality be a case of very early APTDD". Spoladore (2013, p. 29) then gives details about her patient Serge, suggesting that "his autistic-like behaviours originated from early trauma" rather than being "biological ASD" (autism spectrum disorder) and that Serge's presentation "was consistent with the diagnosis of APTDD as proposed by Reid (1999) in many aspects".

Reid makes the hypothesis "that an experience of trauma in the first two years of life may be a precipitating factor in the development of autism" (Reid, 1999, p. 93) in a sub-group of children, so that for this sub-group, the factor of trauma "may have combined with a biological or genetic predisposition in the infant which the traumatising event has then served to activate." She is specific about predisposing biological factors, Reid (1999, p. 106) indicating that based on their case histories, "many of the children in this sub-group, especially in those cases where the traumatising event was primarily psychological, seemed to have been particularly thin-skinned, hypersensitive from infancy, and therefore especially vulnerable to the emotional atmospheres of their environments." She underlines (ibid, p. 94) "that it is the *impact of trauma in infancy* which precipitates an autistic withdrawal, leading to developmental delay" and for this "proposed variant of autism", suggests the name APTDD (Autistic Post-Traumatic Developmental Disorder) (italics from original).

This provides only a brief summary of the work done on trauma as a precipitating factor in the development of autism and in the development of Asperger's. We would probably do well to keep our minds open about the possibility of trauma in the development of Asperger's, and to be particularly open to the ideas about *cumulative trauma* proposed by Khan.

Splitting in Asperger's

To return now to the main line of discussion, consider Dan as he was described in Chapter Six. Like Alan, Dan was also highly prolific in how he experienced the split in his self and in his internal objects. His ways of experiencing these splits included warrior *vs.* priest in the dialogue we overheard, as well as King Kong *vs.* humanity, Martin Luther King *vs.* Malcolm X, Attila the Hun *vs.* Rome, and others. The fundamental cleavage, however, was between bully aspects (as represented by humanity, Malcolm X and Rome) as opposed to victim aspects (as represented by King Kong, Martin Luther King and Attila the Hun).

Similar to Matt, Thomas described his split self in terms of pussycat *vs.* tiger. For Thanos, his representation of the split self was more complex, but centred on Turkey and Bulgaria *vs.* Greece, with the complicating aspects just described.

The original contribution by Freud to the concept of splitting of the ego occurs in the two papers "An outline of psychoanalysis" (1940a) and "Splitting of the ego in the process of defence" (1940e). The ego splits under the pressure of contrary reactions to a conflict (between a demand by an instinct and the prohibition by reality), the conflict being generated by a psychical trauma. The splitting results from "disavowal" of a portion of reality (thus introducing another defence mechanism) and refusal to accept instinctual prohibitions, along with a recognition of reality and the danger (of castration) that it implies. These two contrary reactions to the conflict "persist as the centre-point of the splitting of the ego" so that there is "a rift in the ego which never heals but which increases as time goes on" (Freud, 1940e, p. 276). The two attitudes maintained by those who split their egos, disavowal of the female's lack of a penis along with recognition of this fact, are said to "persist side by side throughout their lives without influencing each other" (Freud, 1940a, p. 203).

Kernberg summarises Freud's position by stating that Freud "defined splitting of the ego as the lifelong co-existence of two implicitly conscious contradictory impulses which did not influence each other" (Kernberg, 1976, p. 21). This permits us to contrast Freud's observations made with fetishists to what we observe in the splitting of the self of Asperger's children. In these children, it is my consistent observation that both sides of their split self are quite conscious of each other, and moreover that both aspects of their split self have a strong impact on each other and even struggle openly with each other. Recall that this was seen with especial clarity in the case of Matt. When the tiger aspect of his split self was unleashed, it both protected but also overwhelmed and terrified the antelope part. In turn, the antelope part attempted to restrain and inhibit the tiger part, mostly in the form of self-punishment (that is, giving himself detentions at school).

Kernberg's (1976) way of characterising splitting of the ego approximates to some degree what we observe in Asperger's children. We can refer to the experiences reported by Matt as our example of psychodynamics in Asperger's.

Kernberg (1976) notes the "alternating activation of contradictory ego states" involving "mutual denial of independent sectors of the psychic life" and he goes on to say "that there exist alternating 'ego states', and I use the concept 'ego state' as a way of describing these repetitive, temporarily ego syntonic, compartmentalised psychic manifestations" (Kernberg, 1976, p. 20). Importantly, he continues by noting that in splitting of the ego, what "are completely separated from each other are complex psychic manifestations, involving affect, ideational content, subjective and behavioural manifestations" (1976, p. 20). He also notes that there is a "specific, well-structured alternation between opposite, completely irreconcilable affect states" (1976, p. 23). A related observation is made in Bokanowski and Lewkowicz: "When a patient separates from a painful and unbearable emotion, he is also splitting from the part of the self capable of having that emotion" (2009, p. xviii).

Kernberg provides the following very helpful summary:

> It was as if there were two selves, equally strong, completely separated from each other in their emotions although not in the patient's memory and alternating in his conscious experience. It was this successive activation of contradictory ego states which I would refer to as an example of splitting of the ego. (Kernberg, 1976, p. 23)

I strongly agree with Kernberg in reference to the experience of Asperger's children, which regularly involves their having two selves which are of similar strength, though one part of the split often predominates or is experienced as the more central and more frequent ego state. The two parts of the split self are well aware of each other and are regularly in competition with if not overtly hostile to each other. One part, the "stronger" part, can also be experienced as having protective qualities. The behaviour of both parts is retained in memory. One part of the split can be activated and can come into play quite suddenly (and the other part can be suddenly deactivated). This occurs most frequently when the Asperger's child is in a situation of interpersonal conflict which feels threatening or overwhelming and potentially traumatic to him.

What is split and kept apart in the two ego states which comprise the two parts of the split includes (as Kernberg has noted): the *matrix of affects* central to each ego state (ferocious rage *vs.* anxiously yearning neediness, for example), the *ideational content* typical of each ego state ("I'll get them before they hurt me", *vs.* "I really wish I could make a friend" for example), the *subjective self-experiences* of each ego state or each aspect of the split self (as being strong and unassailable *vs.* being weak and intimidated, for example), and the characteristic *behavioural manifestations* of each state (angrily throwing pieces of chalk at peers *vs.* crying and guilty, despondent self-punishment, for example). Using the generic bully/victim to characterise the split, the first of each of these examples would be the exclusive characterisation of the bully ego state, and the second of the victim ego state.

What prompts the sudden and sometimes rapid shift from one aspect of the split self to the other aspect? Splitting of the self permits the Asperger's sufferer to avoid, although only temporarily, two groups of painful emotions. But the Asperger's sufferer has to switch back and forth between the two emotional matrices which are embedded in the split self. In some ways, it is almost like constantly jumping back and forth between the frying pan and the fire. The frying pan represents the emotional matrix which is part of the victim side of the split—usually including as part of this matrix anxiety, fearfulness, shame, vulnerability, and often guilt and self-denigration. The fire is the bully side of the split, usually in its emotional matrix including rage, hatred, vengefulness, vindictiveness, arrogance, and cold-hearted contempt.

In addition to the metaphor "from the frying pan into the fire," another comparison also reflects the situation of the Asperger's person. This is the metaphor of the "hot potato"—when a person tries to hold onto an object which is intolerably hot by quickly passing it back and forth from hand to hand. This seems to me close to the situation experienced by many Asperger's children. Both sides of the split are likely to have emotionally intolerable aspects for the person. When one side of the split starts to become psychically intolerable and overwhelming, a brief respite is possible by switching to the other side of the split. The material provided by a number of the patients you have overheard—and the descriptions given by Matt are especially suggestive—indicate that situations of high stress may promote a switch to the other part of the split.

Projective identification into remote objects

For Asperger's children, projective identification usually functions in the service of splitting and helps to maintain the split. Splitting as "maintained by means of projective identification" is not unusual (Ogden, 1982, p. 105). Projective identification in Asperger's children can be used in an attempt to rid the child of the more troubling aspect of the split self (usually but certainly not always the bully aspect) thus fostering the illusory experience of a single and unitary self (which is frequently but not always the victim self).

Projective identification in the treatment of Asperger's children is, in my experience, often quite muted in the experience of the therapist as the therapist being their target, especially compared to the roar of projective identification the therapist often experiences with borderline personality patients (This is less true with those Asperger's children who fall within what I later (Chapter Thirteen) will call the uninhibited/ aggressive type). The reason for this is that Asperger's children employ projective identification mostly with what I will call *remote objects*. These objects are remote in time, remote in space, remote in cultural distance, remote in emotional distance, or remote in any combination of these. For examples of projective identification into remote objects, we need only consider Anthony and the Hulk *vs*. Bob Banner (remote in being cartoon figures), Israel *vs*. Palestine (remote in space), or Matt and his Calvin *vs*. Hobbes (other cartoon figures), tiger *vs*. antelope (remote in being animals), Dan and his Attila the Hun *vs*. the Romans (remote in time, space, and culture), King Kong (a fantastic and thus remote animal), and Captain Jean-Luc Picard *vs*. the alien "Q" (remote in time and space, and for the alien "Q", also remote in culture, thinking, emotionality, and species). Most frequently, there are projective identifications into the therapist which involve the victim aspect of the split and which provoke a concordant countertransference experience in the therapist of sadness, sympathy, and protectiveness toward this victim aspect. As noted earlier, a concordant countertransference derives from what Racker (1974, p. 134) referred to as a concordant identification by the therapist, this involving, according to Ogden "the therapist's identification with the patient's unconscious experience of self in the internal object relationship that is being played out in the transference" (Ogden, 1982, p. 72).

I now express my deep gratitude to Dr. Nilde Parada Franch (2008) for her comments on the paper I presented on my patient Dan, whom you heard about in Chapter Six. I'm specifically indebted to her for the concept she called projection into "distant" objects. I have here slightly modified this concept and referred to it as projective identification into *remote* objects. In the following few paragraphs, I have paraphrased her comments on my presentation of Dan, interspersing my own comments among hers.

It is quite frequent, she writes, for Asperger's patients to project feelings, thoughts, ideas, and sensations into "distant" objects. Such objects may include animals, alien beings, and historical figures. They do not project into ordinary people such as friends or parents. They seem to need to place feelings, attitudes, thoughts, and intentions very far away from themselves and also far from the relationship with the therapist.

In spite of remaining alert in my countertransference experiences for any indications of projective identifications in their transferences from my Asperger's patients, I have experienced only sparse indications of this happening. Often, I have had the sense of being protectively insulated from their projective identifications, as if my being a recipient of such projective identifications would be "too close for comfort" and too risky both for them and, in their fantasies, too risky for me as well. Perhaps part of this risk would be that they would experience me as (and pressure me to act like) a heartless and cruel bully.

Dan looks for people from another world or from a different period of time as targets for the projective identification of aspects of his internal world. Both Dan and Thanos repeatedly stated they would feel more comfortable living in the past. Perhaps using alien or remote objects as recipients of their projective identifications contributes to Asperger's children feeling so different from others and having such difficulties interacting with peers.

Resentment, vindictiveness, and hostility in Asperger's

Many Asperger's children, including Dan, show a strong identification with those who are excluded, rejected, bullied, and abused. Dan's identification with King Kong includes this aspect, but it also includes intense feelings of being usually treated unfairly by life, and feelings of resentment.

The resentful person, notes Dr. Parada Franch, is "stuck to a past where bills have not yet been paid". Resentment calls forth a wish for revenge, with the resentful person feeling free of responsibility, and as having the right to torment and punish others. For example, in my dialogue with Dan which you overheard, he reported on an "initiation" given to a child in grade five, one in which Dan "fazed him out" and frightened and humiliated him to the point that this child left the school. Dr. Parada Franch suggested this was an instance of the resentful side of Dan, the bully side of the split being in charge, so that he considered it "his right to torment and punish others, in revenge". In his bullying and sadistic attitudes, there seemed to be no feelings of shame, regret, embarrassment or culpability. "It was as if he was talking about a third person, not himself. Feelings were not connected with his consciousness." She then adds "how intense is the splitting of his self. He is not capable of identifying himself with bullied, abused people. He is totally identified with the bully, the abuser, in a very cold way. His attitude is one of total arrogance".

This description perfectly captures how the bully part of the bully/victim split operated in Dan. It also captures the way this aspect of the split in the self operates in most and perhaps all Asperger's children.

A third and final digression is now needed. This digression involves the work of Kancyper (2009) on splitting in connection with feelings of rancour, vindictiveness, and vengefulness. Consider a brief comment by Adamo (2012, p. 64) about the literary productions of her Asperger's patient: "The prevalent feeling is rancour". Asperger's children, as part of the victim aspect of their split selves, regularly experience a sense of being victimised, bullied, misunderstood, emotionally abused, and persecuted. They feel dealt with in an unfair, unjust, and discriminatory manner. This regularly activates (as part of the bully aspect of their split selves) feelings of self-righteous and arrogantly superior vindictiveness, vengefulness, and retaliatory rancour—a state of mind in which the talion principle predominates. One might even say that it is the talion principle squared that takes over, so that the revenge to be exacted will not be equal to but must greatly exceed the injury felt to have been done. As Kancyper (2009, p. 116) writes, "rancour is deeply entrenched in, and feeds itself on, the hoped for pay-back time", this payback for Asperger's children involving payback with the accumulated interest which has built up over long years of experiencing mistreatment, victimisation, and abuse.

One Asperger's adolescent whom I'll call Jack, age thirteen, told me about his experience of being "betrayed" by a girl who was in one of his classes (You will hear more about Jack in Chapter Sixteen). He spoke of feeling he had established a connection with this girl during the social event for new high school students organised by his school. A few days after this social event, when Jack spoke to her at the beginning of the class, she completely ignored him. This "betrayal", he felt, merited revenge. When I encouraged Jack to speak about the way he imagined taking revenge, there was no hesitation on his part. He said: "I would burn her alive." I then naïvely (and I think in a self-defensive attempt to minimise for myself the extent of his vindictiveness) commented "you'd get even with her." He looked at me as if I were crazy. "Get even?" He asked me sarcastically. "Are you kidding? I'd give her back a lot more pain than she caused me so she'd understand. Burning alive is the slowest and most painful torture I know". It is this kind of revenge fantasy that regularly appears with Asperger's children. Jack felt that burning his peers alive would be appropriate for many, even most of his peers. He clearly expressed the feeling that the destruction of the entire world would also be appropriate, whatever that might mean for him. He also spoke of fantasies of revenge against his perceived tormentors with gleeful and joyful delight, and with an enthusiastic arousal that bordered on the sexual.

Kancyper (2009) writes about "resentment and splitting of the ego" in the context of trauma, which may open the question of the experience of trauma (perhaps cumulative trauma) for Asperger's children. Whether or not experience of trauma is part of Asperger's, Kancyper's descriptions of the resentful and rancorous person are highly applicable to Asperger's children. He notes that "for the resentful individual, splitting is a defence mechanism as well as the state of the ego" and that "two psychic attitudes are established within the ego, attributes that oscillate …" (Kancyper, 2009, p. 119). Exactly so. The resentful individual, he adds "is usually stuck in obstinate rancour" which provides the person "with narcissistic satisfaction as it promotes the elation of self-esteem" (ibid, p. 118) as well as serving defensive aims.

Kancyper (2009, p. 118) is also beautifully able to capture the predominating state of mind of many Asperger's children. This state of mind is that the other has something I desire (for many Asperger's children this often being friendship, recognition, and empathic understanding) but the other "won't give it to me. That's unfair. I'm just an innocent victim, because it's obvious I'm not getting what I'm entitled to". This sense of being treated unfairly and made into an "innocent victim" is central in Asperger's. Kancyper continues: "With this belief the individual feels he has a right to legitimise his blind repetitive revenge" (ibid, p. 118). These comments apply exactly to Jack, to Dan and to many if not all Asperger's children.

The experience of time in Asperger's

Kancyper is additionally helpful in contributing to our understanding of the experience of time in Asperger's. He states that "The experience of time sustained by the power of rancour is the constant brooding over an affront that never ends" adding that the resentful person "has an urgent need to feel vindicated, as he believes he has suffered an affront that deserves punishment. Hence, the present and the future are mortgaged" (Kancyper, 2009, p. 117) to the extent that one aspect of the past, the experience of being victimised, "has taken control of the three dimensions of time".

Building on Kancyper's comments, I suggest there can be emotional experiences of time as having three dimensions, two dimensions, and one or even zero dimensions. The experience of time in three dimensions (as a kind of sphere surrounding one) is possible in healthy individuals. There is the possibility of growth backwards (integration and elaboration of one's past), forwards (into the future with creative plans, projects, and anticipations), downwards (incorporating dream and other unconscious aspects) and upwards (in the form of an adaptive and social morality). Growth of this kind is a three-dimensional flowering or blooming, like the expansion of a bud into an unfolding blossom.

Time can also be experienced in two dimensions, as a kind of planar surface, permitting movement backwards (in memory), forwards (in anticipations), and sideways (as recursive repetitions or repetitive cycles). This is the context of time seen as an ebb and flow (like tides) or as a flowing river as in the old hymn, "time like an ever-rolling stream".

Time can also be experienced as having one dimension (as linear) or in the extreme, as having zero dimensions (as being like a point). The experience of time in Asperger's is frequently punctiliar (single points in time) or punctilinear (a series of points distributed along a line). It is experienced as a line in which one can only travel to specific points backwards in time, and specifically to experiences of being hurtfully bullied and degraded, or else experienced forwards, in the form of anticipations of future points in time when there can be massively destructive retaliation and revenge against those perceived as bullying. In some children, time is often compressed into points of zero dimensions, namely those points where experiences of being hurt and abused coalesce with phantasies of sadistic and overwhelming revenge. Time becomes a sadomasochistic kind of black hole which compresses together masochistic experiences of being unjustly and constantly abused by others, with erotically stimulating sadistic phantasies of destructive and total revenge. The latter aspect Kancyper describes as "the repetitive, and even insatiable, compulsion of revengeful power" (Kancyper, 2009, p. 117) deeply coloured by "aggression at the service of Thanatos" (ibid, p. 118) and by "thanatic narcissism" (ibid, p. 120), the latter referring to destructive revenge fantasies which also bolster self-esteem.

Kancyper is also helpful in setting out the problem children with Asperger's present to us—"how to combat resentment within the analytic situation, as both resentment and its implacable need for revenge are regressive and repetitive aspects of thanatic narcissism" (Kancyper, 2009, p. 120). Hand-in-hand with this problem is how the therapist can help in undoing the compressed, black hole, punctilinear, zero dimensional, and sadomasochistic experience of time, which blocks emotional growth and nails emotions, palms and feet, to the single issue of being a bully or else a victim.

Treating splitting and projective identification in Asperger's children

Returning again to the central theme, consider Dan once more. Dr. Parada Franch makes suggestions about the handling of the split in Dan's self and the handling of his projective identifications. She suggests that bringing together the victimiser and the victim aspects of the split requires the construction within Dan of a containing mental space through identification with a therapist who is neither cowed by fear of Dan's malignant victimising aspect nor seduced by his own therapeutic desire to save the victim part of the patient.

It is here that I suspect some degree of projective identification may sometimes be at work within the therapeutic situation. For the Asperger's child, this may take the form of urgent wishes for acceptance by peers and for friendships. In the therapist, the resonating and corresponding experience may take the shape of therapeutic ambition and impatience and the impulse to return the patient's projective identifications into remote objects too directly and too quickly to the child.

Dr. Parada Franch suggests that Dan needs to have enough experiences with an idealised or good enough object in his interactions with the therapist to construct a containing space in his own mind, so that there develops space for projection of his malignant aspects into the therapist. This certainly feels correct and appropriate to me.

She also suggests that the therapist needs to contain and maintain awareness in his own mind of his perceptions of Dan's victimiser aspects, and also "his [the therapist's] own wishes and internal pressures for pointing out and interpreting them." Instead of quickly interpreting, the therapist needs to contain this knowledge for a while, "waiting for the time the patient will be ready enough to act these aspects in the transference" (Parada Franch, 2008, p. 2).

These comments are apposite and, in my experience, are applicable to the treatment of all Asperger's children.

In summary, the psychodynamic functioning of Asperger's children regularly, perhaps universally and pathognomonically, includes splitting and projective identification working in tandem. The self is split into bully and victim aspects. There can be rapid fluctuations as to which aspect is behaviourally activated. Both aspects of the split are conscious, and the two aspects have strong impacts on each other, frequently of a mutually opposing or even hostile nature. They constitute mutually exclusive ego states or self-states. The matrices of typical affects, typical patterns of thought, typical subjective attitudes, and typical behaviour patterns of the two aspects of the split are mutually exclusive and usually opposed.

Splitting of the self is regularly augmented and supported by projective identification. However, the projective identifications used by the Asperger's person seldom target familiar people, including the therapist (at least for much of the therapy). Instead, there are frequent projective identifications into remote objects.

CHAPTER TEN

The anxieties and defences of Asperger's children

Anxieties in Asperger's children

The primitive anxieties of the emerging self to which autistic children are prone have been described by a number of therapists. Among such fears are included fear of falling and fear of spilling out ("The terror I feel will just spill out, or maybe I will fall into nothingness" quoted in Mitrani & Mitrani, 1997, p. 119). There are "primitive terrors of annihilation and nonexistence" (ibid, p. 120), "terrors of falling, feeling lost in space, with no anchor or walls to serve as boundaries" (ibid, p. 121), "the terror of hopelessness and the fear of dying" (ibid, p. 132). There is also fear of dissolving, including for one patient fear "that everything would spill out and she would just dissolve" (ibid, p. 133). One writer refers to "terrors of leaking away and dissolving" as well as anxieties about fragmentation (ibid, p. 65). Another therapist notes that "In the 'autistic-contiguous position', the disruption is to the sense of existence with fears of dissolving, disappearing, or falling forever" along with "terrors of nothingness and meaninglessness" (ibid, p. 153). There are fears of being dropped and "profound annihilation anxieties" (ibid, p. 327). One therapist describes "anxieties of falling forever and disappearing in the dark" (ibid, p. 332). There are "annihilation anxieties dating from the very beginning of life [which] are sensed in a bodily manner" (ibid, p. 334). Other similar descriptions involve "the bodily sensations of falling forever and spilling out into annihilation" (ibid, p. 359), and the comment that for autistic children, "the bodily anxieties are those of falling endlessly and liquefying" (ibid, p. 386). Durban (2014) refers to

> losing shape, spilling over, freezing, burning, liquefying, having no skin or membrane, falling forever, being full of black devouring holes, having parts of the body torn off, losing dimensionality and being welded with the environment with no differentiation or contour. (Durban, 2014, p. 188)

Rhode includes "fear of liquefying, spilling out, and falling forever; the fear of unregulated bodily states such as burning and freezing" (Rhode, 2011b, p. 289). She also includes losing parts of the body and losing limbs. These anxieties she refers to as the "existential fears of annihilation that are so characteristic of children on the autism spectrum" (Rhode, 2011a, p. 263). I will also refer to these kinds of anxieties as "existential anxieties".

If the core primitive anxieties in autistic children include fear of falling forever, of liquefying and spilling out into nothingness, of annihilation, of being lost in unbounded space, and of dissolving, then questions are raised about Asperger's children. Because these children are "on the spectrum" of autism, are Asperger's children as a consequence also prey to the same anxieties or to very similar ones such as autistic children experience? Whatever the answer may be to this question, what *are* the core anxieties most often detected in the therapy of Asperger's children and adolescents?

My experience with Asperger's children and adolescents suggests that these primitive anxieties just described lurk in the background for Asperger's children, as they may for all people, even those who are "normal-neurotic", and perhaps especially for those who have suffered traumas involving the early loss of emotionally intimate others. This may be the case, for example, with Holocaust survivors, as suggested by the work of David Rosenfeld and Bianca Lechevalier (both contributing to Mitrani & Mitrani, 1997). Both of these writers suggest that Holocaust survivors employ autistic encapsulations. Rosenfeld (in Mitrani & Mitrani, 1997, p. 170) comments on "autistic encapsulation in the treatment of survivors of the Nazi Holocaust" and Lechevalier similarly notes "the existence of autistic enclaves" in some survivors and "the encapsulation of trauma in the survivors of the holocaust horrors" (in Mitrani & Mitrani, 1997, p. 336). Asperger's children may also have these kinds of autistic encapsulations in response to infantile traumas.

Shortly, we consider some of the more autistic-like defences against primitive anxieties that can be identified in the functioning of Asperger's children. Before this discussion, we can consider the most typical anxieties that seem to be present in the functioning of Asperger's children and adolescents. By and large, the anxieties of these children tend to be "object relational" in nature, but with "existential anxieties" lurking in the background.

A typical psychoanalytic developmental hierarchy of anxiety types, proceeding from the most primitive to the most highly developed, would likely produce a sequence along the following lines: disintegration anxiety or annihilation anxiety, persecutory anxiety, fear of loss of the object (separation anxiety, including anxieties around separation and loss), fear of loss of love, castration anxiety, and finally superego anxiety (depressive anxieties and especially guilt). (This particular hierarchy of anxiety types is a modified form of "A developmental hierarchy of anxiety" contained in Gabbard, 2005, p. 250). One might also include what is called predator-prey anxiety between the first two types.

My impression is that the most typical anxieties experienced by Asperger's children are likely to involve the second and third types of anxieties listed above, persecutory anxiety and separation anxiety, with predator-prey anxiety and annihilation anxiety lurking in the background, predator-prey anxiety taking the form of bully-victim anxiety. Some of the specific anxieties that I have observed as experienced by Asperger's children include the following: being totally isolated in a state of friendlessness; disappearance as an object of human desire into a state of anonymous and isolated loneliness; complete aloneness with no hope of emotional contact with others; having no access to any other living creature capable or desirous of understanding you or extending any empathy to you; and degeneration into alien and unhuman otherness. These anxieties I take to be "object relational" anxieties that are forms of autistic annihilation anxieties which centre on disappearing or suffering annihilation as far as being a human object is concerned; of suffering endless separation from others. They are anxieties about lacking any possibility of engaging emotionally with other humans.

An illustration of these anxieties comes from my very first diagnostic interview with Dan (whom you heard about in chapter Six). At the end of the interview when I was attempting to set up therapy sessions for Dan, I asked him what he wanted to get out of our proposed therapeutic endeavour. In his intellectualised manner behind which it was not difficult to hear his barely restrained sadness and anxiety, he told me that "I want to learn several things." He then gave me a list of five things he wanted to learn. "First", he told me, "I want to learn why I'm different— I can't understand why people are so different from me." He continued: "Second, I want to learn what is different between me and other people. How are other people different from me?" He added: "What is it that's different about other people?" And: "How do I work or cooperate with other people?" Finally, he asked: "How can I get to understand other people?" These overlapping questions repeatedly emphasise a mental struggle most if not all Asperger's children feel very strongly: they are highly aware that in a number of ways they seem to be very different from their peers. They have difficulty understanding their peers, and are well aware that their teachers, peers and often their parents (not to mention their therapists) find it difficult to understand them as well. This often shades into the feeling that they are almost a different species from most human beings, sometimes accompanied by the defence of asserting arrogant superiority over other people, and sometimes accompanied by terrible anguish, often by both. A light scratch on the surface of these anxieties usually reveals more primitive existential anxieties just underneath them. These anxieties are best expressed in the form of a question: "Do I really exist at all as a human being or am I condemned to be forever a stranger to others; lonely, isolated, and shunned, never achieving full existence as human?"

In tandem with and blending into these separation and annihilation-related anxieties, the Asperger's child typically experiences anxieties with a distinct persecutory flavour. These anxieties include: fear of total and brutal rejection by others; fear of being treated in a cold, unempathic, unjust, and unfair manner both by other people and by almost all societal institutions; being bullied, harassed, hounded, and excluded by others; fear of being treated with hostile and complete contempt and dismissiveness by others and as a result feeling worthless, unwanted and contemptible. Many anxieties in this group tend to be defended against by the use of projective identification by Asperger's children, usually projective identification into peers and into authority figures.

I now want to suggest that Asperger's children can be differentiated from children with "pure autism" or "classical autism" by using the distinction between "relational anxieties" and "existential anxieties". This is of course a rough-and-ready and an approximate distinction, but I think one with considerable heuristic and practical value. It might also be of some value to think of "existential anxieties" as involving what I will call "*separateness* anxiety", whereas relational anxieties involve "*separation* anxiety", this being one type of anxiety falling under the rubric of "relational anxieties". In the following few paragraphs, I use a recent and extremely helpful paper by Mitrani (2014—though *all* of her writings are helpful) to expand on these assertions.

Consider existential anxieties. Mitrani (2014, p. 3) summarises these anxieties, as initially outlined by Frances Tustin, as involving "*raw and unmitigated panic equated with the elemental sensations of falling out of control, of discontinuity of being, of nothingness, dissolution, and evaporation— of being a no-body-nowhere*" (italics in the original). This brief summary, involving sensations of "discontinuity of being" and of "nothingness" should suffice to explain the use of the phrase "existential anxieties". Mitrani goes on to note that these anxieties are evaded through autistic defences, involving autosensual or adhesive manoeuvres. Adhesive equation is employed as an autistic defence, as "a protection from the life-threatening awareness of two-ness and the overwhelming ecstasy of at-one-ment" (ibid, p. 3). It is this life-threatening awareness of two-ness that I referred to as "*separateness* anxiety". Mitrani also notes that in an autistic state, awareness of others as other is limited, and much of the time, self, and other "remain largely undifferentiated" (ibid, p. 3).

Using this groundwork, providing an illustration might be helpful. I have written about my high-functioning autistic patient Sam (Holloway, 2013) whom I have now had the privilege of seeing in treatment for seven years. Sam has to a large extent been able to emerge from his autistic state and to relate to others, including me, *as* other. But he still has a tendency under stress to utilise adhesive equation and to treat others in an undifferentiated manner, functioning as part of himself or his skin surface. To give a single example: Sam has recently begun university and has experienced "frosh week" (often called fresher's week) for new students there. He showed me numerous photos on his mobile phone of him hugging a surprising number of female students who were participants in or organisers of these celebrations. In Sam's photos, the expressions on the faces of the young women Sam was hugging conveyed a sense of genuine delight and enjoyment. Sam can be very considerate, so that professional staff at his high school described him as "cooperative, delightful, and sweet". I expect that the young women who allowed Sam to take photos of him hugging them perceived his sweetness. What I expect they did *not* perceive is the autistic aspect of Sam's desires for hugs, the reassuring adhesive equation of skin-to-skin or at least body-to-body contact afforded by the hugs he obtained. I understood the hugs to be in the service of counteracting the anxieties Sam experienced as a result of him being away from his home for the first time and in a completely new environment. As with many aspects of how Sam now functions, the relational or object-related and the residual autistic aspects are both present. As a result, physical body-to-body contact with peers becomes for Sam almost a fetishistic activity. He shows me pictures of himself with male peers as well, their arms linked together over their shoulders. At the same time, a strong element of object relatedness is also present, so that Sam is able to tell me about some of the individual personality characteristics of the peers whose pictures he shows me.

Sam experiences his greatest emotional turbulence and anxiety in connection with issues around separation and loss. A couple of months before his episodes of hugging during university frosh week, Sam had brought to me his anxieties around graduating from his high school at the end of grade twelve. "I'm going to miss them" he said about the other students, and added, coming close to tears, "most of them I'll never, never even *see* again!" He told me how he wanted to avoid the "meltdown" (his word) he had suffered at the end of the previous school year (grade eleven), when he had a minor breakdown. During this meltdown, he had burst into protracted and inconsolable crying and wailing, falling on the floor and writhing in emotional pain, to the extent that it required an hour for his teachers to console him.

The understanding I developed of this incident (and other incidents of separation and loss he had told me about) was that two layers of anxiety were involved in Sam's experiences. One layer was composed of separation anxiety as traditionally understood in psychoanalytic theory—the pain resulting from separation from another or others experienced as needed and narcissistically supportive and valued whole objects. This layer of anxiety was part of Sam's non-autistic aspect of his personality functioning (as Anne Alvarez has suggested is part of the autistic child's repertoire, along with the autistic part of his personality).

In another layer of his personality and the anxieties contained in it, Sam experienced both his school (a small and specialised private school) and the other students there as an integral part of himself he could not do without; as undifferentiated aspects of his own self and his own functioning. It was as if Sam experienced his losses as brutally painful emotional eviscerations and somato-psychic amputations, without bene-fit of anaesthetic; as the tearing away of essential parts of his everyday physical and mental functioning. Being separated from his school and his peers was for him a kind of vivisection, comparable to the Aztec sacrifice in which the victim's still pumping heart is cut out of and torn from the body. Just as with the victim of the Aztec ceremony, the loss of this essential aspect involved for Sam fears of dissolution, nothingness, and non-being. This kind of anxiety derives from the autistic part of his personality, and involves a sense of separateness from others that is the same in his experience as being separated from an essential part of the self. From this comes my choice of the label "separateness anxiety" for this existential type of anxiety.

In short: Sam's experiences of separation and loss provoked two lay-ers of anxiety: the relational anxiety traditionally referred to as sepa-ration anxiety emanating from the non-autistic part of his personality, and the existential anxiety I have called separateness anxiety which is a function of the autistic part of his personality. In addition, these two aspects of Sam's personality interact, so that a dialectical relationship is set up between separation anxiety and separateness anxiety in which they feed into and magnify each other. This results in the fragmenting "meltdown" Sam experiences at the end of the school year, in which separation anxiety and separateness anxiety seemed to literally tear apart the autistic and non-autistic aspects of his personality as both aspects are drowned in their own particular and specific anxieties.

Mitrani (2014, p. 4) is once again extremely helpful in elaborating on this. She writes about the different reactions to separations and losses typically seen in persons who operate in an object-related manner as contrasted with those in an autistic state. The object-related person typi-cally reacts to separation and loss with "expressions of neediness and emotional pain" or else with a "tight-fisted control" over the experience of their neediness. The autistic person is likely to react "with total obliv-iousness or complete collapse" (Mitrani, 2014, p. 4). There are also con-trasting reactions seen when the person's defences against awareness of separateness and loss break down. For the object-related person, there are most likely to be "feelings of rejection". For the autistic person, or the autistic aspect of the personality, the end result may be felt as "bodily collapse, as a dreadful sensation of being ripped-off and thrown away, an experience of total and irreversible dejection" (ibid, p. 4).

Mitrani's outline has powerful explanatory value. Jack, an object-related Asperger's adolescent we will hear about shortly, experienced his loss of a hoped-for relationship primarily as a feeling of rejection. This shaded into the existential anxiety of being "thrown away" and treated as non-existent. However, Jack quickly reinstituted an omnipotent and vindictively retaliatory defence—"all those who reject me should be burnt alive".

The situation with Sam was quite different. When he had to separate from his school and his schoolmates at the end of grade eleven, his experience quickly became one of total and catastrophic dejection and complete inability to mourn. The meltdown he described involved bodily (and psychic) collapse which was beyond the ordinary soothing capacities of his teachers. It involved a sense of being amputated and ripped away from his school and his peers, "trashed" and thrown away. The autistic part of his personality took over, and Sam's anxieties became fully existential ones.

My hypothesis briefly stated is that with autistic children, existential anxieties are very much in the foreground and relational anxieties are hardly more than fleeting shadows in the background. As the child starts to emerge from autism (perhaps partly in response to the onset of adolescence) and in proportion to how high-functioning is the level of his autism, separation anxiety and separateness anxiety become more evenly balanced, with both being visible. After seven years of psychoanalytic psychotherapy, Sam has reached the point where relational anxieties, including separation anxiety, seem to outweigh existential anxieties most of the time, this including separateness anxiety, though both forms of anxiety are still quite visible. Usually with Asperger's children, both these kinds of anxieties are also visible. However, the typical structure for Asperger's children is for relational anxieties (mostly of a paranoid-schizoid quality) to be very much in the foreground, with existential autistic anxieties operative in the background and behind-the-scenes.

Consider more closely relational anxieties and how they operate in Asperger's children. Mitrani comments that when true object-relatedness prevails, "anxieties defended against by manic means are either paranoid-schizoid or depressive in nature" (Mitrani, 2014, p. 3) with the primary defences involving "splitting, projective identification, and manic denial", these being the primary defences I have experienced being deployed by Asperger's children. Jack, age thirteen, whom you will hear more about in Chapter Sixteen, became interested in a female peer in his grade nine class. He finally mustered up the courage to speak to her, but in his next session after this encounter with her, he told me:

JACK: She just ignored me, like *total* rejection.
ROBIN: Didn't reply when you spoke to her?
JACK: Total rejection, like all the other kids.
ROBIN: What did you say to her when ...?
JACK: All of them should be burnt alive, like I told you before.
ROBIN: So they'd understand your pain?
JACK: *No*; so they'd *feel* the pain that I feel.
ROBIN: The pain of being rejected.
JACK: Being treated like I didn't exist, like I was nothing.

In this brief therapeutic exchange, we can glimpse the way anxiety operates in Asperger's children. Jack's anxiety initially operates on the relational level, with Jack feeling anxious on the relational level about his difficulties making a connection with another. This seems to operate in a more or less paranoid-schizoid way (*all* his peers reject him) likely involving splitting (his peers are all bad) and the defence of omnipotent and manic retaliation (they should all be burnt alive). In the background, however, lurk anxieties of an existential nature. Not only is Jack anxious about being rejected on a relational level, he also experiences anxieties involving being treated as non-existent, as a nothing and a nobody.

We can now summarise how anxiety may operate with these children. Children within the broad spectrum of autism experience both existential anxieties (originating in the autistic part of their personalities) and relational anxieties (deriving from the non-autistic part of their personalities). Classically autistic children will show primarily and at first exclusively existential anxieties, with relational anxieties being very weakly suggested at best. With high-functioning autistic children, there is likely to be much more of a balance between existential and relational anxieties, with both being observable. There is a quantitative but *not* a qualitative difference in their anxieties as compared to classically autistic children. With Asperger's children, the anxieties we usually encounter are most likely to be relational ones, with a strong paranoid-schizoid colouring. Existential anxieties operate in the background. They are most likely to be triggered in situations of difficulty or stress.

This is a highly schematic description which offers a general template for children on the autism spectrum. It is likely to require modification when applied to real individual children. Nevertheless, it may provide a broad framework for thinking about children "on the spectrum", for making discriminations among their different psychopathological ways of functioning, and, most importantly, for sensitively gearing treatment interventions to how the individual child is experiencing the world.

Defences in Asperger's children

Turning from anxieties to defences, the Asperger's child or adolescent has in my experience a typical structure of defences used to cope with the primitive and powerful anxieties they experience. The sense I have been able to develop of this structure is that it usually includes three levels. These three levels are; first, the key or cornerstone defences which are likely to be a defining feature of this disorder; second, the subsidiary or supporting set of defences which are most commonly used; and third, a number of specifically autistic defences which are sometimes used. This third group of defences may constitute a "fall-back" level of defences for Asperger's children, deployed in situations of elevated stress and perception of threat.

The cornerstone defences have been discussed at some length. The two invariant and perhaps defining defences used by Asperger's children are splitting of the self into bully and victim aspects, and projective identification into remote objects.

Turning to the second level; in the Asperger's sufferers I have struggled to treat, there are six subsidiary defences which have come into view most often. These six defences are: intellectualisation, idealisation, denigration/devaluation, arrogance, manic denial, and projective identification into less remote and more intimate objects. Of the children we have discussed, Dan (Chapter Six) perhaps illustrates the first four defences most clearly.

For a significant minority of Asperger's children, the defence of intellectualisation becomes a very powerful self-protection, so that if it is not included as a cornerstone defence, it is for these children certainly at the forefront of the second level of defences. It is a common observation that younger Asperger's children often speak "like a little professor", and they may construct from their intellectual preoccupations internal intellectual fortresses into which they can retreat, and which both constrain their own expression of feelings within the fortress walls and block their ready access to and appreciation of the feeling states being expressed by others who are outside the intellectual fortress. There are times with some of these children that the therapist gets a feeling that there is sort of an autistic-like "intellectual encapsulation" occurring. Intellectualisation is typically considered to be a relatively high level and neurotic kind of defence. With Asperger's children, I am not so sure about this. The intellectualisation can become so profound that as I have tried to articulate, it functions almost as a protective shell or a carapace such as many autistic children demonstrate, having the qualities of an internal intellectual fortress or a sort of "intellectual encapsulation" of an autistic-like nature. Because of this quality of their intellectualisations, I have a temptation, to which I will only briefly yield, to invent a new name for the powerfully intellectualising defences used by some of these children to constrain, imprison, and strangle their own emotionality and their appreciation of emotions in others—a phrase like "self-encapsulating or self-imprisoning cerebralisation"—a capsule or internal prison in which everything becomes reduced to logical thinking and also sometimes sucked into the bottomless pit of their own very specific interests. One Asperger's adolescent, for example (whom I call Arturo and who will also appear in Chapter Fifteen), had only one very specific and restricted interest in life—knowing about armadillos. In spite of his tender age of twelve years, his incredible knowledge of armadillos actually made Arturo welcome in the "armadillo departments" of a number of zoos. He presented himself in a credible way and had somehow gained access to the armadillo "stud books" and breeding registers for numerous zoos. I was told by his parents that he was once actually consulted by a zoo as to whether they should breed armadillo Henrietta with another armadillo resident at the zoo by the name of George. Poor George! My patient reportedly informed the zoo that Henrietta and George were actually cousins and so should not breed together. His parents reported to me that the zoo chose another partner for Henrietta based on my patient's advice!

Of the patients presented here, the most inveterate intellectualisers were Alan (Chapter Nine), Thanos (Chapter Five), and Dan (Chapter Six). I wonder if it is an accident that both Thanos and Dan were deeply interested in history. Before his distressing and untimely death, Dan had completed his first year in university studying history and politics. Thanos was very deeply interested in arcane aspects of history and particularly in the Byzantine Empire. His knowledge of Byzantine history was incredibly detailed and quite "Byzantine" in its nature. A preoccupation with historical events also seems to insulate these adolescents from what is happening in the present. For Dan, his intellectualisation and employing his detailed historical knowledge fit into a marriage with the additional defence of cynicism, so that he could dismiss his current conflicts about interactions with others by pointing to events in the past and saying, in effect, "it's always been that way and it will never change". He was also very clear that he felt he didn't belong in the present and would have done much better in an earlier historical era. Thanos was extremely conflicted about his university studies, feeling extremely devoted to pursuing history which he identified with his "real self" and pursuing a more "practical" line of study that might lead to him making a decent salary.

The champion intellectualiser among my patients was Alan. He has now become able to talk about some incidents in his life and to be explicit about the feelings these incidents created in him. Recently, he spoke about an incident that happened one winter when he returned home late at night in the dark as the snow was falling and muffling all the usual sounds he was used to hearing, including the sounds of nearby traffic. Previously, he was unable to link this to any specific emotional state. In his recent revisiting of this incident, he was able to describe the emotional aspects—how bleak, isolated, lonely, and depressed he felt, how the falling snow muffling all sound made him feel cut off from the world and totally alone. Over the years, this has not been very common with Alan. He is able to talk about events in ongoing minute and complicated detail, pointing out their philosophical implications and ignoring any attempts on my part to explore the emotions involved by these events. To me, it felt like being dragged down into a bottomless bog of intellectual quicksand, in which any reference to emotions only brought forth more details and more ideas and seemed to pull us further down into the bog of intellectuality.

Many Asperger's children are unable to even put names on the feelings that they are experiencing or be certain they are having feelings at all. A mother helps her baby by gently mimicking the baby's feelings and supplying some kind of label for the feeling—as in a scenario where the baby is frustrated and angry at not being fed quickly enough, and the mother might say something like "Oh, slow, slow mommy! She didn't bring your food in time! That makes you angry, so angry—you had to wait so long!" In a way not too far from this maternal manner, the therapist often has to function in this way for Asperger's children, first identifying that there is a feeling present, and then attempting to apply an appropriate label and an understandable context for what the child is feeling. For some Asperger's children, and Alan is a wonderful example of this, it requires a great deal of patience on the part of the therapist to wait for the child to muster up the courage to step out of their internal fortress of intellectualisation and even acknowledge the frightening dragons of emotionality that await them outside of their fortress.

The defence of idealisation includes idealisation of the self and often of remote but admired real objects. Dan idealised both. He idealised himself as a sort of paragon or ideal student, who complied with what his teachers asked, completed all of his assignments and did so within the allotted time, and did not goof off or create a ruckus that annoyed his teachers as he felt his peers did. (Notice the defence of arrogance working hand-in-hand with idealisation). He also was deeply interested in history and idealised a number of historical figures. His defence of denigration or devaluation tended to be directed mainly at his peers, especially those he perceived as goofing around, not completing their assignments, and as having a hedonistic tendency—as opposed to what *he* saw as his own serious and committed approach. He at times expressed an arrogantly superior attitude towards his peers, making it extremely clear that his serious and dedicated morality was far superior to the hedonistic and pleasure-seeking frivolousness and self-indulgent laxity of many of his peers. His defensive arrogance seemed primarily geared to cope with his inability to establish social relationships with his peers and to cover over and protect his underlying vulnerable and battered sense of self-esteem. Many Asperger's children take on this mantle of arrogant and self-righteous moral superiority.

There is also the defence of projective identification into less remote and more intimate objects. Peers are often the target of projective identifications. But I am thinking of the therapist in particular. I noted earlier how the therapist and others close to the child seem to be insulated from his projective identifications, at least the beginning of therapy. It is a positive sign when the Asperger's child starts to use projective identification with his therapist (and with others close to him). It signals growing trust, a sense that the therapist will be able to contain and detoxify the projective identifications, and usually suggests successful containment and good progress in the therapy.

Manic denial is also frequent in the therapeutic presentation of Asperger's children. There is frequently denial of any moral weaknesses or shortcomings on the part of the child (a form of denial closely linked to and operating in conjunction with a manic and arrogant sense of superiority), denial of weakness, vulnerability, or a sense of loss on the part of the child ("I wouldn't want to associate with my hedonistic and morally corrupt peers"). With some children, there is a fluctuating level of denial of social interests or desires ("All the other kids are interested in is dumb rock music, videos with simulated sex, and dumb jokes about sex—why would I be interested in that garbage?" This is a quote from Jack who appears in Chapter Sixteen).

The third level of defences consists of the kinds of defences typically employed by autistic children; the autosensuous defences which use autistics objects and autistic shapes, and the formation of a protective autistic shell or carapace. This level of defence is important, I believe, because it suggests both continuity and discontinuity between autism proper (including high-functioning autism) and Asperger's. My impression (and it is only an impression which is in need of additional observational evidence) is that all Asperger's children have autistic defences within their defensive repertoire (hence the continuity with autism). However, they typically only deploy and actively use autistic defences when they feel unusually stressed or unusually threatened, especially by potential losses, separations or by perceived rejections by others. Typically, other defences usually tend to be at the forefront (hence the discontinuity with autism).

For the use of autistic objects by an Asperger's child, I will shortly describe at length one of the ongoing behaviours displayed by Matt, whom we got to know about in Chapter Three. I save this discussion for the end of this chapter. Matt made ongoing use of what I have come to regard as "hybrid objects", meaning a physical object which can be used to function both as one of Winnicott's transitional objects *and* as one of Tustin's autistic objects, with alternations between these two functions. This idea is not a new one. It is used by Tustin (1986), by Mitrani (1996), and by Alvarez (1980). Grotstein (writing in Mitrani & Mitrani, 1997, p. 271) notes that Tustin "distinguished autistic objects from transitional objects" with the difference between them being that transitional objects "are used to maintain connections to real objects, whereas the hard and soft [autistic] objects serve to replace them". Tustin (1972, p. 66) distinguishes between an autistic object which is one that is experienced as being totally "me", and a transitional object which she states has an admixture of "me" and "not-me" of which the child is only dimly aware. She goes on to give an illustration of a child early in her second year of life who has "reached the point where the autistic object merges into becoming the *transitional object*". Alvarez describes a toddler who used a teddy bear "less as a transitional object in Winnicott's sense and more as an autistic object in Tustin's sense" (Alvarez, 1980, p. 71). She implies that there can be a dialectical alternation in function wherein the same object can be used in an autistic as well as a transitional manner. We continue this discussion a bit later.

For autistic shapes, we will consider aspects of the history and therapy of Jack, a young adolescent to be described more fully in Chapter Sixteen, "Treatment of Asperger's children—The Toronto experiment". Jack also illustrates the use of a protective autistic shell or carapace in an Asperger's child, though in a mildly attenuated form as part of "the invention of shells, barriers, enclaves" (Mitrani & Mitrani, 1997, p. 197). Jack described his protection specifically as being a *wall*. It seemed to me that this form of autistic defence as it was used by Jack is included among "measures that avoid the perils of separation from the object and its consequences" and that it was geared "to bridge the traumatic gulf that opens between the self and the object" just as such protections function in autistic children (ibid, p. 276, p. 350). I say more about his wall shortly.

As to autistic shapes, Jack was referred to me with a history of having cut himself more than once, cutting into his skin by using a pocketknife. He has not repeated this activity since the beginning of his therapy, and we have only made some occasional references to this behaviour at this point in his treatment. The sense I developed was that Jack's cutting of his skin was at bottom an autosensuous activity which created for him a particular autistic shape of physical pain and the physical sensation of bleeding, into which he could become completely absorbed and could "bury himself", so to speak, using this cutting activity to insulate himself from the emotional pain he was experiencing in his everyday external object relations. His cutting activities enabled Jack to become "enveloped in a world of bodily and tactile sensations" (Mitrani &

Mitrani, 1997, p. 164) and also served counterphobic ends. His cutting was counterphobic against underlying autistic fears of spilling out and leaking away into nothing, so that he could watch his blood ooze out from the cuts he made while still reassuring himself that he would not leak away totally. It also seemed to have another kind of counterphobic potential. It was as if he was making deliberate tears in his skin surface so as to test the protective and containing strength of his own skin surface as a barrier or a wall. Even if he made tears in his skin, he could test its resiliency by tearing it, in order to feel reassured his skin would not rip to shreds and tear away completely, thus leaving him flayed, vulnerable, and as exposed as a snail bereft of it shell.

Jack and I spoke repeatedly about his wall. Our discussions arose in the context of his deep interest in architecture and buildings (the overwhelming preoccupation he has as part of his Asperger's). He spoke of both towers and walls. The conversation between Jack and myself, went as follows. We had been speaking of his lack of trust in his peers:

ROBIN: Well, trust is really important.

JACK: Yeah, but there's not a single kid I really trust.

ROBIN: Even your friend Ramjit that we talked about?

JACK: Maybe—maybe I could trust him.

ROBIN: So with trust, how do you measure …?

JACK: With towers.

ROBIN: You measure trust with … towers?

JACK: Yeah, there are four towers in every structure I have for another person.

ROBIN: Structure?

JACK: Yeah, a structure with four towers, including a tower for trust and a tower for friendliness. Each tower has a level and the level can change quickly. It can grow or it can get less. With Ramjit, the trust tower is pretty high, the highest of any of my friends.

ROBIN: And like I said, trust is really important. Including here—I mean between us. I'm wondering if I'm trustworthy enough for you to talk about the trust tower in *my* structure that you have; I mean how my trust tower is right now.

JACK: Oh, I don't mind talking about it—it's been growing.

ROBIN: I'm doing fairly well?

JACK: Yeah, it's been growing since we first met and it's pretty high right now. But the towers can change their height pretty quickly, so …

ROBIN: So I should go carefully?

JACK: Uh, not really. Because of my wall.

ROBIN: So there's a wall between us right now as we speak together here?

JACK: Yeah, but not just between us. I have a wall between me and everybody.

ROBIN: Okay, but we talked about your classmate Valerie before and I got the feeling you were pretty open with her, told her you liked her and didn't have much of a wall between you?

JACK: You're right, but that was stupid of me. I was really tired and I didn't have much of a wall and now I regret it.

ROBIN: You felt she ignored you, right?

JACK: Damn right!

ROBIN: And that wall between us, that's here, right now, as we speak— can I know about that?

JACK: Oh, man, is it *thick*! You'll never break through that wall, not for *years*. It's incredibly thick.

ROBIN: So we may spend a really long time together, huh? But what if I said I didn't want to *break* through your wall or hurt it in any way? That I feel we all need some kind of protection and I want to respect your wall. That I don't want to *break* through it, but maybe to, uh, find a way around it or, uh, maybe some kind of the door in it you might open?

JACK: Well … (hesitating and considering what I said) it's … it's still going to be a long, long time. I'm not sure it can have any door in it—it's a wall. Well, maybe, but it'll be a long time.

ROBIN: I plan to be around for a while.

This should give the flavour of how Jack viewed his wall. I also felt his emphasis on how *thick* his wall was and how *long* it would take me to break through it was an unconscious question about how long I would actually stick with him. I tried to suggest I was going to stick around for him. My experience with him suggests his use of his wall properly places it in the set of autistic protections referenced above that includes shells, barriers and enclaves. Jack's way of talking about his wall clearly suggested an autistic barrier.

Hybrid objects as defences in Asperger's

Finally, we can consider at some length Matt's use of what I have come to call hybrid objects, with the alternating functions (perhaps better called the dual functions since both seemed to be in play at once or in quick alternation) of a symbolic/transitional object and an autosensuous/autistic object. I consider Matt's use of these hybrid objects at sustained length because I think his use beautifully illustrates how Asperger's children can have one foot in the country of autosensuous non-relatedness at the same time that the other foot is firmly placed in the country of object-relatedness along with a sense of vulnerable object-neediness. In fact, I strongly suspect that these two tendencies played into one another in an alternating manner based on the kind of anxiety that was being aroused in Matt. There was almost a kind of "pendulum effect" it seemed to me, in how Matt used these objects. It was as if powerful relational anxieties ("will I be accepted or rejected?") propelled Matt into the autosensuous and autistic defensive use of his little toy objects, whereas existential anxieties ("do I even exist for others except as a thing to be teased and made fun of?") drove him towards the symbolic/transitional use of his small toys. Form of anxiety and manner of defence seemed to be intertwined. Tustin (1986) differentiates between the two kinds of objects. Autistic objects, she writes, "need to be differentiated from Winnicott's 'transitional object' which, having reached the status of an object, and being a combination of 'me' and 'not-me', can facilitate ongoing psychological development" (Tustin, 1986, p. 128).

Matt had one main preoccupation. This was of a kind very typical for Asperger's children. His preoccupation or obsession was with means of transportation. He was continually collecting information about all kinds of vehicles, cars, buses, airplanes, and most centrally, trains. Because of his Estonian heritage, he had travelled widely in Europe, and described to me at length all the different kinds of trains in Europe, the different gauges of track they used, the train stations he had visited and their peculiar and distinguishing features, and how the different vehicles communicated with one another and responded to signals, especially the trains. His preoccupation with transportation spilled over to some degree into a deep but secondary interest in forms of communication, including computers.

In his therapy, some of these themes were developed as relating to his difficulties with peers. We were able to speak about his difficulty communicating with them, reading the social signals that they sent out, and not being able to empathically transport himself into the worlds and interests of some of his peers, as well as his feelings about the reluctance of his peers to transport themselves into his world and his interests.

Beginning in his first session of therapy, Matt made me aware that most of the time, he would come to his therapy sessions clutching a small, hard toy in his hand. These toys almost invariably related to his preoccupation with transportation. He favoured toy cars. He also brought in various train cars, airplanes, and boats. I tried to observe what he did with them during the session. He would hold onto the small toys throughout the whole session, never putting a toy down or placing one in his pocket. At times, he would vigorously squeeze the toy, rub or stroke it or transfer it from hand to hand. Much of the time, he would simply hold onto it tightly.

Matt would also very frequently describe some aspect of his small toy to me. It was as if he treated these toys as ersatz friends. He would tell me something of their history, or how he and his younger sister had argued about them, or how they had become damaged and hurt. At times, I got the impression that the toys were symbolic self-representations and that it was possible to talk about some of his own issues based on what he told me about his small toys. For example, he told me about one small toy car which in Canada is called a "smart car", a very small and fuel-efficient vehicle meant mainly for use in urban areas. The name he gave to the car was "Smart". We were then able to talk about how, like his car, he also was smart, but quite small compared to others.

In the very first session we had together, Matt introduced me to the small toy he was holding, which he named "little green car". It was a little green car. He pointed out scratches which it had on it. After he told me some things about it, I commented that perhaps it was a bit like him—it was cute and full of energy, but with some hurt aspects. He agreed, but added that it was also nice to have something solid and strong simply to hang onto. In this very first session, two aspects of his toy had been highlighted. I stressed the more symbolic aspects of his toy and treated it as a symbolic self-representation which seemed to have both me and not-me aspects. He accepted this but quickly alerted me to another aspect it had for him, namely its sensual and tactile properties. All his toys were hard objects. In addition to having some symbolic aspects, his experience of the toy was also of its sensual properties, like Tustin described autistic objects as having. Matt said his toy was "solid and strong", and therefore that it was something to "hang onto" in order to reduce anxiety. In his first session, he also described a transportation game he had on his computer called "Trainz", which is a railroad simulator. In this game, he coupled and uncoupled the cars of trains. I referred to his wish to be able to "couple up" with friends and him wondering why they wanted to "uncouple" from him.

In his next session, I noted he had brought a different vehicle with him. He introduced me to this car and told me that its name was "Skyway". Later in the session, he said that he had lots of Lego toys but he hasn't finished constructing many of them and can't bear to throw them out. (I wondered to myself whether this could also refer to partially constructed *internal* objects, part objects, which only captured aspects of others, and were thus not whole objects). His great number of unfinished toys, he told me, feels like a warehouse filling up that crushes him. He also feels neglectful of his toys, like a mother who has too much work and so can't play with her babies. As the treatment proceeded, I learned that his mother was often abroad for fairly long periods of time on business. His parents had divorced, and when his mother was abroad, he would stay with his father. He was very attached to his mother and had difficulty tolerating her being away.

Two themes were introduced in his third session, which have continued through his subsequent therapy. He introduced me to another toy car he was clutching in his hand, which he said was called "Smart". "Smart" has made numerous appearances over time in our therapy sessions. He said that this car was "his best friend". I said I felt a little sad about "Smart" being his best friend because maybe his best friend should be a human being. He immediately looked sad and agreed. As I got to know "Smart" and some of his other toys, the more "transitional object aspects" also seemed to stand out. With "Smart", Matt seems to be dealing with an intermediate area of experience, as Winnicott described, in which the object is not-me, but at the same time is not fully a part of external reality. "Smart" and many of his other hard toys functioned for Matt in an intermediate area of experience to which his inner reality and the external world both made a contribution. In this case, Matt's inner reality makes a large contribution to the way in which he views "Smart"—as being his best friend. However, at other times it is the external physical world properties of the toy, its sensuous and tactile properties, which seem to be most central for Matt.

Recall Matt's own description of the split in his self as one of "tiger *vs*. antelope." When he has "meltdowns" or temper tantrums at school, this is his tiger part. When it gets out, he told me, "all hell can break loose". Antelope is the sad, hurt, non-autistic part which is fearful of the tiger part. Antelope does "self-detention" as a punishment for what the tiger has done and it tries to keep tiger in its cage. Antelope wants to show off, to have others see how good it is and how skilled it is. But when the others fail to notice these things, the feelings Matt then experiences feed tiger and make it stronger. Tiger feeds on feelings of being hurt, misunderstood, and teased. Tiger can also take bites out of antelope. Antelope may secretly admire tiger. Tiger seems to represent a more autistic aspect of his personality which has very little tolerance for frustration and is easily provoked to temper tantrums. It seems to be this tiger aspect of the split which is most closely linked to the autistic object aspect of Matt's toys. Antelope seems to represent a more advanced and object-related part of his personality, but it is extremely timid, fearful, and vulnerable. The antelope part of the split is most closely linked to the transitional object aspect of Matt's toys.

I now describe a few more examples of Matt's use of toys over about a year of his therapy. He came with a small hard toy which he called "Cargo Express", because it is a vehicle used for transportation of goods. He referred to this toy as his "long-lost friend". He had apparently lost this toy for quite some time in what he referred to as "an abyss" at his home. We discussed this "abyss" to some extent and how sometimes it might feel like a place where a person could go to be safely alone, and at other times it might feel like a place where you were cut off from others. In the back of my mind was Tustin's notion of "the black hole", but I did not feel Matt's material justified any mention of this.

He began another session by speaking of the small toy airplane he had brought with him. He said he had fixed it with crazy glue, but some parts of it had again started to become loose. We spoke of the expression "having a screw loose" and what that might feel like for his toy airplane.

He brought a small jet airplane with him to one session, which he called "Small Cessna". He said it was different from other jets because it was smaller. Because he had compared "Small Cessna" to other jets, I was able to talk about him comparing himself with other kids. He was well aware that he seemed to have different interests from the other kids at school. He might be interested in trains, whereas they seem to be interested in other things such as the latest pop song.

In his first session after a summer vacation, Matt spoke of wanting to sit in the same chair and not a different one. I replied that sometimes having things predictable and the same might make him feel more comfortable. He said he had seen a smart car outside on the way into my office. He had also taken his smart car "Smart" on his summer vacation visit to Estonia. I said that having familiar and predictable things with him was also comforting.

Matt brought another toy airplane with him to one session. When toward the end of his session I spoke about the timing of his next session, he wanted to know what toy he should bring with him. He said if he knew what toy to bring, this would help him decide what he might talk about. He seemed to be giving a transitional object significance to his toys in that they apparently helped him get into the intermediate area of experience represented by free association and fantasy.

Matt brought a small toy boat with him to one session. He said that it was originally designed as a gunboat, but he had made it into a cargo ship. I said that a gunboat might feel it had some protection, but could also feel threatened by enemies. A cargo ship, while not feeling so protected, might feel it was doing a good job in the world. Matt then spoke of a new kind of submarine, which could operate in "stealth mode". I took him up on the issue of stealth mode, saying perhaps this was something that could be helpful to him sometimes. Perhaps sometimes he could be quiet and unobserved in his classroom and hope that this might avoid trouble for him. He agreed that sometimes he did go into "stealth mode".

Matt began one session by showing me the "toy" he was clutching in his hand—it was the old CPU ("central processing unit") he had taken from his dad's computer. I silently wondered about him holding on to something perhaps symbolic of paternal phallic power. He made reference to both his father and his stepfather. I commented that perhaps it felt good to have something powerful like his dad's CPU that he could keep with him. We then talked about his own CPU, meaning his brain, and some of the things we hoped might happen, such as connecting up his emotional circuits and getting the tiger part and the antelope part to work together. He was then able to speak specifically and I felt rather courageously about some of his fears. When it is dark, he told me, he is afraid of monsters and aliens and he has to keep on his light.

I wondered about him possibly feeling like an alien, feeling different from other kids and feeling alienated from what they did. He sadly agreed. He then spoke of fears about what he referred to as "structural collapse". I said there was probably a word for this as it applied to human beings, and the word was puberty. Puberty involves incredible structural changes in a person and the structural collapse of how we were as children. I could see that this reference was making him anxious. He went on to talk of a movie in which a male robot gets covered in trash but falls in love with a female robot called Eve. He described another cartoon situation in which a cat was not being taken care of and therefore blew a fan across its litter box so the owner would know to help it and take care of the poop. I said that when you have to take care of a poopy situation, it's important that others should understand and try to help you cope with the poopy stuff. Matt agreed. At the end of this session, he referred to himself as being cute and he put on his baby voice. I got the feeling that this was a form of clinging to his cute child self while fearfully avoiding his burgeoning pubescent self. His hard toy, the CPU, seemed to have both transitional and autistic aspects. Its transitional function seemed to be to help him hold on to reassuring and powerful aspects of his father while still maintaining separateness from the father. There also seemed to be a regression from more libidinal themes (the robot falling in love) to anal or even more primitive themes (covered in trash, poopy stuff, structural collapse). His clutching of the CPU, turning it in his hands and rubbing it, seemed to provide a more autistic and autosensuous form of soothing as he confronted the more primitive themes.

Matt brought with him a train engine which he said was called "cuddly engine". Cuddly engine was like one he had seen on vacation in Estonia. This engine was friends with some of his other toys, such as "Smart" the smart car and "Cargo Express". Cuddly engine seemed to have some significant transitional aspects—it was a hard object, but was also cuddly. His fantasy was that it was friends with some of his other toys, and this seemed to be in the transitional world of imagination.

Three more examples follow taken from psychotherapy sessions over a period of five months. How Matt held, clutched and turned these objects in his hand throughout our sessions suggested all had the autosensuous properties experienced as a result of the use of autistic objects. At the same time, all three seemed at least in some degree to involve self-representations. Matt brought in a small toy truck. He spoke of very small vehicles such as this small toy truck and ultralight aircraft, as compared with very large vehicles such as the jet airplane he had flown on a computer game which is a flight simulator. The comparison of sizes made me think of his small stature compared with other kids his age who were much larger. I had it in mind to raise this issue, but Matt went on to other themes. He brought in what he specifically said was a Pacific Union train engine. He said that it was cute and that he had another orange train that was very much like it. He said that he had stepped on this train and had broken all four windows in it. He said he was not sure he had forgiveness from it. We again did not get to deal specifically with some of the issues that seem embedded in his description of the train engine. The fact that it was cute certainly reminded me of Matt. I had the feeling that he was talking about broken or damaged aspects of himself for which he felt some responsibility. He brought in another train engine that he said had become disconnected from its other cars and was now by itself. Picking up on this theme of connection/disconnection, I wondered if this train car might be able to connect with the other cars again. I had in mind his disconnection from peers and wish to be connected with them. He replied that getting it connected again would be more difficult, but then went on to another theme so that we did not come back to connection/disconnection.

In his classical paper "Transitional objects and transitional phenomena" (1951, included in 1975), Winnicott specifically indicates that the transitional object to which the infant becomes attached can include a hard toy. He notes that boys "to some extent tend to go over to use hard objects" (1975, p. 232), and refers to transitional phenomena as comprising what he calls "an intermediate area of experience which is not challenged". This intermediate area of experience is said to include the arts (which I take to mean literature, music, dance, and the figurative arts) as well as religion. The notions of "intermediate" and "transitional" refer to phenomena which have aspects of both inner and outer reality but cannot be exclusively confined to either and which also shift back and forth between and thus make transitions between inner reality and outer reality. Consider a Salvador Dali painting as an example. Nobody would "challenge" it because it is not a photographically accurate representation of reality. The attitude towards it would likely be a contemplative one, taking into account both Dali's feverish imagination and inner world as well as his painting technique and style, use of colours and so on. In creating such an object, the artist is forced to make repeated transitions between the inner world of imagination/representation and the outer world of artistic style, technique, and materials. Dali imagines and visualises, for example, his soft watches as they droop and dribble. But he must also buy the appropriate canvas, coat the canvas with gesso, choose which paintbrushes to use, decide how thickly to use the paint (maybe some impasto technique—perhaps use a palette knife), how to mix and apply the colours and so on. In creating his painting, he will repeatedly transition between his own inner imaginative world containing the soft, honey-like watches which attract bees—as opposed to how he will use his real life materials to represent what he imagines— does he use cobalt blue or cerulean blue; short, stubby, and crosshatched brushstrokes or long flowing and graceful ones? And so on.

Transitional objects as Winnicott describes them seem to involve a number of transitions between different but related polarities. One central transition as noted just above is that between the polarity of internal world and external world. A closely related polarity also just described is that between fantasy/imagination *vs.* style and materials (materials including paint and paintbrushes in art; rock, chisels, and hammers in sculpture; words and literary tropes in literature; musical instruments and their auditory characteristics in music, and so on). Two other polarities are those of me *vs.* not-me and symbiosis *vs.* separation/autonomy. The last noted is of course in the language of Mahler and not Winnicott, but is strongly implied in how Winnicott writes. Symbiotic aspects are implied in the infant's use of the transitional object, such that it must be physically with the infant in many circumstances, can never be washed or significantly altered by reality and in some ways is a substitute for mother and mother's breast. However, it is also the first not-me possession and is clearly distinct from the mother and her breast for the infant, thus suggesting the beginnings of separation and autonomy.

Tustin is extremely helpful in distinguishing between transitional objects and autistic objects in reference to the polarity me and not-me. She writes that the transitional object "is a combination of 'me' and 'not-me' and helps to link the two together. The transitional object is a *bridge* to the 'not-me'; autistic objects are a *barrier* to it" (Tustin, 1990, p. 99). She elaborates this further when she states that the main function of autistic objects is one of *evasion* in that "they are a protection against, and an escape from, the 'not-me' outside world, whereas the main function of the transitional object is to help the child to tolerate, express and manage his feelings in relation to it" (Tustin, 1992, p. 132). As a result, "transitional objects are a *bridge* to the 'not-self' mother; they enable the child to wait until she comes; they keep her alive in his mind". Autistic objects constitute "a *barrier* between the child and the nurturing people who want to help him" (ibid, p. 132). Mitrani echoes this distinction, referring to transitional objects as a combination of 'me' and 'not me' "that constitutes a bridge that links the two together during physical absence," whereas autistic objects are "barriers to the awareness of 'not me' and as such are an impediment to growth and development" (Mitrani, 2015, p. 192, n. 5).

Transitional objects are transitions which occur in the intermediate area between the polarities of the subjective and what is objectively perceived. The importance and significance given to the transitional object by the infant is highly subjective, but it is also a real and objective thing which can be forgotten, lost, damaged or subject to any of the vicissitudes of real objects. A similar comment applies with equal force to a Dali painting. It has a high degree of subjective significance for Dali and for many viewers of his paintings. It is also a real physical object which can be damaged or destroyed. Transitional objects also shift between what is within and what is without.

The transitional object is also endowed with a symbolic and representational aspect. It stands for the maternal breast, indirectly for the external breast and the infant's experience of it and more directly for the internal representation of the breast. It has relationships to both.

Transitional objects partake of illusion. What Salvador Dali paints are also surrealistic illusions if judged by the yardstick of ordinary everyday reality.

Winnicott (1975) notes that the transitional object becomes vitally important to the infant at certain times such as going to sleep, "and is a defence against anxiety, especially anxiety of depressive type" (Winnicott, 1975, p. 232). The way Matt used his small, hard toys strongly suggested this kind of defensive aspect. He was especially prone to bring them to therapy sessions when his mother was out of town on business. They seemed to serve as defences against the experience of grief, separation anxiety, sadness, and depression at the missing mother as well as other depressive anxieties such as fantasies around how his own inner destructiveness (the tiger part of his ego split) may have driven the mother to go away.

For Tustin, his perception of horrible dangers prompts the autistic child to use auto-sensuousness in generating autistic objects. Autistic objects (along with autistic sensation shapes) generate a sensual and protective shell, making the child feel strong and safe. The crucial feature of the autistic object is not any feature of the object itself, but the sensations the object creates on the child's skin. The sensations could be ones made by a small metal "car hidden in the hollow of the hand" or by "hard metal trains and cars" (Tustin, 1992, p. 95, p. 112). Autistic objects are used obsessively and in idiosyncratic ways for the child. They may be pressed very hard into the hand and be experienced as a part of the body. They are not associated for the child with fantasies but function only to create sensuous experiences. For the autistic child, an autistic object is primarily if not exclusively a sensation or set of sensations. Autistic objects are used in a repetitive and ritualised manner. Autistic objects are also interchangeable in the sense that their important feature is not any characteristic of the objects themselves, but the sensations they produce. One autistic object is easily replaced by another, provided it produces the same sensations for the child. There is no representational aspect to an autistic object. Tustin (1992, p. 114) describes an autistic child who used a small metal car not to *represent* his feelings about his home and himself, but to *be actual parts* of these things.

"Hardness" is said to be a typical feature of most autistic objects. This sense of hardness gives the child the feeling that the autistic object keeps him safe. Hardness, writes Tustin "helps the soft and vulnerable child to feel safe in a world which seems fraught with unspeakable dangers, and about which he feels unutterable terror" (Tustin, 1992, p. 115).

Autistic objects are experienced as being a part of the child's body. They tend to be "clutched or squeezed tightly so that they leave an impression behind" (Tustin, 1990, p. 40) with a sense on the child's part that the hardness and impenetrability of the object will become part of their body. The autistic object is experienced as keeping the child safe. Autistic objects are described as being "me" objects that help the child feel safe and which "shut out distressing flashes of awareness of what is felt to be the dangerous 'not-me', which seems to threaten both their existence and their safety" (Tustin, 1990, p. 99). Because they are experienced as being part of the child's body, they shut out awareness of bodily separateness, and defend against the existential anxiety I have referred to as separateness anxiety. "They are hard objects that are clutched tightly. They make the child feel hard, impenetrable, in absolute control, and thus safe" (Tustin, 1990, p. 151). Tustin (1992, p. 133) states that hard autistic objects "completely obstruct awareness of the 'not-me'" and she adds that the autistic object

> is used in two-dimensional states of awareness, in which there is no knowledge of outsides or insides. It is a surface which can be grasped and which, in the delusion of fusion, can seem to enplate the child in a protective shell. (Tustin, 1992, p. 133)

Autistic objects also insulate the child from the experience of object loss and any sense of separateness. The autistic object is always present in an autosensuously gratifying manner and the child is therefore not stimulated to call absent people or objects to mind.

Tustin notes that autistic objects tend to be used when there is frustration and resulting temper tantrums. "When frustration impinges, tantrums pound through muscle and vein and cause the child to fear total annihilation. To counteract this deadly terror he clutches a hard autistic object" (Tustin, 1992, p. 123). Matt's classroom tantrums seem to match Tustin's description.

Whether we call an object transitional or autistic is a *functional* distinction, that is, *it depends completely on how the child uses the object*. The qualities of the object itself play only a minor role in the distinction. For example, it is typical to think of a transitional object in terms of a soft toy such as a teddy bear, and is typical to think of an autistic object as being hard. Neither of these are essential features. The essential feature is how the child uses the object, regardless of the physical properties of that object.

I refer to the toys Matt brought to his therapy sessions as being "hybrid objects". This is simply to notice that Matt used these objects in two different ways at the same time. He made use of his small toys as transitional objects while at the same time making use of them as autistic objects.

Matt used his small toys in a transitional object modality. He had fantasies of these toys interacting with and being friends with each other, and he also experienced them as being personal friends as well—his best friend, his long-lost friend, and so on. He had a fantasy as to whether or not one toy might forgive him for damage he had accidentally inflicted on it. I tended to make interpretations based on his toys as being symbolic self-representations. Most of the time, Matt accepted my comments and sometimes was able to add to them. He tended to bring in small toys most frequently when his mother was away on business, just as a small child might cling more strongly to their beloved stuffed animal. The transitional qualities of his objects included their functioning in an intermediate area of experience, that of fantasy, having qualities from both his internal world and from the external world, and functioning as "not-me" objects which still had some "me" qualities.

There was also considerable evidence that Matt used his small toys in an autistic object modality as well. Recall that his primary interest and strongest obsession was with means of transportation. All the toys he brought in fit with this strongest obsession, with the exception of the CPU of his father's computer, which fit in with his secondary obsession with communication. He specifically pointed out to me how he wanted his toys as something to hang onto. Having observed numerous young autistic children and their handling of small toys they needed to keep with them, how Matt handled his small toys seemed quite similar. He seemed to experience them as a source of autosensuous stimulation. As noted, he brought the small toys more frequently when his mother was away, and his handling of these toys seemed to help him blot out to some extent his awareness of her absence and his separation from her. At these times, his toys seemed to function as "me" objects which diminished at least some aspects of his awareness of reality. Matt would clutch his toys tightly. There was a ritualised aspect in how he brought them to his sessions or needed to have them with him when he took trips abroad. The sensuous experience of his toys seemed to offer Matt some degree of escape from everyday reality.

Most of the time, these two different modalities of handling his toys seemed to be present at the same time and, with some shifts back and forth, to have roughly equal importance to him. In this sense, functioning for Matt in two different modalities at the same time, the toys he used seemed to be true "hybrid objects".

Many aspects in Matt's psychotherapy suggested the presence of a split in the ego or the self. This was mainly in terms of antelope *vs.* tiger. Our understanding of antelope and tiger built up over the course of Matt's therapy so that we ended up with a detailed and quite complex picture of many aspects of how these two parts of his personality interacted with and impacted on each other. To give the simplest of summaries: tiger seemed to represent a more autistic-like aspect of Matt's personality functioning whereas antelope seems to represent a more highly developed aspect capable of object relations but accompanied by a great deal of neediness, anxiety and timidity. To frame this in a more Kleinian manner using Ogden's notion of the three positions of autistic-contiguous, paranoid-schizoid, and depressive; tiger seemed to reflect a combination of the autistic-contiguous and paranoid-schizoid positions, whereas antelope seems to reflect mostly the depressive position but sometimes shading into more paranoid-schizoid issues. Tiger had very low frustration tolerance, would easily disintegrate into temper tantrums, and seemed to represent a kind of protective autistic shell which kept other people at a distance from him. Tiger seemed to need mother's physical presence in a reassuring way and to become very disturbed when she was absent. Antelope was very frightened of tiger, and as the names clearly suggest, his antelope part was fearful, skittish, and quick to take flight. However, it was also needy, dependent, and timidly hopeful of supportive object relationships from others. Antelope was closely attached to his mother and very much missed her when she was away. Antelope was also capable of depressive anxieties in that it had questions about whether its bad behaviour caused his mother to go away on business and caused his peers to distance themselves from him. Antelope was quite capable of guilt, and Matt in his antelope guise expressed a great deal of guilty worry about the emotional damage tiger may have wrought—both to himself and to others.

When he was describing the tiger aspect, Matt seemed to use his toys more as autistic objects. He tended to rub them, stroke them, clutch them forcefully or pass them from hand to hand. His use of objects in a transitional mode was more object-related. It also gave Matt scope for the use of the intermediate area of experience which is called fantasy. When they were used as transitional objects, Matt could describe friendly relationships between different toys and how they could be connected or disconnected with other toys. Sometimes the two aspects of autistic *vs.* symbolic/representational/transitional were difficult to separate. My own tendency may have been to promote and pursue the transitional aspects of how he used objects and to wishfully underestimate how much he used them as autistic objects. Consider a single example. As noted, one "toy" he brought to a session was the old CPU from his father's computer. Well, here we are in the Oedipal, aren't we? He has his father's CPU, which for Matt was certainly a potent object. But not so fast! Matt also clutches the CPU in a way that could suggest he experiences it as almost at an adjunct to or a bit of his own body. It may be important not to lose sight of the autistic-contiguous aspects of the CPU.

Recall Matt's very first session, to which he brought "little green car". My immediate response was to see this in a transitional/symbolic light as a kind of self-representation. Although Matt agreed with me, he added a correction or at least an amplification to how I was seeing things. His addition was that it was also nice just to have something solid and strong to hang onto. In retrospect, it was as if he needed to let me know about the more autistic-like aspect of his "little green car", in addition to the transitional aspect which I had latched onto. I now wonder in retrospect whether I might have missed something else. The paternally protective aspect of my countertransference, leading me to see him as anxious, helpless, and vulnerable, may have covered over for me that aspect of his transference in which he saw me as anxiety-provoking because I might react to him just as he perceived his peers had done. For Matt, I may have been protective, but possibly also threatening. There were times when Matt seemed to go into anxiety states which prevented him from talking to me. I wonder whether one autistic-like aspect of his use of small, hard toys might have been to sometimes help insulate him from fully confronting my existence as a separate object.

Matt's use of small, hard toys points to a possibility—the possibility that the Asperger's child has one foot in the world of autistic autosensuousness and the other foot in the world of object relatedness. Matt used his toys both as autistic objects to fend off existential anxieties as well as symbolic/transitional objects to cope with object relational anxieties.

Summary

In this chapter, I have given an outline of the main types of anxiety experienced by Asperger's children, and the main defences they typically use in the attempt to cope with their anxieties. I suggest they experience relational anxieties and existential anxieties. Relational anxieties are usually very much in the foreground, with existential anxieties bursting out when the child is under stress. The defences these children tend to use occur in three layers. The first level or layer is comprised of the primary or cornerstone defences of splitting of the self and projective identification into remote objects. The second level includes intellectualisation, idealisation, denigration, denial, and other defences. The third level is comprised of specifically autistic defences, including the use of psychic walls or internal fortresses, autistic shapes, and autistic objects as these defences have been described in the work of Frances Tustin.

CHAPTER ELEVEN

Defences in Asperger's children continued—should we call it splitting or dissociation?

We now embark on a discussion that for me has some echoes of fruitless philosophical verbal controversies around which is the appropriate conceptual label that is to be applied to certain phenomena. This difficulty in how we should describe and label a phenomenon also involves something quite common in the field of psychoanalysis, namely clashes between different psychoanalytic schools along with both the theoretical and the interpersonal loyalties these clashes typically involve. I suggest it would not be unusual for a person identifying with the object relations school to march under the banner of splitting, whereas a person adhering to the relational school would tend to raise the flag of dissociation. Nevertheless, whatever the philosophical overtones of the differences in how we label phenomena, I believe substantive differences are involved in whether we see Asperger's children as strongly manifesting the defence of splitting of the self or whether we view this as dissociation, or if we might see both defences as being implicated. To lay my own cards on the table face up, I feel a great deal of sympathy for both schools of thought, but have not sworn an undying oath of fealty to either school. As a result, I hope I can bring to the following discussion a significant degree of sympathy for both splitting and for dissociation as ways of understanding Asperger's children.

Bromberg on dissociation

The work carried out by relational psychoanalysts and especially by Philip Bromberg (1998, 2006, 2011) raises a number of issues highly pertinent to our attempts to understand Asperger's children and their typical ways of being and psychodynamics. In what follows, I focus on Bromberg's most recent (2011) contribution. At the centre of Bromberg's work stands a highly creative triptych consisting of three closely related and dialectically interacting claims. These three fundamental claims are as follows. First, he asserts that *everyone* has experienced some kind of trauma to some degree during the course of his or her growth and development. Experiences involving trauma and being traumatised are, according to Bromberg, universal and unavoidable aspects of becoming human.

Second, because of the universal experience of being traumatised, dissociation takes centre stage as the key and central defensive operation used by most if not all people. Many other defences are also used, including that of splitting. The key, however, is that "mental functioning is inherently a dialectic between dissociation and conflict and cannot justifiably be seen as based on conflict alone" (Bromberg, 2011, p. 77). In other words, dissociation is the main and likely the only self-protective process or defence that is deployed in an attempt to deal with trauma, whereas other defences such as splitting are employed to deal with intrapsychic conflict, according to Bromberg. Part of this way of looking at things is that conflict is viewed as a significant developmental *achievement*, a sort of developmental pinnacle. The aim of therapy is to allow the patient to achieve a state in which internal conflict becomes central and the focus of treatment. Before this is possible, however, the patient's use of dissociative functioning must first be addressed and a voice be given to the different self-states which are sequestered from each other as a result of this dissociation.

This leads on to the third and final panel in Bromberg's triptych of mental functioning. Following from and fully integrated with the first two assertions is the third assertion that a unitary core self which gives healthy people a single central identity simply does not exist. All people are composites or have composite selves, formed by alternations between different alters or different self-states. Every person is therefore a medley, a pastiche or a potpourri of mutually exclusive self-states. In normal, healthy and adaptive functioning, the use of dissociation is not disruptive and as a result, the transitions between different self-states are not abrupt shifts but smooth, seamless and largely unnoticed transitions. At the other extreme, we enter the territory of dissociative identity disorder in which the alters or different self-states are radically different. There is no unitary core self but a disjointed series of self-states with the transitions between them being abrupt and potentially destabilising. This third claim raises an interesting question which I feel unready to deal with at the present time. This question is how to adequately distinguish among three significantly overlapping theoretical constructs: split-off parts of the self (which has long been part of Kleinian thinking); autistic enclaves, cysts or encapsulations (which has become central in the thinking of those who follow Tustin in dealing with autistic states); and different self-states or alters (central to the thinking of Bromberg and others). Are these simply alternative ways of trying to describe *the same* basic phenomenon, the fruitless philosophical verbal controversies I noted above, or do they represent different psychological patterns with considerably different clinical and treatment implications? I incline to the latter view, but I am so far not fully certain about these distinctions.

I now want to consider each of Bromberg's three foundational claims at greater length, and start to tease out possible implications of these claims. These claims have the potential to change how we understand Asperger's children. Underlying this is the main question I feel we need to wrestle with. The question: is one of the central defensive processes used by Asperger's children best seen as splitting of the self (which according to Bromberg implies internal conflicts) or would this better be seen as dissociative processes at work (implying experiences of trauma and different self-states)? Or, are these two defensive processes really no more than alternative ways of describing the same underlying process, so that at least for Asperger's children, splitting of the self and dissociation among different self-states amounts to the same thing?

A subsidiary question relates to projective identification and its status. The answer to this subsidiary question is that Bromberg apparently takes projective identification to be "a core element in the process of enactment" (Bromberg, 2011, p. xxx) and on the next page, Schore, in his Foreword to Bromberg's book writes that "subsymbolic communications of 'not—me' states (mutual deep projective identifications) are subcortical nonconscious communications between … the patient and therapist" (2011, p. xxxi). Projective identification can be considered as being an important defensive and communicative process for Bromberg (see Bromberg, 2006, p. 185).

Consider Bromberg's (2011, p. 13) treatment of the concept of trauma. He considers it *not* to be something unusual and extraordinary, "not as a special situation but as a continuum" and in addition, if "we accept that developmental trauma is a core phenomenon in the shaping of personality then we also accept that it exists for everyone and is always a matter of degree" (ibid, p. 14). Even a secure attachment offers the person stability only to a degree, meaning that "everyone is vulnerable to the experience of having to face something that is more than his mind can deal with" and as a result, being vulnerable to what Bromberg refers to (using the terms synonymously) as "developmental trauma" or else "relational trauma" (ibid, p. 14). Bromberg is crystal clear that developmental trauma is a universal experience—"a core relational phenomenon and invariably shapes personality in every human being" (ibid, p. 32). In addition, developmental or relational trauma "is always part of what shapes early attachment patterns (including 'secure attachment')" and it is as a result "an inevitable aspect of early life to varying degrees, and is of significance in all analytic work". Further to this, "attachment-related trauma is part of everyone's past and a factor in every treatment experience, but for some patients it has led to a dissociative mental structure that virtually takes over personality functioning and mental life" (ibid, p. 99).

Bromberg refers to a patient who suffered "the cumulative trauma of neglect and disconfirmation" this as a result of "personal invalidation" by her mother along with the frustration of her "normal developmental need for an interested mother" (Bromberg, 2011, p. 111). The mention of "cumulative trauma" of course brings to mind Masud Khan's (1963, 1964) seminal works using this concept. Bromberg also refers to "the trauma of nonrecognition" (2011, p. 93) as a result of the childhood experience of "being valueless as a source of pleasure to a needed other" (ibid, p. 94) as well as to developmental trauma resulting from consistent and cumulative "nonrecognition and disconfirmation" of the child's self-experience (ibid, p. 4).

Bromberg's view is that developmental trauma is a universal and a core relational experience that shapes both early attachment patterns as well as adult personality functioning. Tustin was equally clear about her view that "autism is a reaction to trauma" (Mitrani & Mitrani, 1997, p. 12), with autism resulting from a situation which is biphasic in nature; a first phase in which the infant is undifferentiated from the mother and in a state of adhesive equation with her, then followed by a second phase including "the shock of the *traumatic awareness in infancy of bodily separateness from the mothering person*" this awareness being both "*premature and traumatic*" (ibid, p. 259). Both theorists strongly emphasised trauma. But are their theories applicable to Asperger's?

The traumatic origins of autism are strongly debated; to give only one example, debated by Grotstein in his contribution to Mitrani and Mitrani (1997, pp. 257–290). His stance is that a traumatic origin for autism is "problematic", autism being "a nontraumatic disorder of development" (ibid, p. 282). However, the neurobiological impairments that are part of autism for Grotstein still render autistic children "more prone to being traumatised in attempting maturation" (ibid, p. 282).

If it is accurate to say that suffering some kind of developmental trauma is both a universal and a core relational experience, then it seems to me that Asperger's offers, *because of* the neurobiological impairments that are part of it, a very fertile ground for specific traumatic experiences. Among the neurobiological impairments afflicting the Asperger's infant, we are likely to discover heightened sensitivity and therefore vulnerability to being overwhelmed by and traumatised by different kinds of environmental stimuli, perhaps sound in particular (see Chapter Thirteen for a fuller discussion). The Asperger's infant is also likely to be compromised in his ability to participate in establishing a "rhythm of safety" with his mother (see Mitrani & Mitrani, 1997, p. 376), and in the production of consistent and interpretable behavioural cues his mother can use to sort out his "emotional location". Her difficulty in emotional location of and subsequent connection with her infant is likely as well to impede, at least at times, her capacity for reverie and her ability to function as a "good enough container" for her Asperger's infant.

The end result of this may be as Bromberg suggests; a cumulative developmental trauma deriving from gaps in the mother's capacity for reverie and in her resulting ability (sometimes) or inability (at other times) to exercise a good enough containing function for her infant. Over time, the infant's normative tendency to split the maternal object into good and bad mother aspects may be augmented by and dovetail with his unpredictably shifting experience of her as a good enough or a not good enough container, this in turn being as a result of her own struggles to comprehend and connect with her biologically compromised infant.

I have here used the language of splitting. Could it also be that some of the Asperger's infant's self-states derive from experiences traumatic enough that they are dissociated rather than split off? And this raises the additional problem of spelling out the differences (if there are any) between "split-off parts of the self" and "dissociated self-states". Bromberg writes about dissociated self-states as if they were completely isolated from each other, mutually cut off, segregated, insulated, sequestered or quarantined—choose your metaphor. To quote an example from Bromberg he writes:

> When dissociation is enlisted as a defence against trauma, the brain utilises its hypnoid function to limit self-state communication, thereby insulating the mental stability of each separate state. Self-continuity is thus preserved within each state, but self-coherence across states is sacrificed and replaced by a dissociative mental structure that forecloses the possibility of conflictual experience. (Bromberg, 2011, p. 161)

Bromberg also notes (ibid, p. 42) that "When dissociation is operating, each state of consciousness holds its own experientially and encapsulated 'truth'".

Along with this, Bromberg also understands dissociation as a basic and universal mode of defence, extending "his trauma-dissociation model ... to the treatment of all patients" and asserting that dissociation is "observable at many points in every treatment" (ibid, p. xxv). Furthermore, dissociation "is a healthy, adaptive function of the human mind—a basic process that allows individual self-states to function optimally" and *not just defensively*, under appropriate conditions (ibid, p. 48). While referring to both pathological dissociation and to normal dissociation, Bromberg refers to the latter as "a hypnoid brain mechanism that is intrinsic to everyday mental functioning, assures that the mind functions as creatively as possible, selecting whichever self-state configuration is most adaptive to the moment" (Bromberg, 2011, p. 161).

Kleinian writers often treat split-off aspects of the ego as if they were completely sequestered and unavailable to consciousness, very similarly to how Bromberg writes about dissociated self-states. Bromberg (2011) invokes the language of "me" and "not-me", so similar to how Tustin describes the functioning of autistic children, in order to describe the functioning of self-states. The currently active self-state is experienced as "me" and all other self-states as "not-me". He comments that:

> The mind recruits its self-states into a covert survival team. Its members are aware of one another only on a need-to-know basis and they exercise their skills through their insulation from each other. Each self-state has its own task and is dedicated to uphold-ing its own version of truth. (Bromberg, 2011, p. 30)

Bromberg makes it clear that prior to treatment, different self-states have zero to minimal awareness of each other. He states, for example, that the mind/brain tries "to shut down experiential access to self-states that are disjunctive with the dissociatively limited range of the state that is experienced as 'me' at a given moment", so that there is a "rigid sequestering of self-states" (ibid, p. 15).

Bromberg is clear that self-states can be adversarial with each other, moving "from being separate but collaborative to being inhospitable and even adversarial, sequestered from one another" (ibid, p. 69) and that "self-state collisions are inherent to routine mental functioning" (ibid, p. 31). He notes that the capacity of one self-state "to recognise other parts as 'me' is always relative" (ibid, p. 150) and that self-states are such highly individualised "modules of being" that each one is "configured by its own organisation of cognitions, beliefs, dominant affect and mood, access to memory, skills, behaviours, values, actions, and regulatory physiology" (ibid, p. 73). The overall impression is that self-states are highly individualised in their functioning, strongly sepa-rated from one another (*sequestered* and *insulated* being his preferred metaphors in the previous quotations), and that they can be adver-sarial and can have "collisions". If I have understood Bromberg cor-rectly in the quotations previously given, I think he would agree that by and large, different self-states are quite unconscious of each other, one of the goals of treatment actually being to increase mutual self-awareness among the patient's different self-states. As the quotation last given above makes crystal clear, different self-states are structured, organised, and function in very different ways. However, they can be mutually "inhospitable", they can be "adversarial" and they can have "collisions" as Bromberg writes in some of the quotations given above. What is he getting at?

It seems to me that Bromberg wants to avoid conflict language, to avoid saying that self-states are "in conflict", or "have conflicting values" or "conflicting motivations". Dissociated self-states for him preclude the experience of intrapsychic conflict, so that therapeutic work must first be done in lessening the power of dissociation and making different self-states more aware of each other and thus more capable of cooperation. This for Bromberg is a prerequisite for intrapsychic conflict to be experienced and to be worked on therapeutically.

As our discussion proceeds and our understandings of Asperger's children move toward centre stage, it might be useful to select two "prime examples" of Asperger's children to anchor the discussion. I have chosen to use Matt (Chapter Three) and Thanos (Chapter Five) as these examples. Matt described his two "self-parts" (whether we end up calling them splits in the self or self-states) as being antelope and tiger. It was Matt who provided me with these names for his different ways of functioning, the different aspects of his self, derived from a nature programme he saw on television concerning predator-prey relationships in Africa. Thanos also provided his description of his different "self-parts", his description being based on an Internet game in which he played different roles for different countries. Thanos supplied the names, but how each part functioned was clarified from "co-constructions" to which both of us made contributions. These different parts included the Greek part (civilised, highly intellectual, arrogantly superior, and victimised), the Turkish part (uncivilised, angry, vindictive, and bullying), and a Bulgarian part (primitive, impulse-ridden, corrupt, and corrupting, and wallowing in masturbatory self-indulgence).

Two features stand out as characterising their different aspects of their self or their self-parts for both Matt and for Thanos. First, these different parts seemed to be fully, or at the very least moderately, conscious of each other and also of the fundamental differences in how each other tended to function. Some therapeutic work was required to clarify the *details* of how the different parts functioned. Little work was required for either patient to accept the existence of and to elaborate on the interactions between each of their different self-parts or self-aspects. This same comment holds true of every Asperger's child, adolescent or adult, I have been privileged to work with.

Second, a regular feature of the different parts was inhospitable and adversarial interactions and what Bromberg has referred to as "self-state collisions". In fact, it would be difficult to avoid the formulation that the different self-parts were, for Matt and for Thanos (and for all the other Asperger's patients I have worked with) in *direct conflict*. To give the barest of examples, Matt's antelope part would impose "self-detentions" and other forms of self-punishment when his tiger part had lost control. Thanos' Bulgarian part attempted from the way he experienced things to pervert, subvert and corrupt his other parts, especially the haughtily superior Greek part by, from his point of view, dragging his other parts down into a filthy and rancidly polluted mire of chronic and compulsive masturbatory self-indulgence. It was the awareness, of each part of Thanos' self, of the wishes, intentions, needs, and activities of the *other* parts that seemed to strongly motivate these internecine conflicts.

On these two points, consider Bromberg's "trauma-dissociation model", as Schore refers to it (Bromberg, 2011, p. xxv, although "trauma-dissociation-sequestered self-state model" might be a more complete designation). This model does not seem to fit very well with Asperger's as far as I have been able to observe it. The different self-parts of Asperger's children seem to have *at the very least* a moderate degree of consciousness for each other and *not* to be totally sequestered from each other as they would be in Bromberg's model. They also seem to engage in direct, head-on conflicts with each other, as opposed to simply "colliding" because they function so differently. But we can directly compare the Bromberg "trauma-dissociation model" with what I suggest Kernberg might refer to as his "conflict-splitting model", but what I will come to call the Kernberg "trauma-splitting model".

The trauma-dissociation model and the trauma-splitting model

Kernberg's (1976) ideas about split apart ego states overlap significantly, but also incompletely and confusingly, with the ideas and conceptualisations of Bromberg (2011) about self-states. I outlined Kernberg's (1976, p. 20) position previously, and will only briefly summarise it here. For Kernberg, when the ego is split, the result is the "alternating activation of contradictory ego states" which he characterises as "compartmentalised" (with Bromberg preferring the different metaphors of the states being mutually "sequestered" or "insulated" from each other). Kernberg refers to the states as being "temporarily ego syntonic," with Bromberg preferring to refer to the temporarily ego syntonic aspect as being the current 'me' self-state. Kernberg goes on to describe split- ting of the ego as involving the complete separation from each other of a number of psychic manifestations, "involving affect, ideational content, subjective and behavioural manifestations" (Kernberg, 1976, p. 20), and as specifically involving a "specific, well-structured alter- nation between opposite, completely irreconcilable affect states" (1976, p. 23). Bromberg (2011, p. 73), as I have previously outlined, echoes Kernberg very closely. For Kernberg, affect states are separated from each other, as (similarly) for Bromberg "dominant affect and mood" are separated for different self-states. Turning from affect to thinking, for Kernberg it is the ideational contents of different ego states that are separated, whereas for Bromberg it is the "cognitions, beliefs" of differ- ent self-states. Turning finally to overt behaviours, Kernberg writes of a separation between different behavioural manifestations for different ego states, and Bromberg echoes this by writing about the separation of "behaviours, actions" in different self-states.

For Kernberg (1976, p. 23), splitting of the ego results in the crea- tion of "two selves, equally strong" which are activated successively so that they alternate in the person's conscious experience, and are "completely separated from each other in their emotions although not in the patient's memory". Here, I believe, we have a crucial point of disagreement between Kernberg and Bromberg. For Kernberg, the dif- ferent parts of the split ego, the different ego states, are not separated in memory. All the different ego states have access to more or less the same "pool" of memories. For Bromberg, the different self-states have differ- ent "access to memory", with the current "me" self-state monopolising this access.

On this specific point, based on my experience with Asperger's patients, the Kernberg "trauma-splitting model" (to be more fully describe shortly) represents the data more accurately than the Bromberg "trauma-dissociation model". Dissociation into different self-states on the Bromberg model separates and dissociates the access to memory of different self-states, not to mention their awareness of one another. Splitting of the ego into different ego states or self-states *does* sepa- rate emotional experience, but *does not* separate memories or access to memory. The split-off ego states or self-states of Asperger's children are separated, compartmentalised, sequestered or mutually insulated *affectively* (again, choose your metaphor), but are *well aware of each other* and seem to have the same access to memory, at least as far as I can tell to this point.

Before rounding out this discussion, it would be valuable to consider specific criticisms Bromberg (2011, p. 76) makes about the interpretation of splitting in general and what Kernberg suggests about "interpreting the splitting" in the transference of borderline patients, which, Bromberg states, "frequently makes things worse". Things are made worse according to Bromberg, if I understand him correctly, because the interpretation of splitting is, in effect, to accuse the patient of "avoiding conflict" by an inconsistent and split apart way of experiencing the analyst, as all good and idealised at one point and as all bad and denigrated at another point. For Bromberg, what is really happening, if I understand Bromberg's point of view, is that "strong dissociative processes" are in action, so that the patient can only experience the analyst as a function of the one self-state which is currently the "me" state and which can "exist experientially" at a particular time. The interpretive framework (as employed by Kernberg) is based on what Bromberg calls "conflict theory" and for Bromberg it suggests there is an internal conflict between good and bad which the patient defends against experiencing and avoids by using splitting. This undermines for Bromberg the more accurate and relevant interpretive framework. This accurate interpretive framework suggests that the patient has just switched self-states because of anxiety and so can at the moment only see the analyst through the lens of the current self-state.

If I have understood Bromberg correctly, I offer the comment that his whole critique of splitting (on pages 76–77 of his superb 2011 book) seems to me to be based on an assumption which is erroneous. This assumption is that splitting is always and only a part of conflict theory and is a defensive process directed uniquely against conflict— specifically the conflict between good and bad internal representations of the mother (and representations of others as well as development proceeds).

To me, it makes much more sense to understand splitting as a defence directed against trauma or the cumulative and (for the infant and the adult borderline patient as well) the terrifying potential for trauma. The threatened trauma would be that the internal bad mother could pollute and even destroy the internal good mother, leaving the infant to confront a relational situation in which the infant is essentially alone with a hostile, destructive bad mother. If such a configuration were to arise for the infant (or for the adult borderline patient in reference to their analyst), the result would likely be overwhelming anxiety, the experience of complete helplessness and horrible trauma. If good and bad aspects can be split apart and experienced separately, however, then the "dosages" of bad mother can perhaps be titrated sufficiently so that the possibility of overwhelming trauma and anxiety might be avoided. Contra Bromberg, therefore, I suggest that splitting is primarily *a defence deployed to forestall the experience of overwhelming trauma*. This is what leads me to what I call the Kernberg "trauma-splitting model" as likely to be the best way of understanding the psychodynamics of Asperger's children.

But don't rule out dissociation

I want to make it clear that I am *not* arguing we should reject Bromberg's understandings when we consider Asperger's children. Precisely the contrary! I express the hope that my colleagues (and myself) will continue to search for evidence to see if Bromberg's work does offer a potential to understand Asperger's more completely, especially because Bromberg's emphasis on trauma fits so well with the possibility that Asperger's children regularly suffer from developmental trauma, perhaps of a cumulative nature.

Before completing this discussion, I want to provide some suggestions from other sources that thinking of Asperger's children as primarily using dissociation as a major defence could make considerable sense. Bion (1967, p. 69) makes some interesting comments comparing splitting with dissociation. The problem is that I am not certain Bion is using the term "dissociation" in the same sense that more recent theorists such as Bromberg are using this term. Bion comments that "Freud used the terms splitting and dissociation indifferently", but that it seems to him the phenomenon he has observed in disturbed patients are "best described by the term 'splitting' as it is used by Melanie Klein, leaving the term 'dissociation' free to be employed where a more benign activity is being discussed" (Bion, 1967, p. 69). He then goes on to be more specific: dissociation "appears to be gentler and to have respect for natural lines of demarcation between whole objects and indeed to follow those lines of demarcation to effect the separation; the patient who dissociates is capable of depression" (ibid, p. 69). With Asperger's children, we are not concerned with lines of demarcation between whole objects, but with lines of cleavage between different aspects of the self or self-states. Nevertheless, we can build on what Bion suggests here. Can we understand splitting as a process which is "less benign" and in a sense more violent, tearing internal objects or the self apart, for example into good and bad or bully and victim aspects? Can we also understand dissociation as more benign and less violent in its functioning, separating, and insulating from one another parts that are already differentiated? Does splitting forcefully create lines of cleavage (in internal objects or in the self) whereas dissociation relies on pre-established lines of cleavage and demarcations of personality aspects which are already in formation? Perhaps another way of raising this question is whether dissociation steps in and uses lines of cleavage previously carved out by the process of splitting. I have no easy answers to the questions just posed, except to suggest they are worth considering.

There are certainly psychoanalytic commentators who specifically suggest that Asperger's children use the defence of dissociation. Levy (2011) is one such commentator. He advocates the use of psychoanalytic play therapy with Asperger's children to promote improved "socio-emotional" functioning, this being accomplished "by the process of containing, regulating, and repairing the treatment relationship, the engendering of experimentation, and promoting the formulation of new self-states" (Levy, 2011, p. 80). He points to the possibility of the child "experiencing new or dissociated self-states" in the therapeutic play relationship. He also suggests that the therapeutic relationship established in psychoanalytic play therapy promotes greater "identity complexity" for the child because "unformulated and dissociated self-states become further elaborated, more flexibly experienced, and better integrated within the child's personality" (ibid, p. 80). Comments such as those quoted from Bion and from Levy indicate that an open mind about the role of dissociation in the psychodynamics of Asperger's children is indicated.

To complete this discussion: as I now see things, the experience of (cumulative) trauma is likely to be a regular feature in the development of Asperger's children. These children are likely to defend against the experience of overwhelming trauma by deploying splitting, which then leads to one or more splits in the self. As a result of this splitting of the self, Asperger's children are likely to develop at least two, and very frequently more, self-states, the two most common of these being the victim and the bully self-states. These self-states are "compartmentalised"

(Kernberg) or "disjunctive and mutually sequestered" (Bromberg). These different self-states also "alternate" (Kernberg). However, the different self-states of the Asperger's child tend to be quite aware of each other. They are often, perhaps always, locked into chronic mutual conflicts with each other. The different self-states are split apart in their emotional experiences and affective functioning, their habitual ways of understanding and thinking about interpersonal relationships, some of their typical ways of behaving, and in at least some aspects of their moral judgments and superego functioning. They are *not* split apart, however, in their access to memory. In fact, as clinical examples such as the experiences of Matt demonstrate, the different self-states seem to be *quite well informed* of the doings of the other self-states.

PART II

THEORISING ABOUT THE
AETIOLOGY OF ASPERGER'S

CHAPTER TWELVE

Towards an understanding of the aetiology of Asperger's disorder

If we attempt the difficult task of feeling our way into the emotional atmosphere of the mother–infant dyad in which the infant is destined to develop Asperger's disorder, the following may emerge. Consider the infant pole of the dyad: the infant comes into the world with atypical neurological structures. The details of just what structures are atypical, how these atypical aspects lead to atypical functioning, and how the atypical functions develop over time—all of this needs clarification. I have a suggestion towards such clarification, though it is supported by only minimal evidence. I requested the mothers of two of my patients, Dan and Matt, to fill out a standard toddler temperament questionnaire (McDevitt & Carey, 1978) in retrospect many years after the period of their toddlerhoods. On the nine standard aspects of toddler temperament measured by the questionnaire (activity level, rhythmicity, approach/withdrawal, adaptability, intensity, mood, persistence, distractibility, and threshold), Dan and Matt had closely matching scores on three aspects. Both measured as having low activity level, a tendency to withdraw rather than to approach, and a very low level of intensity. These findings may suggest that even early in life, there is a tendency for Asperger's infants to "down-regulate" and to withdraw from stimuli.

One salient and important (if not the most important) atypical feature is the Asperger infant's inability to transmit an infant's usual repertoire of nonverbal cues to the mother and to receive and visibly respond to the mother's ministrations to the infant. The most important aspects of the mother's ministrations include her capacity to introject her infant's moments of agitated negativity, to accept his projective identifications, detoxify these aspects in her reverie, return them to the infant in a detoxified and digestible form, and thus to act as a good-enough maternal container for the infant (Bion's model is primary here).

As to the maternal pole of the dyad: the mothers of Asperger's children have without exception seemed to me to be more than "ordinarily devoted" to their infants. These mums regularly give the impression of being excessively competent in what they do for their Asperger's children, but in a manner that is over-involved and strongly coloured by anxiety. Some examples include Dan's mother, who drove him a long distance for his therapy sessions, repeatedly took him a long distance to hospital for numerous tests and procedures related to his metabolic disorder, and took him to several universities to investigate in detail what accommodations he could receive because of his Asperger's and how the university might respond supportively to his social deficiencies. She met with me on a number of occasions to express her anxieties about Dan and to get my opinion. Matt's mother, a single mum, brought both Matt and his younger sister to their respective therapies at different locations. She repeatedly expressed her anxieties about Matt's difficulties in coping. These examples could be multiplied so as to include every one of my patients whom you have heard about. A comment by Pozzi is apposite here. Pozzi (2003) notes that children on the autism spectrum

> require something different from ordinary maternal care or a containing, "good enough" mother. They seem to require the mother to take in, contain and divest of pain the entire child, not merely a part. Such infants seem to require superhuman mothers who could only exist in an ideal world. (Pozzi, 2003, p. 1336)

A caveat is now needed. My suggestion that the mothers of Asperger's children are often highly competent needs to be modified by referring to their occasional excessive involvement with their children, sometimes to the point of enmeshment with the child to the extent of creating a *folie a deux*. The best example is provided by how Thomas and his mother interacted (Chapter Four). Not only did he lie on my couch with his head in his mother's lap as she stroked his hair, but mother and son also had identical reactions as to how the school treated him. Both felt the school was negative, judgemental, punitive, and unempathic towards Thomas. His mother made numerous complaints to the school and the officials responsible for it. Her competence in supporting Thomas slid into anxious over-involvement, emotional enmeshment, and anxious over-protectiveness. The mothers of Asperger's children are, in general, highly competent and extremely devoted. However, their devotion can sometimes become excessive and counterproductive.

The mother–infant dyad for Asperger's children

So, if there is a typical mother–infant dyad for Asperger's children, it may consist of an infantile partner with unusual difficulties in both transmitting the expected infant cues to the mother, and in receiving her efforts at containment in a way the infant can experience as sooth-ing—and so that the mother can also experience the infant's ability to be receptive to her efforts as an affirming responsiveness to her care. The maternal partner may tend to be strongly motivated to care for her infant as well as being very solicitous (sometimes over-solicitous) towards her baby. Her response to her apparent failure to read her infant's cues, her growing uncertainty about the baby's emotional states, and her experi-ence of lacking encouraging and affirming responses from her baby in a way that is predictable—all of these difficulties tend to have a typi-cal result. The result is a huge increase in the mother's anxieties, regu-larly accompanied by a (sometimes frantic) redoubling of her efforts to understand her baby's needs and emotional states. When this is success-ful (which happens only sporadically and unpredictably), it enables the infant to affirm for his mother the appropriateness of her interventions. The infant can do so by showing calmer and more engaged behaviours towards her. The mother's wish for this affirmation and confirmation from the infant is only sporadically gratified.

And so a vicious interactional circle tends to arise. The infant per-haps experiences the mother as responding disruptively, as having dif-ficulty interpreting his weak, variable, atypical or defective cues and as being unwilling or unable to provide the containing and detoxifying functions he so much needs (The male pronoun is used because by far the majority of Asperger's children are boys). For her part, the mother tends to experience her infant as unpredictable, confusing, unrespon-sive, ungratifying, and highly anxiety-provoking.

But this scenario of the "vicious interactional circle" is, I suggest, at best half of the story. The cues sent by the Asperger's child may be weak or inconsistent or atypical, but they are not mostly absent (The absence of identifiable and comprehensible cues may sometimes be the case in the development of autistic infants). The Asperger's infant does not (as again may sometimes tend to be the case for autistic infants) give up hope. He continues to struggle to send out cues and signals to the mother, and continues to have some degree of hopeful expectation of her appropriate responsiveness. Indeed, the infant may in some ways sense her sustained and even desperate attempts to "read" him correctly and respond to him helpfully. The infant may also in some ways be able to sense the growing desperation and anxiety in how the mother is approaching him, so that there may be times her anxiety has the infantile equivalent of a smothering, drowning or devouring impact. Nevertheless, it seems that the Asperger's infant does not give up hope, and continues to strive for connection with the maternal partner of the dyad. And, importantly, among the frequent misfires in establishing a regulating and understandable mutual connection, there will also be reasonably frequent successes as well. These successes may have an almost tantalising impact on both the infant and maternal partner, because of the frequency of the misfires. But there will probably be sufficient successes so as to maintain the hope of establishing connections and a continuing effort by both partners toward the establishment of regulating and containing connections. The result over time may tend to be a relatively stable kind of oscillation between the misfires of vicious circle failures to connect, alternating with successes at mutual connection, regulation of the infant and maternal containment of him.

This kind of oscillation may serve to exaggerate both tracks of Grotstein's "dual track theory", in which "the baby functions with both a feeling of separation and with a beneficial adhesive identification at the same time" along with "oscillation between moments of normal fusion and moments of partial awareness of separateness" (Haag, 1997, p. 384; p. 375).

The connected and the disconnected mother

It is this oscillation between the two states of connection and misconnection (and all the primitive emotional baggage that comes in its wake) that may set the stage for developments in the child's inner world that are key elements in the development of Asperger's disorder. The experiences of the infant within the mother–infant dyad tend to precipitate out, as the inner world of the young child starts to take on a definite shape, in the form of an internal structure specific to Asperger's. Without initially relying too heavily on the defence of splitting, the Asperger's infant has an especially powerful experience of a "binary mother"—an experience of two different kinds of mothering. This experience is later subject to extensive defensive splitting as well. There is on the one hand the mother of misfires in the dyad, the mother perhaps experienced as intrusively anxious, overwhelming, and unable to connect with and contain the infant. Perhaps this "bad mother" aspect could be referred to as *"the disconnected mother"*. There is also sometimes a very different experience of a mother who can successfully connect, contain, and detoxify, thus enabling appropriate regulation within the mother–infant dyad. Call this "good mother" aspect *"the connected mother"*. States of the early self may tend to vary in tandem along with the infant's experience of the mother— "connected mother" experiences leading to relatively contained and regulated experiences of the infantile proto-self. Similarly, experiences of "the disconnected mother" are likely to lead to disregulated, uncontained, threatened, overwhelmed, and anxious experiences of the early infantile self.

The protected self and the overwhelmed and vulnerable self

As the child's internal world becomes structured, the internal object of "the connected mother" is established, and with this internal object as a core, the self-representation of *"the protected self"* also precipitates out. Another internal object, "the disconnected mother" is similarly linked to the self-representation of *"the overwhelmed and vulnerable self"*. From this primal dichotomy eventually emerge all the other many dichotomies that so strongly characterise the psychodynamics of Asperger's children. These dichotomies typically include ones such as those between fair/unfair, just/unjust, protective/threatening, friendly/ persecutory, friend/foe, accepting/rejecting and so on. Examples are numerous. For Matt, the dichotomies would include antelope/tiger, participant/spectator and resident/immigrant. For Thanos, they would include Turkish/Greek. For Thomas, there would be pussycat/

tiger. For Dan, we find Malcolm X/Martin Luther King. There are numerous others.

Bully and victim in Asperger's

One dichotomy that in my experience is a very regular if not invariant feature in Asperger's children is that between bully and victim. It seems to me that it would be an unwarranted and inaccurate oversimplification to simply link the bully aspect to the internal representations of "the connected mother" and "the protected self" and to link the victim aspect to the internal representations of "the disconnected mother" and "the overwhelmed and vulnerable self". The latter part is probably accurate. The sense of being bullied, misunderstood, badly treated, and victimised likely builds in a fairly direct manner on the sense of self as overwhelmed and vulnerable and the important other as disconnected and in a state of unempathic separation from the self. The Asperger's child seems to find it quite easy to fit this structure of internal representations of "the disconnected mother" and "the overwhelmed and vulnerable self" with many of his experiences in the rough-and-tumble interactions of the child's world. The sense of other children being disconnected empathically and being uncaring bullies seems for them to fit quite easily with the internal object I have called "the disconnected mother". It will then very easily evoke the self-representation of "the overwhelmed and vulnerable self". These internal representations almost seek out exemplifications in the outer world. The Asperger's child can very easily discover external situations which seem to fit very well with their internal objects. Asperger's children quickly find what they expect.

The bully aspect of the split self, however, seems to be a later and more complicated defensive development. Projective identification (or, synonymously, identification with the aggressor) seems to be very much in play, so that the Asperger's child seems to be rapidly able to identify his own aggressive, vengeful, and enraged aspects with the hurtful and abusive aspects to be found in the bullies he encounters. However, this may fail to account for one aspect regularly observed in Asperger's children. These children speak of bullying and being bullied, of themselves as bullies and as victims, as if these two aspects are completely walled off from one another in terms of their affective impact. The experience of having been bullied and victimised does not seem to contribute any degree of empathy or compassion when they assume the role of bully. Indeed, as they describe their own experiences, they seem to assume the role of bully with a kind of lascivious, victorious, and gleeful enthusiasm. There seems to be a split in the self between the victim aspect and the bully aspect so that neither impinges on or influences the other emotionally or behaviourally.

I suggest the following. The bully aspect is a defensive development in response to the sense of being a victim. It does not derive developmentally *directly* from the internal object of "the connected mother" and linked self-representation of "the protected self". However, it piggybacks, so to speak, on these representations. When the Asperger's child has assumed the role of the bully, he can then feel safe and protected. This sense of safety and protection links up to and evokes the self-representation of "the protected self". This in turn activates the linked internal object, that of "the connected mother". The child is able to feel powerful, in control, protected, and in connection with a strongly supportive internal object. The original powerful experience of a "binary mother"—of two different kinds of mothering—leads to a split in the early self which is continued as "the protected self" and "the overwhelmed and vulnerable self". The dichotomy of bully/victim, and all the other dichotomies common to Asperger's children, utilise and build on, and also strengthen, this split in the self.

The Asperger's child *unconsciously provokes* the bullying he fully expects. The bully aspect of the Asperger's child may employ projective identification in the attempt to dispose of his persecutory anxieties by projecting these into and "lodging" them in another child (who is likely to be a bully), or evacuating them into another child for disposal. The bully chosen by the Asperger's child is likely to find this attempt at projective identification intolerably irritating. The other child may then attempt to eliminate this irritation by returning it to the Asperger's child in the form of acts of bullying. Asperger's children *create* in others what they *expect* from them.

Michael relating to his mother

This way of understanding the typical unfolding of mother/child interactions with Asperger's infants is a pastiche of reconstructions from numerous patients. It requires further confirmation (and likely emendation) based on the observations of other therapists, and hopefully from infant observation and mother/infant therapy as well. I now cite one suggestive piece of evidence provided by my Asperger's patient Michael, age twenty-one, whom you did not hear about previously.

I had met with Michael's mother a few times during the assessment of Michael before his treatment began (when he was seventeen years old) and had received a number of anxious emails from her during Michael's subsequent treatment. She held a prestigious job in academia and seemed to be effective and well-respected in her academic position.

Michael, very much against his mother's advice, decided to pursue a career in "event planning" offered by a local college. His mother was strongly and vigorously opposed to this decision. Marshalling evidence from thorough psychoeducational testing she had wisely and efficiently arranged for Michael during high school, she maintained Michael would be able to do well in the planning aspects of event planning, but would not succeed in the important interpersonal component of this field because of his quite limited social skills. During the frequent morning rides she gave Michael on the way to her work, she would repeatedly inveigh against his choice of studies, trying to persuade him to change to something less socially demanding and more in line with his cognitive abilities as they manifested in the testing she had arranged. Based on Michael's reports about their interactions and the anxious emails she sent to me, his mother seemed to be quite accurate in her evaluations, in her usual logical, carefully reasoned, and not openly emotional manner.

The more his mother argued against Michael's choice of career, the more he felt narcissistically injured by her assaults on the choice he had made, the less understood and supported he felt by her, and the more he dug in his heels and opposed her suggestions, in an increasingly hostile way. Eventually he decided to move out of his mother's house, and into the house of his father, who was divorced from his mum. The matrimonial split between the parents thus served to reinforce the defensive emotional split he made between them.

In his therapy sessions, Michael repeatedly described his experience of his mother as her being intrusive, overbearing, coercive, controlling, pig-headed, unempathic, unreceptive to his point of view, unrelentingly demeaning of his abilities, and totally deaf to his wishes. She was certainly a "bad mother" as Michael saw her. My colleague Dannette Graham raises a very useful question here. Was it the case that Michael evacuated his anxieties into his mother by using projective identification? Did she then try to contain these anxieties by her exercise of "nagging counter-control" over Michael, such that she then played out in her actual relationship with him the internal bully aspect of his internal split, and he played out the misused victim aspect in response?

As his therapy proceeded, we were able to struggle with these experiences of his mother repeatedly. I began by suggesting that his mother seemed to be quite anxious about him and his future, that she seemed to be driven by an anxiety-ridden form of caring for him, and that parental anxiety could be experienced by children as unrelenting and smothering. At first, Michael was reluctant to view his mother in this light. Over time, though grudgingly, he accepted the idea that his mother was anxious about him. He even accepted the idea that she cared about him, though her manner of caring was soaked with anxiety. He began to accept rides to school with her again, and even allowed her to arrange for him a meeting with one of her academic colleagues who was an expert in his chosen academic area of event planning.

This type of mother/child dynamic is, in my experience, not unusual, and is even typical with Asperger's children. The mothers are almost always devoted, to the point of being anxiously and intrusively over-devoted. Their sons not infrequently develop hostile or distancing attitudes towards the mother and sometimes towards both parents, as Dan for example felt distanced from both of his parents and from his siblings as well. Michael has split the internal mother, with the "bad mother" becoming predominant. Michael's situation captures the dynamic I am suggesting—the experience of a split in the internal mother with the "disconnected" mother predominating, and this aspect being connected with a sense of the "overwhelmed self"— overwhelmed in respect to the mother's anxious over-devotedness (which was experienced by Michael as intrusiveness).

Understanding in Winnicott's idiom of the good enough holding environment and in Bion's idiom of container/contained and maternal reverie

Up to this point in the discussion, I have tried to feel my way into the vicissitudes of the early relationship between the Asperger's child and his mother by using my own particular idiom and language. However, this whole discussion might fruitfully be seen through a number of different lenses and using different languages to talk about what is going on—different idioms. In Chapter Nine, for example, I briefly considered the idiom used by Khan (1963, 1964) which involved the mother's role as a "protective shield" for her infant with a pattern of significant but minor breaches in the protective shield contributing to cumulative trauma for the infant. We might very fruitfully recast the previous discussion in the idiom of Winnicott by talking about the mother's failure or inability to provide a consistent and good enough holding environment for her infant. We might also recast the discussion in the idiom of Bion by talking about container/contained and maternal reverie. I want to briefly suggest how the early relationship between the Asperger's infant and his mother might be viewed if we look through the lens provided by Winnicott and how it might be viewed if we look through the lens provided by Bion.

Winnicott's ideas about maternal holding are well described by Mitrani (1996, p. 118) and by Ogden (1994, 1997). For Mitrani, maternal holding protects the infant against "awareness of the earliest unintegration anxieties", those of dissolution and evaporation, permits a gradual development of the infant's phantasy life, and opens the road for the infant to develop an internal psychic space which in turn permits normal processes of projective and introjective identification. Good enough maternal holding allows the infant to begin to experience moments of separateness from the mother.

However, as Ogden notes, failure by the mother "to provide a good enough holding environment (whether primarily the result of the inadequacy of the mother or a reflection of the hypersensitivity of the infant) is experienced by the infant as the terror of impending annihilation" (Ogden, 1994, p. 177, n. 4 and 1997, pp. 186–187, n. 5). Using Winnicott's idiom, the mother of the hypersensitive Asperger's infant strives mightily to provide her baby with a good enough holding environment. Some of the time, her efforts at holding are able to reach the level of being good enough. But the infant's "sensory hypersensitivity" (Rhode, 2011b, p. 288) and difficulties sending out appropriate cues to his mother frequently defeat her best efforts to provide good enough holding, leading to her experience of sometimes being inadequate. The fears of annihilation mentioned by Mitrani and Ogden then assail the infant, and his experience is of a mother whose holding is decidedly not good enough. The oscillation between good enough holding and not good enough holding by the mother then leads to the situation I have previously described.

Turning to the lens provided by Bion, Bion (in *Transformations*) makes a comment which I think captures exactly the predicament experienced by the Asperger's infant and his mother. Bion's comment is:

> The mother's inability to accept the projective identifications of the infant and the association of such failure with disturbances in understanding is matched by complications arising through the existence of an extremely understanding mother, particularly understanding by virtue of ability to *accept* projective identification. (Bion, 1965, p. 62)

In so far as I can putatively reconstruct the situation that typically arises between the Asperger's infant and his mother, *both* of these situations as Bion describes them above arise, and they alternate with each other in an oscillating manner. The mother struggles to make contact with her baby through the fog and the static deriving from his impaired ability to emit and to receive the typical nonverbal communications between mother and infant. This impairs the infant's ability to use projective identification as a means of communicating with his mother.

In her attempt to be (and to feel like) an adequate container for her infant, the mother strives to see through the fog and to listen through the interfering static so that she can detect and accept projective identifications from her infant. She attempts to become a "super mother" and sometimes she succeeds. In Bion's language, she is then "an extremely understanding mother" who is able to both detect and accept her infant's projective identifications. She is able to function as an adequate container—sometimes—but for the infant, not reliably so. She can sometimes be the attuned, containing, adequately responsive, and what I have called the "connected" mother. The infant may internalise this as his wished-for expectation.

However, the mother cannot reliably and consistently function as a super mother. She will fail—unpredictably and more often than most mothers—to detect and therefore to accept her infant's projective identifications. The infant may then experience the black hole of the "no-breast", and may react in a number of ways, including the infantile equivalent of frustrated rage, hatred, and destructiveness. The mother is now an inadequate and smashed container, who is misattuned to the infant and helpless to respond to him adequately. This state I have referred to as the "disconnected" mother.

The initial experience of the infant of a "split in his containing reality", this oscillation of good breast and no-breast, good container and smashed container, sets the stage for a number of future developments.

First, it may make the infant highly selective in how he employs projective identification. Frustration and rage at the mother's failure to function for him as a reliably "good enough container" may contribute to a later reticence to risk projective identification with those close to him (including the therapist at first) and to restrict his use of projective identification to remote objects.

Second, the "split in reality", in his containing maternal reality, anchored in the infant's own neurological limitations, may create fertile ground for the later split in the self. Perhaps, to give one example, the frustrated rage directed at the no-breast, misattuned mother later on feeds into the bully part of the split in the self. It might also be that the infant's repeated disappointments in the apparent disappearance of the attuned and connected mother (in how he experiences the mother) contributes strongly to later limitations in the reality testing of the Asperger's child and adolescent. These are limitations which prompt Asperger's children to quickly *impose* the representation of mean, teasing, unempathic, and cruelly rejecting bullies onto other children, and even to inveigle other children to realise this "bully template" by using projective identification. In this way, Bion's comments about the mother accepting or being unable to accept the infant's projective identifications may be very helpful to our understanding.

Mitrani (1996) is helpful as usual. We need to consider the mother's function as a container for her infant's projective identifications, exercising this function through her capacity for reverie vis-à-vis her infant. This is described in exquisite detail by Mitrani (1996) under the headings of "Maternal containing" (pp. 119–120) and "Deficiencies in maternal holding and containing" (pp. 120–123). I provide only a brief summary of what she describes and attempt to relate reverie and containment to the mother infant-dyad with Asperger's infants.

Mitrani (1996, p. 121) summarises the container function of the mother and her three closely related aspects: reverie, alpha function, and maternal feedback. Reverie implies the ability to detect and to be receptive to the projective identifications of the infant, "the receptivity of the container to the projected distress of the baby" (Mitrani, 1996, p. 121) or the "capacity of the mother to be open to the baby's projected need" (Grinberg, Sor & de Bianchedi, 1977, p. 56). The second aspect is the containing mother's alpha-function, the "transformational capacity of the container or its ability to detoxify or render meaningful those projected aspects of the infant's experience" (Mitrani, 1996, p. 121). Grinberg, Sor and de Bianchedi comment that: "The mother who functions as an effective container of the infant's sensations can successfully transform hunger in satisfaction, pain into pleasure, loneliness into company, fear of dying into peacefulness (Grinberg, Sor & de Bianchedi, 1977, p. 56)". The third aspect described by Mitrani (1996, p. 121) is maternal feedback to her infant, this being "the mother's active return to her infant of mitigated and modified emotional experience".

A summary quite similar to Mitrani's is provided by Levine and Brown. They summarise the containing function of the mother in the following way.

> According to Bion, in healthy development the mother, through her *reverie* functions as a *container* for her infant's projections of painful, unrepresented experience (the *contained*), and uses her *alpha function* to transform the projected contained into an *emotional thought* (Bion, 1962), which she can represent to the infant. (Levine & Brown, 2013, p. 201)

Applying this lens to the Asperger's infant, I suggest that the infant's hypersensitivity to some aspects of sensory stimuli combined with the neurological differences he may have interfere with the expectable "projections of painful, unrepresented experience" into the mother. This has the impact of making maternal reverie more problematic for her, and sometimes disrupting her capacity to act as a good enough container for her infant.

Parada (1996, p. 779) also summarises this situation well. Failure in communication between mother and infant may be induced by "sensory deficits of various kinds in the baby" which has the impact of preventing the mother "from receiving and tolerating the baby's projections and from being in contact with his anxieties" with the result that "the child frustrates the mother's capacity for reverie or puts it out of action".

CHAPTER THIRTEEN

The sensory vulnerability of Asperger's children

It may be that the Asperger's infant is, in a sense, too preoccupied to be able to receive and process the nuances of his mother's communications with him or to send communications to her in any but the most primitive, basic, and importuning manner. It may also be that the Asperger's infant is preoccupied because he is born with a thin sensory skin and hyperacute sensory equipment. His infantile experience of the world may thus tend to be one of sensory bombardment, flooding, and inundation. The sensorium may thus tend to be experienced as persecutory in nature. Sensations in most (if not all) modalities may need to be constantly muted and warded off, or at least modulated in a downward direction so as to be less intense and overwhelming. A number of clinicians comment on the sensory vulnerability of children on the autism spectrum. An example is Pozzi (2003, p. 1333), who writes of these children having "a deep sensory openness which he experiences as a bombardment of sensa". These children were also described as

> having to deal with an unmitigated sensory input before their
> neuro-psychological apparatus is equipped to cope with or process
> strong emotions. As infants it is likely that they have experienced an
> assault on their senses from which they have protected themselves

by erecting shells, barriers and encapsulations, and these have the
effect of cutting them off from direct engagement in human relations. (Pozzi, 2003, p. 1333)

Ogden (2008, p. 223) makes similar helpful suggestions. The earliest
sensation-based experience of the infant as part of his autistic-contiguous
level of functioning, he says, can "devolve into pathological autism as
a consequence of a combination of constitutional and environmental
problems." The constitutional problems of the infant include "constitutional hypersensitivity to stimuli (i.e. an inadequate capacity for filter-
ing and ordering stimuli)" which can at times be so severe that "even
good mothering is not sufficient to filter and organise experience." The
infant with such constitutional difficulties is in such a "raw" and metaphorically skinless state that "he cannot tolerate the unexpected," and
thus withdraws from the unpredictability of human interaction into an
inner world governed by autistic defences.

I have heard repeated descriptions by Asperger's children and adolescents that bear out these comments. They often begin by saying that
they cannot tolerate participating with classmates in sports or physical
education activities in the school gymnasium. When asked what makes
this so, they answer with comments such as: "It's the *noise*! And the
echoes! I can't hear what *anyone* is saying. It drives me *crazy*! It's like
having jet airplanes taking off inside my head! I can't do *anything* when
that noise is going on. I don't know how the other kids can *stand* it—but
they *tease* me about it!" This is but one example of the hypersensitivities
these children have. Other children are sensitive to the tags sewn into
the back of their shirts. They cannot bear to wear garments with any
irritating tags still inside and touching their necks, so their mothers get
used to cutting out all neck area tags without even thinking about it.

If such a constitutional hypersensitivity to stimuli is the case, then
the Asperger's infant (and perhaps the autistic spectrum infant in general) may become preoccupied with avoiding, muting, or warding off
sensations of various kinds. The mother may try her best to be helpful
by functioning as an auxiliary stimulus barrier for the infant. It seems
likely that the Asperger's infant is able to form an internal good and
helpful object. However, the overwhelming stimulation experienced by
the infant cannot always be mitigated by the mother, so that persecutory sensory flooding may be experienced as connected with the bad
and betraying internal mother who repeatedly seems to overwhelm the

infant. The Asperger's infant may tend to focus on avoiding persecutory overstimulation and will thus have much less "mind space" to engage in the give and take and the nuances of nonverbal dialogue with the mother.

Mother/infant dialogue may also be compromised by a lack of basic trust on the infant's part. The Asperger's infant may tend to experience the mother as unpredictably unable to prevent the infant from being overwhelmed by stimulation, or even as the mother herself in some measure being the source of the persecutory stimulation. The Asperger's infant may thus be reluctant to engage with his mother, or even come to avoid engaging with her.

Later transference paradigms reflect the split in the infantile self. The therapist may experience the split self in the form of a transference paradigm in which the therapist is seen as uniquely good and idealisable, with no negative qualities admitted. Such was my experience with Dan. Or else, the therapist experiences a flip-flop between the protected self/therapist as a good object and the overwhelmed and vulnerable self and the therapist as a bad and likely persecutory object. Switching between these two transference paradigms may be initiated by the child or adolescent perceiving the therapist, even in the smallest way, as either being protective or else as unprotective and intrusive. In the uniquely good transference, the therapist may have a powerful countertransference experience of wanting to be considerate, nonintrusive, careful, cautious, protective and sympathetic. This was my experience with Dan. It may represent the therapist's response to the child's intense need to hold onto a benevolently protective other as well as a sense of the self as protected and safe, with the overwhelmed and vulnerable self remaining split off from the analytic situation and experienced only outside the therapy (at school, with peers, and so forth). It is often the case, as suggested by Parada Franch (2008), that the Asperger's child tends to project feelings, thoughts, ideas, and sensations into "distant" and therefore safe objects.

It may be that the primary neurological deficit in the Asperger's infant is the inability to modulate sensory input as a "neurotypical" infant might, perhaps combined with sensory hyper-perception. One result of this is that the mother, however effective she tries to be as an auxiliary stimulus barrier for the infant, cannot but fail in trying to be protective. The mother comes to be internalised as unprotective, bad, and even persecutory. The infant struggles to preserve some sense of being safe and protected. This is achieved by a splitting of the early self into "protected self" and "overwhelmed and vulnerable self" fragments. The internalised bad mother, the unprotecting mother, is linked to the overwhelmed and vulnerable self by the infant.

An additional consideration may be relevant. Let's suppose that the Asperger's infant is precipitated into a state of overstimulation by—that he experiences being bombarded by—sensory input experienced by most infants as being quite tolerable. Let's further suppose that these sensory inputs, at least sometimes, include the typical visual and verbal displays used by good enough mothers. If the Asperger's infant experiences typical visual and verbal displays used by mothers as being overwhelming, then he may try to turn away from and avoid the mother's displays. This may leave the mother with two alternatives. One is to modulate her displays downward so that they are less intense and therefore manageable by her infant. As Alvarez notes, issues around "intensity, overload, over-sensitivity and over- and under-stimulation" are crucial for autism spectrum infants in terms of how and whether "experience can be taken in or introjected" (Alvarez, 2005, p. 8).

If the mother of the Asperger's infant is able, in response to her infant's initial avoidance, to modulate downward the intensity of her communicative displays, then the way may be open for a positive experience by the infant. He may have an experience of the mother as protective. The other alternative for the mother is to increase the intensity of her communicative efforts in an unfortunately mistaken attempt to break through to him and to establish contact. If his mother chooses this approach, then the Asperger's infant may begin to experience her as overwhelmingly intrusive and even persecutory. Perhaps even a vicious circle of increasing avoidance by the infant followed by increasing intensity by his mother may be set up.

Another scenario is also possible. In this scenario, the Asperger infant's mother starts to experience uncertainty and anxiety about her communicative connection with her infant. She tries to modulate her communicative intensity so that it oscillates both upward and downward in a manner experienced by her infant as confusingly unpredictable. Perhaps both mother and child are thrown into a state of mutual anxiety, with the infant anxiously avoiding his mother and the mother anxiously groping for communicative contact with her infant. This kind of scenario might increase the possibility of splitting in the early self along with splitting of the associated internal objects. Thus, one aspect becomes the protected self with an internal soothing and idealised (m)other, the second aspect being the overwhelmed and vulnerable self structured as related to an intrusive and persecuting (m)other.

Dan as a case example

Now consider Dan and whether these suggestions about an early splitting of the self might have any explanatory value for his situation. What Dan brings into the transference is his protected self, accompanied by an idealised representation of the therapist who is seen as understanding and caring. The overwhelmed and vulnerable self is certainly part of his treatment, but only outside the consulting room and outside the transference. Dan's peers certainly tend to be seen as bad objects (lazy, egocentric do-nothings with a perverted sense of values focused on immediate gratifications) as are his teachers (only concerned with their own needs and not those of their students), his siblings (whom he sees as selfish and egocentric) and to some extent his parents (out of touch with him and his needs). The therapist, however, must be experienced as a good object who can be understanding of Dan. The therapist must be insulated against the possibility of being perceived or experienced as being unempathic, intrusive or uncomprehending. The aspect of the protected self must be guarded and sustained at all costs. There is perhaps projective counter-identification by the therapist with the "Peter Pan" aspect of Dan (what I've called the protected self) which yields countertransference feelings of a mothering nature (the figure of Wendy in the Peter Pan story) so that I want to be tender, careful, delicate, cautious, and protective with Dan. (For the concept of projective counter-identification, see Grinberg, 1962 and especially 1979, and for an example in the context of child psychotherapy, see Cecchi, 1990, p. 404). In other words, my whole affective stance towards him is cautious, dampened down, and carefully modulated so as to dovetail with the needs of the protected self/Peter Pan aspect of Dan. My own characterological tendency toward diffidence is exaggerated by the needs of Dan's protected self and the projective identification into me of these types of needs.

The aspect of the overwhelmed and vulnerable self/Captain Hook in Dan takes on characteristics of self-righteous, almost antisocial resentment. Society and all its institutions, especially the educational ones, come to be experienced by Dan as morally corrupt, unjust, unfair, discriminatory, abusive, and intrusive. I have also referred to this as the "Malcolm X" aspect of Dan that totally rejects the social status quo and sees the only solution as being to live apart from society. The other aspect (which I have variously called the protected self, the Peter Pan aspect and the Martin Luther King aspect) still maintains hope, however fragile that hope may be. For this aspect, the possibility of community and mutual endeavour still seem to be open or at least to be wished for. These objects are all what Parada Franch (2008) referred to as "distant objects".

PART III

THE DIAGNOSIS OF ASPERGER'S CHILDREN

CHAPTER FOURTEEN

The differential diagnosis of Asperger's children

Diagnosing Asperger's

We can make diagnoses in two different ways—from the outside or from the inside. Fargione says it well. "Tustin distinguished between autism as defined by the DSM, which uses external descriptive features as the basis for classification and autism as understood by psychoanalysts who look for the internal processes that give rise to the syndrome" (Fargione, 2013, p. 187, n. 1). The DSM in its three most recent incarnations (American Psychiatric Association, 1994 for the DSM-IV, 2000, for the DSM-IV-TR and 2013, for the DSM-5) makes use of lists of "external descriptive features" which in philosophy of science would be called "observation statements", these presumably having the scientific advantage of consensual observation and consensual confirmation. The psychoanalytic form of diagnosis from the inside, which is based on internal processes within the person, is perhaps best represented by the PDM or *Psychodynamic Diagnostic Manual* (PDM Task Force (2006) *Psychodynamic Diagnostic Manual*. Silver Spring: Alliance of Psychoanalytic Organizations). Sadly, both the DSM using external descriptive features as the basis for classification and the PDM which should look for the internal processes that give rise to the syndrome are utterly deficient and completely inadequate when it comes to the diagnosis of Asperger's disorder.

In the rest of this chapter, I hope to provide some initial antidote to what is in my view the grotesque deficiencies of both the DSM and the PDM. I hope to outline the obvious deficiencies in both these publications as they now stand. I then hope to suggest how these deficiencies might be remedied. I will spend time suggesting how a DSM-type list of "external descriptive features" of Asperger's could at least be made more adequate than now appears in either the DSM-IV or the DSM-5. Because lists of external descriptive features are of much less interest to psychoanalytic therapists than underlying internal processes, I spend more time considering how the internal processes in Asperger's children (mainly splitting and to a lesser extent projective identification, as well as the types of underlying anxiety) enable us to specify three different kinds of Asperger's in children and adolescents, and how this specification in turn may help us to develop more specific treatment approaches to these children. As Rhode (2011b, p. 288) comments, "the intimate psychodynamic knowledge of a child acquired during therapy can make a contribution to diagnostic classification".

It might be useful to begin an approach to diagnosing Asperger's by using a joke which was first related to me by an adolescent patient. Here is the joke:

QUESTION: "What is the difference between *ignorance* and *apathy*?"
ANSWER: "I don't know and I don't care".

This joke functions by operating on two levels at the same time. One level is the *literal* or overt level. The literal level is that the joke teller neither knows nor cares about the question that has been posed. If you stay on this level alone, the whole joke gets lost.

The joke also functions on a second, slightly more *covert* level. On this level, the hearer becomes aware that "*I don't know*" in fact defines *ignorance*, and "*I don't care*" defines *apathy*. In this way, it effectively answers the question that has been posed. The humour of the joke derives to a large extent from the contradiction between the two ways in which the answer can be interpreted on the two different levels, so that the question is *both* rejected and answered by the same words.

This joke leads us to some important information about Asperger's disorder. First, you would predict that an Asperger's child, or adult for that matter, might not get this joke. Someone with Asperger's might get stuck on the more literal, overt level of the answer. They might conclude that the joke teller neither knows nor cares about the question that has been asked. The person with Asperger's could fail to appreciate or to mentally process the more covert level of the answer. The Asperger's child possibly would not understand this joke as a joke. He would thus be unable to share in the mirth and laughter of his peers. He (the male pronoun because more males than females suffer from Asperger's) would possibly feel cut off, shut out, and isolated, saying to himself: "I just don't get it". After having this experience repeatedly, he might begin to feel depressed.

This joke also hints at a crucial difference between the Asperger's sufferer and those who suffer from other forms ASD or autism spectrum disorder, including "high-functioning autism" or "HFA". The difference between Asperger's and HFA may be precisely the difference between *ignorance* and *apathy*. The Asperger's child usually very much *wants* social interaction with peers, but seems completely *ignorant* of the social skills necessary to bring friendships about. Over time, the Asperger's child develops an awareness of being different from his peers, and he experiences a significant degree of pain if he is not accepted by them. This at times eventually leads to comorbid mood and depressive disorders.

Instead of ignorance about how to develop social relationships, the HFA child often shows *apathy* or indifference towards others, with little or no interest in developing peer friendships. The HFA child may be quite content to play alone for long periods of time. Note that this proposed difference between Asperger's and HFA is definitely not a hard and fast one. We *do* meet HFA children who are described as being affectionate with their parents, and who may begin to develop some interest in peers after placement in a daycare setting. Adolescence seems to provoke HFA sufferers into strong interest in peer relationships, and I report on two such adolescent patients I had the opportunity to treat in Holloway, 2013. Also, some Asperger's children *are* content to be alone and aloof, and want to be so. My patient Dan was one such adolescent who expressed a strong inclination to live by himself for the rest of his life. I suggest that this aloofness in an Asperger's child is a *secondary* and defensive or self-protective aloofness resulting from repeated painful experiences of rejection by peers, and that there will be some time earlier in the child's history when the child *did* want peer relationships. Below, I suggest that these Asperger's children can be viewed as having an "inhibited/avoidant type" of Asperger's in which external others tend to be shunned and there is a pseudo-autistic stance toward others.

Because of their repeated experiences of rejection by others, they may be seen as "burnt-out Asperger's" children. As an initial hypothesis I suggest that *"ignorance* vs. *apathy"* is a useful differentiating feature between Asperger's and HFA.

In discussing this issue with colleagues, some have disagreed with the "ignorance *vs.* apathy" distinction. For example, some have commented that "I am seeing a high-functioning autistic child who very much wants to play with me", or else "I see a child with Asperger's who doesn't want to interact with other children, and remains by himself every recess at school". I strongly believe and accept such statements. But I wonder if the friendliness shown by the HFA child is "secondary" in the sense that this apparent friendliness happens after a long period of intense interventions from professionals, and whether the HFA child might still at times "disconnect" and drift off into his "own little world". This was certainly my experience with Sam (as reported in Holloway, 2013) as he started to emerge from his autistic state. I also wonder whether the isolation of the Asperger's child is also "secondary" in the sense that the Asperger's child had once in the past sought for connections with others, and to have friends, but has suffered so many hurtful and humiliating rebuffs that he now protects himself by resorting to isolation. These are hypotheses which need to be substantiated or disproven. The evidence needed may well come from the early histories of these children—was there a time when the now aloof and isolated Asperger's child sought friendships, and was there a time when the peer-seeking HFA child was isolated and disconnected?

This difference between Asperger's and HFA is mentioned frequently in literature. Klin, Volkmar and Sparrow note "the greater desire and motivation for social interaction in patients with [Asperger's]" (Klin, Volkmar & Sparrow, 2000, p. 44) as compared to those with autism. They state that Asperger's children can be differentiated from autistic children in that Asperger's children may have "marked social isolation" but "they are usually not unaware of or disinterested in others" and often make "constant but inappropriate approach to others" (ibid, p. 38). In contrast, those children with HFA "are more frequently described as withdrawn and are more likely to be seen as unaware of or disinterested in others". Another similar comment is that

> individuals with [Asperger's] experience social isolation but are not withdrawn or devoid of social interest; in fact, they often

approach others but in eccentric ways. Their interest in having friends, girlfriends/boyfriends, and social contact may in fact be quite striking. (Klin, Volkmar & Sparrow, 2000, p. 59)

My own experience confirms that, with few exceptions, Asperger's children very much want, and at times are painfully desperate and needy for, peer relationships. One final quotation (ibid, p. 62) is very similar to my suggested "ignorance *vs.* apathy" differentiation. In this quotation, it is noted that the Asperger's child "often has a wish for social interactions but an inability to engage in them", whereas in autism one notes "the centrality of social avoidance".

Wing (in Klin, Volkmar & Sparrow, 2000, p. 425) notes *four* subtypes of "quality of social interaction" in the PDD ("pervasive developmental disorder") population. Her subtypes of social interaction are: (1) aloof and indifferent to others, (2) passive acceptance of social approaches, (3) active but odd and inappropriate approaches to others, (4) high-functioning individuals who have acquired social rules through intellectual learning rather than through interaction and who apply the rules rigidly. It seems to me that (1) and (2) would apply more to autism, (3) and (4) more to Asperger's. Even in these four subtypes, the ignorance *vs.* apathy distinction appears to be present.

I approach Asperger's from the point of view of "object relations", that is, taking into account the *internal world* of the child that facilitates or impedes the forming of human relationships. Asperger's disorder and other disorders on the autism spectrum have often been referred to as "disorders of empathy"; as "disorders of affective contact"; or as disorders in the ability to form a "theory of mind" that is, to comprehend and act on the concept that others have minds just like oneself. Each of these aspects is clearly important. However, I suggest that each of these aspects is included in the notion that autism spectrum disorders, including Asperger's, are essentially *disorders of human relatedness.*

Was Asperger's disorder a valid and viable diagnosis in DSM-IV?

Let's consider whether Asperger's disorder was a valid and viable diagnosis as it was formulated in DSM-IV. The evidence strongly suggests that it was not. A paper by Mayes, Calhoun, and Crites (2001, p. 208) is entitled "Does DSM-IV Asperger's disorder exist?" Mayes and colleagues point out that contrary to the DSM-IV, definitions of Asperger's proposed by numerous authors "have all included language abnormalities as a symptom". If we search the literature, there is abundant evidence for this statement. Three examples would be the definition by Gillberg and Gillberg (1989) which includes "speech and language peculiarities", that by Szatmari et al. (1989) which includes "odd speech", and that by Tantum (2000, p. 377) which includes "impaired speech and language". By not including among its diagnostic criteria for Asperger's any impairment in speech and language, DSM-IV was clearly out of step. This difficulty is mentioned repeatedly in the literature. To give just a single example, Klin Volkmar and Sparrow in *Asperger Syndrome* (2000, p. 12) note that: "Among the behavioural features of individuals with [Asperger's], possibly the most conspicuous aspect of their presentation is the severe deficits in the social use of language despite relatively formal language strengths." Because of the relative strengths in the formal aspects of language, they say, there is no attempt in the DSM-IV "to include abnormalities of communication in the definition of the condition".

Mayes, Calhoun, and Crites (2001) further suggest that the DSM-IV requirement for a diagnosis of Asperger's that there is an absence of early speech delay "may be ... meaningless". The literature is ambivalent, with some researchers reporting *early* speech development in Asperger's children, and others finding speech *delays* in at least some Asperger's children.

It is a significant problem that in the DSM-IV, the diagnostic criteria for autistic disorder and for Asperger's disorder overlap quite significantly. Those criteria in the areas of "impairment in social interaction" and "restricted repetitive and stereotyped patterns of behaviour" are in fact *totally identical*. As it was defined in DSM-IV, Asperger's had two main sets of diagnostic criteria, which were *identical* to those of autism. The only differentiating feature was a lack of speech or cognitive delays in the Asperger's group. This completely fails to differentiate Asperger's and HFA.

In their research, Mayes, Calhoun, and Crites (2001, p. 263) considered a sample of 157 children who had received diagnoses of autism or of Asperger's. *All* of these children had impairment in communication (along with social impairment and repetitive interests). On this basis, all of the 157 children "met the DSM-IV criteria for autistic disorder and none met criteria for Asperger's disorder". This included all those children in the sample with both normal intelligence and no history of early speech delay, which are the DSM-IV requirements for Asperger's. Mayes and colleagues (2001, p. 268) arrive at a clear conclusion, that: "a diagnosis of Asperger's disorder is impossible using DSM-IV criteria". They then pose a crucial question (2001, p. 269). Can Asperger's disorder be re-defined in the DSM system "so that it is accurately and meaningfully differentiated from autism" or is Asperger's simply identical to high-functioning autism? The DSM-5 solution would seem simply to give up on defining Asperger's, and to dump it into the category of ASD (autism spectrum disorder) without even attempting to differentiate it—an extremely unhelpful "solution" to the problem.

A paper by Klin and Volkmar (2003, p. 7) arrives at a similar conclusion. The authors note that the DSM-IV definition of Asperger's disorder "has been consistently criticised as overly narrow, rendering the diagnostic assignment of [Asperger's] improbable or even 'virtually impossible'". These two authors in their chapter on diagnosis in the book *Asperger's Syndrome* (2000, p. 44) note that both ICD-10 and DSM-IV "appear to differentiate [Asperger's] from autism almost solely on the basis of the onset criteria" [no early onset of language or speech delays] so that "diagnoses of autism rather than [Asperger's] might often apply". They also note the significant problem in DSM-IV of a "failure to specify differentiating diagnostic features … because identical criteria are used for both conditions". Szatmari in his chapter on diagnosis in *Asperger's Syndrome* (2000, p. 407) joins this chorus, and states that the DSM-IV criteria for Asperger's "are virtually unworkable". Szatmari and his group in their study of outcome in autism and Asperger's elaborate on this claim, stating that: " the DSM-IV criteria for Asperger's disorder are essentially unworkable, largely because the children with a clinical diagnosis of Asperger's disorder also meet DSM-IV criteria for autism" (Szatmari et al., 2000, pp. 1985–1986).

Could the DSM-IV be revised so as to produce a valid diagnosis of Asperger's disorder, as a separate diagnostic category from HFA or other forms of autism spectrum disorder? I think it could be so revised. I suggest that the minimal revisions needed to rescue the DSM-IV definition of Asperger's disorder and to make it a valid diagnosis include the following: (1) some acknowledgement that Asperger's children *want*, (or at the very least *have wanted* at some time) and often *seek out* social relationships, even though they cannot successfully *maintain* these relationships; (2) recognition that *all* Asperger's children have difficulties in communication, in the *pragmatics* or actual use of language, even though their grammar and vocabulary are perfectly preserved (this is *not even mentioned* in the DSM-IV); (3) recognition that motor clumsiness may be a diagnostic aspect in many if not all Asperger's children. In the DSM-IV (American Psychiatric Association, 1994, p. 76), this is briefly mentioned under "associated features" where it is noted that: "motor milestones may be delayed, and motor clumsiness is often observed". But there is *no mention* of motor difficulties in the actual diagnostic criteria; (4) eliminating as far as possible the significant diagnostic overlap with other disorders, especially with autistic disorder (as noted, in the DSM-IV, the Asperger's symptom lists for impairment in social interaction and for stereotypies are *identical* to those of autistic disorder, the only real distinction being no delays in language or cognitive development); (5) removing the overly stringent requirement that there is no significant delay in language acquisition or in cognitive development as a *necessary* diagnostic criterion for *all* Asperger's children by acknowledging that these criteria may apply to some, or even to most, but not to *all* Asperger's children, and (6) removing the requirement that a diagnosis of autistic disorder negates that of Asperger's by *giving Asperger's precedence* when both diagnoses apply.

What the DSM-5 might have done with Asperger's using external descriptive features

Following are my suggestions for what could have been the DSM-5 criteria for Asperger's disorder. As they stand, these criteria are likely too lengthy and cumbersome to be easily used clinically. But to make an adequate diagnosis of Asperger's using external descriptive features as the basis for classification, at least *some* of these criteria should have been included in the DSM-5. The DSM-5 criteria would then need to be refined and reduced in number in order to be used in the DSM-6. Here are the proposed DSM-5 criteria:

List 1: Proposed DSM-5 diagnostic criteria for Asperger's disorder.

- **Diagnostic criteria for 299.80 Asperger's disorder**

A. In the context of a *person who desires or has at some time desired age-appropriate social interaction*, there is an impairment in initiating and/or sustaining such social interaction, as manifested by two or more of the following:

1. mild to marked impairment in the use of nonverbal communicative behaviours such as eye-to-eye gaze, contextually appropriate facial expressions, contextually appropriate body postures, and contextually appropriate gestures used to regulate social interaction;
2. failure to develop or sustain desired peer relationships which are appropriate to the person's cognitive and developmental level;
3. failure to spontaneously share enjoyment, interests (*excluding* a single or perseverative interest) or achievements with other people;
4. lack of or impairment in developmentally appropriate social or emotional reciprocity with peers, including impairment in the capacity for empathy (e.g., deficiency in age-appropriate sensitivity or tact).

B. Restricted, repetitive and stereotyped patterns of behaviour, interests, and activities, as manifested by one or more of the following:

1. encompassing preoccupations with one or more stereotyped and restricted patterns of interest that are abnormal either in intensity or focus (noting that in children, "abnormal" intensity or focus of interest in, for example, dinosaurs or popular card games may be indistinguishable from "normal" intensity and focus);
2. insistent and apparently inflexible adherence to specific, non-functional routines or rituals (e.g., the person insists on always taking exactly the same route to a known destination);
3. stereotyped and repetitive motor mannerisms.

C. In the context of well-preserved *syntax and semantics* of language (with functioning at least in the "low average" range on standardised tests), delays or impairments in the *phonology and/or pragmatics* of spoken language, as manifested by at least one of the following:

1. impaired speech prosody (patterns of stress and intonation), such as a constricted range of intonation patterns that is used with little regard to the communicative functioning of utterances (e.g., "sing-song" speech or flat, monotonous speech);
2. speech which appears to be tangential and circumstantial, conveying a sense of looseness of associations or incoherence;

3. lack of coherence and reciprocity in speech as a result of a one-sided and egocentric conversational style;
4. marked verbosity, including incessant, unrelenting monologues about a favourite but restricted topic of interest, without apparent reference to the reactions of the conversational partner(s);
5. failure to suppress the vocal output accompanying internal thoughts (e.g., blurting out socially inappropriate comments);
6. failure to appropriately modulate the volume of spoken language in accordance with the context (e.g., speaking out loudly in libraries or during religious services);
7. a literal or concrete understanding of language, including an inability to appreciate humour, sarcasm, irony, or metaphorical speech;
8. stilted, formal and pedant speech (e.g., a child may speak like "a little professor").

D. At least two of the following additional characteristics:

1. verbal IQ at least in the "low average" range as measured by standardised IQ tests;
2. verbal IQ is significantly higher than performance IQ as measured by standardised IQ tests;
3. there is no clinically significant delay in language acquisition (e.g., single words used by two years of age, communicative phrases used by three years);
4. there is no clinically significant delay in cognitive development or in the development of age-appropriate self-help skills, adaptive behaviour (other than in social interaction), and curiosity about the environment in childhood;
5. there is motor clumsiness as manifested by delays in fine motor skills, gross motor skills, visual-motor coordination or awkwardness of gait. (Examples include delayed acquisition of motor skills such as pedalling a tricycle, catching or kicking a ball, holding a pen or pencil, printing or writing; rigid gait, odd posture);
6. difficulties in regulating in an age-appropriate manner the expected physical proximity between two persons, as culturally appropriate according to the situation (e.g., being "right in your face" at a first introduction);
7. a history of precocious development of speech, which exceeds age-expected motor development, including a history of talking before walking. That is, as an infant, the person speaks early and walks late;

8. in children, a preference for relating to adults rather than to peers. The child may be perceived as "charming" by adults but as "odd" by peers.

E. The disturbance causes clinically significant impairment in expected age-appropriate social, occupational, or other important areas of functioning.

F. If criteria are also met for DSM-5 Autistic Disorder, *the diagnosis of Asperger's Disorder takes precedence.*

In work leading up to the next DSM after version 5, the DSM-6, we would have to consider a number of criticisms of these proposed DSM-5 criteria. The DSM-5 list contains too many alternatives. There are eight alternatives under both language impairments and under additional characteristics. Research would need to reduce the length of these lists by eliminating those criteria that are less discriminating. Some of the symptom alternatives border on being too complex to readily interpret and apply in a clinical setting. There is redundancy among the lists of criteria. Section D of the proposed DSM-5 "additional characteristics" is a garbage can of criteria which likely apply to most Asperger's children, but may well not apply to all. For example, the DSM-IV requirements of no delays in speech or cognitive development have been relegated to this list. Nevertheless, it would be interesting to see whether criteria such as these can establish Asperger's as a valid, viable diagnostic entity separate from HFA and other related diagnoses.

Note that Szatmari in *Asperger Syndrome* (2000, p. 405) suggests that sometimes "it is more important to evaluate the *usefulness* of the diagnostic distinctions rather than their validity". It may be the case that the diagnosis of Asperger's remains a *clinically useful* one, even if its validity as a separate diagnosis based on observable external characteristics cannot yet be appropriately established.

Is there consensual agreement on a set of differentiating observable external symptoms or descriptive features for Asperger's?

The brief answer to this question is "no". Prior to the DSM-IV in 1994, there were a number of similar but not completely overlapping lists of symptoms, such as those by Szatmari, the Gillbergs, Tantum, and others. With the advent of the ICD-10 and the DSM-IV in 1994, we have a common symptom list, but one which is virtually unworkable, and at the very best, glaringly inadequate. This is a difficulty which has bedevilled and continues to bedevil research into Asperger's (especially now that it has been removed from DSM-5), as well as any attempts to outline the epidemiology, course, prognosis, and aetiology of Asperger's as based on external descriptive features. Prior to 1994, it is impossible to compare studies of Asperger's because each study has a somewhat different list of criteria for Asperger's, some lists being more stringent and others considerably laxer. We therefore cannot make any comparisons across studies, cannot pool data from different studies, and cannot do meta-analyses of studies. It is unclear whether the "Asperger's" of one study is the same clinical entity as the "Asperger's" of another study.

The situation changed very little in 1994. We did have the DSM-IV criteria, but these were so inadequate as to make research difficult at best. Uncertainty continues because some researchers, frustrated by the inadequacy of DSM-IV, have used "modified" DSM criteria in the attempt to better differentiate "true" cases of Asperger's. Having modified the criteria, we once again cannot make comparisons across studies. The use of the inadequate criteria of DSM-IV in doing a study must raise questions about the validity of the study being done.

To put it briefly, the situation with research into Asperger's and of even adequately defining Asperger's on the basis of observable external characteristics or descriptive features has been one of controversy, chaos, ambiguity, and uncertainty. This situation might have improved with the advent DSM-5, but has actually been considerably worsened by this unfortunate document, at least unfortunate for Asperger's. In the DSM-5, all forms of autism are unceremoniously dumped into a single, undifferentiated glob called "ASD". This glob may be useful to a few constipated statisticians in their dusty corners, but it is counterproductive for frontline clinicians who actually want to treat these children and who need *finer distinctions* rather than unwieldy and undifferentiated diagnostic globs.

The search for defining observable characteristics and symptoms of Asperger's continues. Deficiencies in language use and deficits in motor skills have both been suggested as crucial for this. Ozonoff and Griffith in *Asperger Syndrome* (2000, p. 75) ask:

> What are the diagnostic bell ringers of [Asperger's]? It has been suggested that motor deficits may be central to [Asperger's],

although there is not, as yet, consensus on this. Some diagnostic systems and clinical descriptions consider motor dysfunction to be a core symptom of the disorder, … whereas others [such as DSM-IV] regard it as an associated characteristic that may or may not be present. It has also been proposed that visual-spatial deficits may be characteristic of [Asperger's]. Both motor and visual-spatial dysfunction are appealing core symptoms of [Asperger's], as they appear to distinguish it from HFA, which is usually described as having superior abilities in these areas. (Ozonoff & Griffith, 2000, p. 75)

These authors also note that some researchers cite "evidence of visual-motor integration, visual-spatial perception, nonverbal concept formation, and visual memory deficits in subjects with [Asperger's]," whereas "those with HFA did not demonstrate such impairments" (Ozonoff & Griffith, 2000, p. 83).

Attwood (undated: p. 1) concludes that "between 50% and 90% of children and adults with Asperger's Syndrome have problems with motor coordination" but that "there continues to be some confusion as to whether motor clumsiness should be a diagnostic criterion" for Asperger's. My proposed solution to this difficulty was given in the above suggestions for DSM-5, namely, that if fifty to ninety per cent, but not all of those with Asperger's show the symptom, then it could be included in a list of non-mandatory symptom alternatives. Among the motor coordination problems which Attwood lists as occurring in Asperger's are the following: ungainly walking and running, difficulty accurately catching and throwing a ball, and also in kicking a ball, poor manual dexterity in handwriting, lax joints, and difficulty in copying rhythms.

Ghaziuddin and Gerstein (1994) in their paper entitled "Is clumsiness a marker for Asperger syndrome?" give the answer "no" to the question posed by the title of their paper. They compared a small group of people with Asperger's with a group suffering from HFA using a standard test, the Bruiniks-Oseretsky test, to assess clumsiness. They found that: "Both groups showed problems with coordination and the distribution of standard scores was virtually identical. This suggests that motor clumsiness, as measured by tests of coordination, may not reliably distinguish [Asperger's] from HFA" (Ghaziuddin & Gerstein, 1994, p. 519).

Poor manual dexterity and difficulty with handwriting have been noted frequently in Asperger's children. In spite of these difficulties, I have noted that *some* Asperger's children seem to be quite good at drawing. I'm not sure how to explain this. Lesinskiene (2002, p. 90) in her paper entitled "Children with Asperger's syndrome: Specific aspects of their drawings" makes some interesting observations. In her very small sample of nine Asperger's children, she states that: "All children showed good abilities in drawing." In her opinion, "Analysis of free drawings [of these children] was found to be a helpful tool in understanding the inner world and the dynamic changes during the therapy process of these children." She feels that beginning with drawing a picture "is a good way to start communication and friendly relations with [Asperger's] children." She adds (2002, p. 92) that most of the free drawings of these children "reflected [the] narrow interests of [Asperger's] children" and that Asperger's children "did not like drawing people".

In my experience, some but not all Asperger's children are good at drawing. One child I worked with actually had a special interest and skill in making elaborate drawings. This particular child *did* like drawing people, or at least human-like figures, but only in the context of his complex and elaborate fantasy world involving goblins, demons and the like. I felt that his drawings certainly did give me access to his inner world, and were also very helpful in communicating with him.

Another "diagnostic bell ringer" for Asperger's suggested by some, is the specific pattern of strengths and weakness in language found in Asperger's. Ghaziuddin and Gerstein (1996, p. 585) have written a paper entitled "Pedantic speaking style differentiates Asperger Syndrome from high-functioning autism", with the title indicating clearly what their position is. They state that: "pedantic speech is common in [Asperger's] and may help differentiate [Asperger's] from high-functioning autism." They go further to suggest "that pedantic speaking style may be used as a diagnostic feature of [Asperger's]" (ibid, p. 593). Asperger's, they say, "has aptly been described as a key to the puzzle of autism." Though most agree about the clinical usefulness of the Asperger's diagnosis, "its diagnostic validity and its distinction from HFA are still not established" (ibid, p. 593). They note that, for DSM-IV, one of the few distinctions between Asperger's and HFA is "relatively normal language development" in Asperger's, a diagnostic criterion which "is largely dependent on parental recall." The last sentence of their paper is: "Use of a criterion, such as pedantic speech, that is not dependent on parental recall, may provide a useful method of establishing the diagnostic validity of [Asperger's] and its possible distinction from high-functioning autism" (ibid, p. 593).

It would be encouraging to be able to agree with Ghaziuddin and Gerstein (1996). The problem with their suggestion is a problem which they allude to in passing but do not discuss in their paper; that is, "pedantic speech is *common* in [Asperger's] (my italics)." I would agree that pedantic speech is *common* in Asperger's. The problem is that it is *not universal in Asperger's, and therefore cannot be used by itself as a defining or a differentiating symptom* for Asperger's. It is an important *suggestive* symptom of Asperger's, but it is not a *mandatory* symptom. We do not need to discard this *possible* symptom of Asperger's, however. As with the other *possible but non-mandatory Asperger's symptom* of motor clumsiness, I suggest that pedantic speech should be included in a list of non-mandatory symptom alternatives which *taken together* might help to define Asperger's. This is what I have done in the proposed DSM-5 definition.

Differential diagnosis of Asperger's based on observable external descriptive features

In making a differential diagnosis of Asperger's disorder, the clinician must be able to differentiate Asperger's from at least the following similar or symptomatically overlapping diagnostic categories: (1) high-functioning autism (HFA), (2) pervasive developmental disorder not otherwise specified (PDD NOS), as it appeared in DSM-IV, (3) deficits in attention, motor control and perception (DAMP), (4) nonverbal learning disabilities (NVLD), (5) semantic-pragmatic disorder, (6) schizoid personality disorder, (7) schizotypal personality disorder, and (8) obsessive-compulsive disorder (OCD). In what follows, I confine my brief consideration to just HFA/PDD NOS and to schizoid or schizotypal personality disorders.

HFA and PDD NOS

The most difficult differential diagnoses, and the most controversial, are those between Asperger's and high-functioning autism, and Asperger's and PDD NOS. Many would *not* make a differential diagnosis between Asperger's and HFA, saying that they were really one and the same. Prior to the DSM-IV in 1994, the most likely diagnosis open to an Asperger's child would have been one of PDD NOS. Asperger's has an *inadequate* definition in the DSM-IV, whereas PDD NOS is a "garbage can" category with *no* formal definition. It would thus seem impossible to validly differentiate between them.

Klin, Volkmar and Sparrow in *Asperger Syndrome* (2000, p. 330) note that: "The differential diagnosis of [Asperger's] involves primarily … HFA and … PDD NOS." They continue: "[Asperger's] differs from HFA in that the onset is usually later and the outcome more positive. In addition, social and communication deficits are less severe, motor mannerisms are usually absent whereas circumscribed interests and verbosity are more conspicuous [and] motor clumsiness is apparently more frequent" in Asperger's (ibid, p. 331).

Considering PDD NOS, Klin, Sparrow, Marans, Carter and Volkmar in *Asperger Syndrome* (2000, p. 331) correctly note that "the distinction between [Asperger's] and PDD NOS is problematic because, essentially, the latter is a residual category with no defining criteria". It is impossible to differentiate between two diagnostic categories when one remains undefined and, as has been noted, the other is inadequately defined. Nevertheless, Klin and colleagues go on to do just this, stating that Asperger's "differs from the much more common PDD NOS in that social, emotional, and communicative deficits are more severe and outcome is poorer in [Asperger's]" (ibid, p. 331). How they reach these conclusions about an undefined diagnosis the authors do not say.

One common approach is that because of the "absence of strong validation data for [Asperger's]" a conservative approach may be to "regard autism and [Asperger's] along a continuum, possibly with individuals with autism representing the more cognitively challenged and those with [Asperger's] representing the more cognitively able" (ibid, p. 4).

One possible psychological distinction between HFA and Asperger's disorder is the different profile of each on intelligence tests. "Individuals with [Asperger's] were more likely to exhibit Verbal IQ scores greater than Performance IQ; the *opposite* result was obtained in higher-functioning individuals with autism" (Klin, Volkmar & Sparrow, 2000, p. 42). Additionally "individuals with HFA are much more likely to have significant deficits in the areas of verbal comprehension and language" but with nonverbal abilities being "areas of relative strength" (ibid, p. 48). It is noted that with Asperger's, peaks are obtained in verbally mediated tasks, such as the Information subtest of the WISC (Klin,

Volkmar & Sparrow in *Asperger Syndrome*, 2000, p. 315). It is further suggested that Asperger's children may do better on a *verbal* task involving understanding of social conventions such as the Comprehension subtest of the WISC, than on a *nonverbal* task exploring the ability to sequence social situations, such as the Picture Arrangement subtest.

HFA and can also possibly be differentiated from Asperger's in terms of the latter having a relatively intact capacity to form a "theory of mind" that is, the realisation that others have minds just as oneself and the capacity to impute mental states to others and to oneself. HFA individuals tend to perform worse than Asperger's individuals on tests of theory of mind. There is "spared theory of mind performance in most subjects with [Asperger's]" (Ozonoff & Griffith, 2000, p. 85).

As noted: "It has been suggested that [Asperger's] may be no more than high-IQ autism" (Ozonoff & Griffith, 2000, p. 88). Another suggestion, by Szatmari (2000, p. 411), is that autism and Asperger's represent different "developmental pathways or trajectories". Children with autism and Asperger's may share the same aetiological process, but "there may be a difference in either their rate of development or the appearance and disappearance of certain PDD-like behaviours and symptoms" (ibid, p. 411). If Asperger's children develop some functionally useful speech earlier on, this may "put them on a different developmental pathway or trajectory than other children with PDD" (ibid, p. 411). When autistic children develop language, though at a later age than Asperger's children, "they may then join the developmental pathway of the children with [Asperger's]" (ibid, p. 411).

These views are supported by some data in a paper by Szatmari and his colleagues (2000, p. 1980) entitled "Two-year outcome of preschool children with autism or Asperger's syndrome". To find out whether outcome in Asperger's differs from that of children with autism, they compared outcomes of groups of children with these disorders over a period of two years. They found that:

> Children with Asperger's syndrome had better social skills and fewer autistic symptoms 2 years after study enrolment than the children with autism. The differences in outcome could not be explained by initial differences in IQ and language abilities. Children with autism who had developed verbal fluency at follow-up were very similar to the children with Asperger's syndrome at study enrolment. (Szatmari et al., 2000, p. 1980)

They conclude that: "Asperger's disorder and autism represent parallel but potentially overlapping developmental trajectories" (ibid, p. 1980).
    For Ozonoff and Griffith (2000):

> [Asperger's] and autism may differ in their underlying neuropathy. The proposed visual-spatial deficits of [Asperger's] individuals, as well as their difficulty producing and interpreting facial expressions, gestures, and prosody have led to the hypothesis that the right hemisphere is dysfunctional in [Asperger's]. (Ozonoff & Griffith, 2000, p. 89)

Smith (2000, p. 97) states that: "It has been asserted that motor inco-ordination (or "clumsiness") might differentiate [Asperger's] from HFA." It is said to be "commonly accepted wisdom" that "motor skills are unimpaired or even precocious in autism" (ibid, p. 117). This position is criticised on the basis of "lack of any attempt to define operationally the concept of clumsiness" (ibid, p. 98). It is asserted that in individuals with Asperger's, "movements were awkward," and many are said to be "poor at games involving motor skills, and sometimes the executive problems affect the ability to write or draw" (ibid, p. 99). One report states that "ball catching produced the greatest difference between [Asperger's] and non-[Asperger's] individuals" (ibid, p. 104). Her conclusion is that: "The issue of the association of clumsiness with [Asperger's] remains ambiguous" (ibid, p. 106).
    A very similar conclusion is reached by Schultz, Romanski and Tsatsanis (2000, p. 175): "The research literature provides substantial evidence suggesting that motor deficits are frequent in [Asperger's], but there is mixed evidence in support of these deficits as distinguishing [Asperger's] from autistic disorder".

Schizoid personality and schizotypal personality disorders

DSM-IV states clearly that: "there may be great difficulty differentiating individuals with schizoid personality disorder from those with Asperger's Disorder" (American Psychiatric Association, 1994, p. 640). DSM-IV suggests that the difference is that those with Asperger's have "more severely impaired social interaction" along with "stereotyped behavior and interests" (ibid, p. 640) It is of interest that in the ICD-10, Asperger's comes with an exclusion criterion for schizotypal disorder, "but the definition includes schizoid disorder of childhood"

(Wolff, 2000, p. 287). Referring to Hans Asperger's original cases, Wolff (2000, p. 278) states that "our schizoid children were like the children he described", and she adds that: "our children also resembled children given a diagnosis of schizotypal personality disorder". One difference was that "our schizoid young people were, as a group, much less impaired socially both in childhood and in adult groups of patients described … as having Asperger's". In summary, Wolff concludes that "the children we have described could be classified either as having a schizoid/schizotypal personality disorder or as having Asperger's" (ibid, p. 290), according to Asperger's original criteria. It is also suggested that: "the concepts of pervasive developmental disorder and personality disorders of the schizoid/schizotypal kind may not be as discrepant as current classifications suggest" (ibid, p. 291).

Volkmar and Klin in their chapter on diagnostic issues (in *Asperger syndrome*, 2000, p. 29) state that: "The relation of schizoid personality disorder to [Asperger's] has been somewhat controversial." Similarities include "abnormalities in empathy and nonverbal communication," with differences including social disability more severe in Asperger's, outcome less positive in Asperger's, and closer relation to schizophrenia with schizoid personality. The competing claim is also made that "in spite of some differences in severity, children with schizoid disorder and [Asperger's] represent the same group of children" (ibid, p. 406).

For the DSM-IV, Asperger's and schizotypal personality disorder share a pattern of social and interpersonal deficits. DSM-IV, in fact, notes that there may be difficulty in differentiating children with this personality disorder from a "group of solitary, odd children whose behaviour is characterised by marked social isolation, eccentricity, or peculiarities of language, and whose diagnoses would probably include … Asperger's Disorder" (American Psychiatric Association, 1994, p. 643).

Folstein and Santangelo (2000, p. 160) decline to distinguish among the three, stating that: "The similarity between [Asperger's] and schizoid personality disorder and … schizotypal personality disorder makes it difficult to identify [individuals] clearly as [Asperger's], schizoid, or schizotypal".

I can only offer a few personal observations based on my treatment of one schizoid child whom we can call Justin, whom I have had the privilege of treating between eleven years and fourteen years of age (with his treatment ongoing). His period of treatment overlaps with many of the Asperger's children I have previously described.

Two characteristics of Justin stand out for me—avoidance and a kind of hyper-perceptive empathy. In contrast to many (but not all) Asperger's children, Justin prefers, in his own words, to "fly under the radar". He does not want to be noticed in any way by his teachers or come in any way to the attention of his peers. Many Asperger's children are desperate to form friendships. Justin strongly prefers to avoid friendships. Much of his avoidance seems to be based on the fear of potential humiliation that for him would be involved in being noticed by others.

He also seems to have what I call a "hyper-perceptive empathy". When he and I play board games together, he very carefully monitors my facial expression and my behaviour so that quite frequently this enables him to guess very quickly the character whose card I am holding, and he wins the game. He also plays hockey and very much worries about how the other kids on the opposing team might feel. Whereas his own teammates are happy to score as many goals as they possibly can, Justin feels that scoring too many goals against the opposing team may be experienced as demoralising and humiliating by them. He therefore wants to limit the number of goals his team scores. This is totally incomprehensible to his teammates. Both Justin's avoidance and his "hyper-perceptive empathy" seem quite different from what one might expect in an Asperger's child.

Aetiology of Asperger's based on external descriptive features

Anything useful that might be said about the aetiology of Asperger's is significantly constrained by our inability to adequately define Asperger's or to differentiate it from other clinical entities on the basis of external descriptive features. Having stated this caveat, we can make two suggestions about aetiology. The first suggestion is that there is mounting evidence for genetic transmission of Asperger's in families. The second suggestion is that Asperger's is essentially a right hemisphere dysfunction. If, as has also been suggested, autism, including HFA, is essentially a left hemisphere dysfunction, then we may have a clinical basis to validly differentiate Asperger's and HFA.

As with everything else about Asperger's, the suggestion that Asperger's is a right hemisphere dysfunction and autism a left hemisphere dysfunction remains controversial and unproven.

DSM-IV indicates that: "there appears to be an increased frequency of Asperger's Disorder among family members of individuals who have the disorder" (American Psychiatric Association, 1994, p. 76). Some research suggests that "there is an even stronger familial component in [Asperger's] than in autism" (Volkmar & Klin, 2000, p. 58), and that there are similar traits, particularly in the fathers of Asperger's children (ibid, p. 57). Folstein and Santangelo claim that: "[Asperger's] is probably genetically related to autism" (Folstein & Santangelo, 2000, p. 164).

Prognosis of Asperger's based on external descriptive features

DSM-IV simply states that Asperger's "follows a continuous course and … the duration is lifelong" (American Psychiatric Association, 1994, p. 76). Asperger himself initially suggested a good prognosis for the children that he identified, but he became somewhat less optimistic later on in his career. The current climate of opinion tends towards a good prognosis, the prognosis being improved if the Asperger's child is able to form and maintain some kind of peer relationships or friendships.

Klin, Volkmar and Sparrow write that: "The intellectual and language assets of individuals with [Asperger's] are likely to be associated with increased social, vocational, and independent living opportunities" (Klin, Volkmar & Sparrow, 2000, p. 8). These "increased opportunities" may be in *comparison* with those of autistic children.

Wolff (2000, p. 295) states that it is important to "maintain an optimistic stance" towards Asperger's, noting that "the children's adjustment improves with age, once the pressures for conformity, always greatest during the school years, are at an end and the young people can find their own niche in life".

Gillberg (1992) is also optimistic, concluding that: "Oddities of social style, communication and interests are likely to remain, but the majority of this group hold down jobs and it seems that a large proportion get married and have children" (Gillberg, 1992, p. 833).

Tantum (2000, p. 377) makes two helpful comments. He states that: "People with [Asperger's] who make long-term intimate relationships are exceptional, but when this happens it appears to accelerate social development". His overall conclusion is that: "[Asperger's] has a good prognosis … . The primary impairment in [Asperger's] does not seem to worsen and may improve," including "greater expressiveness over the years, a reduction of extreme preservation of sameness, growing intersubjectivity and empathy, and less incoordination." It is also noted that "social contact with peers was associated with good prognosis" (ibid, p. 397).

Attwood (undated, p. 2) makes the intriguing suggestion that "girls have a better long-term prognosis than boys", the reason for this being that girls "appear to be more able to learn how to socialise and to camouflage their difficulties at an early age".

DSM-5 as published in 2013

The standard diagnostic manuals used by clinicians in North America for the diagnosis of Asperger's and of autism spectrum disorders are at best incomplete, and for the psychoanalytically oriented clinician, are in my view frustrating, unhelpful, and highly disappointing. The specific manuals are the DSM-IV (in the form of the DSM-IV, 1994 and the DSM-IV-TR, 2000), the DSM-5 (2013) and the Psychodynamic Diagnostic Manual (PDM, 2006). From a clinical point of view, the DSM-5 is a distinct step backwards from the DSM-IV, as far as the autism spectrum is concerned. The DSM-5 represents a counterproductive and an ignominious retreat in the attempt to provide an adequate diagnostic description of Asperger's, a retreat which literally throws out the baby with the bathwater by eliminating the diagnosis of Asperger's completely. The history of botanical taxonomy is full of "lumpers" (those who lump together related taxons and thus reduce the number of species) and "splitters" (those who make finer and more exact divisions among species and thus increase their number). For the autism spectrum, the DSM-5 is an unhelpful exercise in indiscriminate lumping, so that all syndromes related to the autism spectrum are slopped together into one undifferentiated gelatinous glob which allows one to only play around a bit with degrees of severity. Such lumping may possibly be of value to statisticians or nosological researchers. It is *precisely the opposite* of what is likely to benefit clinicians. In order to gear their treatment efforts as precisely as possible to the wide range of children on the autism spectrum, and to "fine tune" these efforts, clinicians need as much splitting (in the *taxonomic sense*) as our experience in treating autistic people indicates is actually there.

The Psychodynamic Diagnostic Manual, 2006

Even the usually very helpful PDM (Psychodynamic Diagnostic Manual) is for me, an extreme disappointment. It is disappointing to the degree that those who *actually work* in a psychoanalytic way with children on the autism spectrum are likely to feel that it is distinctly unhelpful. The diagnoses of autism and Asperger's are barely mentioned, and then only to lump these together under the rubric of "neurodevelopmental disorders of relating and communicating". In what purports to be a "psychodynamic" diagnostic manual, and which is mostly very helpfully so, when it comes to autism, there is no effort at all to convey any sense that these children even have interesting psychodynamics, let alone to suggest what these psychodynamics might look like. In what purports to be psychodynamic, there is a sudden regressive retreat to a sort of fundamentalist biological psychiatry which is as far from being psychodynamic as our Milky Way is from another galaxy. Psychodynamic clinicians interested in autism and Asperger's are left scratching their heads in confusion and dismay, wondering what could have possibly made purportedly "psychodynamic" writers engage in such a regressive retreat into biological fundamentalism. No mention is made of *any* of the psychoanalytic pioneers who have theorised about or engaged clinically over the years with these children—Tustin, Alvarez, Mitrani, Houzel, Meltzer, and Ogden to mention only a few. The part of the PDM which purportedly deals with autism does not even read like a psychoanalytic work at all. Again, the psychodynamic clinician is left baffled and confused. Did purportedly "psychodynamic" writers engage in a willful retreat into biological fundamentalism for some obscure reason? Surely their ignorance of psychoanalytic writing about autism could not have been so complete as to not recognise or mention even one of the writers just noted above? The apparent total and overwhelming ignorance displayed by the PDM in reference to psychoanalytic writings about the autism spectrum is perplexing to say the least. To summarise my view: all the diagnostic outlines most commonly used in North America seem to leave us totally and completely in the lurch when it comes to diagnosing Asperger's disorder.

A diagnostic system for the autism spectrum

Fortunately for psychoanalytic clinicians, some of the pioneers noted above have used their years of experience with autistic children to make diagnostic suggestions, Frances Tustin and Anne Alvarez in particular. As early as 1972 in her book *Autism and Childhood Psychosis*, Tustin had begun the task of trying to differentiate among types of autism, mentioning "encapsulated secondary autism" and "progressive secondary autism" as two possible forms, among others in the section entitled "Types of Autism" beginning on page ninety-five of her classic book. In what follows, I use Anne Alvarez's (1992, p. 190) suggestion, based on Tustin's work, as to autism proper being divided into two different subtypes—unformed autism in which the children are like "amoebas" and shell-type autism, in which the children are metaphorically "crustaceans".

I also set apart "high-functioning autism" as a separate subtype. In the course of presenting a wonderfully detailed paper on the treatment of a female adolescent with Asperger's, an experienced colleague referred to Asperger's as "a form of high-functioning autism". I have to disagree. In my view, Asperger's is both quantitatively and qualitatively different from "autism proper", including high-functioning autism, though with sufficient overlaps between the two conditions to correctly identify Asperger's as an "autism spectrum disorder (ASD)". I also view high-functioning autism as a distinct type of autism, differentiated from full-blown autism by being quantitatively but *not* qualitatively distinct from full-blown autism.

I'm going to present some very limited evidence suggesting we should distinguish Asperger's from autism (specifically, from high-functioning autism) in the hope that others will outline more evidence confirming, disconfirming or modifying what I will outline here.

What is high-functioning autism? This phrase is used frequently in literature, but to the best of my knowledge, it is nowhere clearly described or defined. I will briefly try to suggest some of the possible defining features of high-functioning autism, underlining again that high-functioning autism differs quantitatively (referring to the quantitative strength of the symptoms involved) but not qualitatively from what I am calling "full-blown" or classical autism.

The "autistic triad" or "triad of impairments" which defines autism for some diagnostic systems consists of three aspects: "the triad of social, language, and behavioral impairment" (Mitrani & Mitrani, 1997, p. 145). Specifically, one finds absence of or significant delays in verbal and nonverbal communication, impairment of social relationships, and stereotyped preoccupations or rituals, often of an autosensuous nature (such as lining up toys in a rigidly invariant order in rows, spinning the wheels on toy cars or flicking lights repeatedly on and off). In each of these three parts of the autistic triad, the child with high-functioning autism tends to function at a higher, more advanced level quantitatively speaking than the functioning of a child with classical or full-blown autism. Although likely delayed, language and some capacity for verbal communication at least of a moderate level will be present in high-functioning autism, as opposed to minimal or no language for classical autism. Social relationships will still be limited or impaired for the high-functioning autistic child. But unlike the child with full-blown autism who may totally shun social interactions, avoid other people, and have no eye-to-eye contact other than fleeting glances from the corners of his eyes, the high-functioning autistic child will show some interest in others and some willingness and ability to interact and communicate with others, at least some of the time. Finally, with the high-functioning autistic child, autistic rituals or stereotyped behaviours are still present, but at least some of these are likely to be less autosensuous in nature and less rigidly stereotyped and mechanically repetitive than for children with full-blown autism. Instead of endlessly spinning the wheels on a toy car as I have seen many full-blown autistic children do, the high-functioning autistic child may produce endless cartoon drawings of people, though these may be quite stylized in nature. This is in fact what I observed with the two high-functioning autistic children I treated at the same time, as fully described in Holloway, 2013.

I now want to describe the (quite limited) evidence I am aware of which to me suggests that Asperger's is distinct from autism, quantitatively and qualitatively, including distinct from high-functioning autism.

This evidence derives from an unusual and very informative experience I was privileged to have. For several years, I had the opportunity of meeting in psychotherapy sessions on consecutive days with Dan (the Asperger's adolescent we met in Chapter Six) and with Sam (the high-functioning autistic adolescent I describe in Holloway, 2013). The respective diagnoses of these two adolescents were as clear and as definitive as any diagnosis could be. Both of these adolescents came from backgrounds of privilege, and their respective diagnoses were made repeatedly over the years by a number of highly experienced professionals. At the beginning of their respective treatments, the evidence accumulated over the years for both of these adolescents was shared with me, and it was in agreement with my own diagnostic evaluations of the two adolescents.

Note that I evaluated Dan as having the "object-shunning" or inhibited/avoidant type of Asperger's. Because these children have "secondary" autistic-like avoidance of interpersonal relationships, presenting themselves as "burnt out" in their attempts to relate to others, this is the type of Asperger's child or adolescent who externally most clearly resembles high-functioning autistic children.

When I presented some of my initial thinking about Asperger's to a group of colleagues, one colleague very experienced with children on the autism spectrum challenged my thinking in a very useful way which helped me clarify a number of issues in my own mind. "You differentiate Asperger's children from high-functioning autistic children on the basis of how they relate to others—or not" she began. "You say Asperger's children always want to relate to others, sometimes even desperately so. But haven't we encountered Asperger's children want to avoid others, who have no friends, and who want to stay away from other people as much as they can?" I quickly agreed that her comment was true. I then suggested that it might be important to look at the history. If the Asperger's child is in the "object-shunning" group, or what I refer to as the inhibited/avoidant type, then the likelihood is that their history will involve the following constellation. At one time, they did seek connections with others. But repeated cumulative traumas of experiencing rejection and rebuff and perhaps also of being bullied and denigrated in the way they experience their relationships then resulted in these children "burning out" as far as seeking external objects was concerned. Put briefly, even with inhibited/avoidant object-shunning Asperger's children, the history, I suggest, will invariably reveal a period of time when they did seek out external objects. And even for high-functioning autistic children, who presently seem to want relationships with peers or other external objects (which was in fact the case for both Sam and Josh, the two high-functioning autistic adolescents I described in Holloway, 2013), their histories will reveal that earlier on, there was a long period of time in which they avoided external objects. At least, this is how it seems to me.

Unfortunately, reality has nasty habits. It tends to blur and dilute the clear, precise, and convenient distinctions we humans would like to make, what Descartes referred to as "clear and distinct ideas", and to substitute for such clear and distinct ideas unclarity and impreciseness. So I rely on my colleagues all over the world to provide whatever evidence is sufficient to confirm, to disconfirm or to revise what I suggest here.

Before leaving the topic of whether or not there is a distinction between Asperger's and high-functioning autism, I want to describe the qualitatively different experiences I had with Dan, the adolescent with inhibited/avoidant Asperger's, and Sam, the adolescent with high-functioning autism. During the years I saw them on alternate days, the emotional experience of what it was like to be with them was quite different. My countertransference to each adolescent had for me very different qualities, and the therapeutic reverie in which I tended to engage with each of them was also qualitatively different—or at least such was my experience.

With Sam, especially early in his treatment, there were frequent occasions during which I felt totally out of contact with him as he silently and compulsively worked at his collections of drawings. For periods of time, I had the feeling he was psychically absent, far away from me in what has been referred to as "an elsewhere state of mind". As in the movie *Gravity* I felt like an astronaut, floating off into nowhere, with no solidity, nothing to grasp onto, nothing to tether me in any way to Sam or to what he was currently experiencing. My therapeutic reverie would decay and evaporate, so that I was unable to hold onto Sam in my mind, and I drifted off into my own narcissistic and autistic-like state of reverie focused on my own concerns. My countertransference included states of feeling isolated and alone, sadly yearning for contact, and struggling to fight off hopelessness. The states of isolation and being cut off from Sam were not continuous, but were frequently interpolated into times of feeling in contact with him.

Both Sam and Dan were silent from time to time, but I experienced their periods of silence very differently. During his silences, I experienced Sam as disappeared, absent, elsewhere. It was very different with Dan.

Dan struggled to communicate with me, and especially at the beginning of sessions, he silently struggled to find what he wanted to say and to organise it. My experiences of his silences were of times when he was struggling—to reorient himself, to reorganise and to come up with ways to make contact with me. I experienced a lively countertransference and an ongoing therapeutic reverie when I was with Dan, never feeling totally cut off or disconnected from him as was the case with Sam. With Dan, the countertransference involved usually feeling engaged, connected, and actively participating with him in a mutual struggle to make sense of his experiences. My countertransference was mobile, shifting from optimistic hopefulness about him to times of gloomy disappointment. My reverie about what he could become and make of himself was always active.

I offer this small piece of evidence that high-functioning autism and Asperger's involve the child in different states of mind, at least at the beginning of therapy. After a number of years of treatment, these two conditions likely become much more difficult to distinguish, one from the other.

In Figure 1 below, under "other autistic disorders", I have placed Reid's (1999b) diagnosis of "autistic post-traumatic developmental disorder" (APTDD). This is based on a number of papers providing evidence that an autistic or autistic-like presentations can appear subsequent to traumatic experiences during the infantile period of development.

I now make some very tentative suggestions about types of Asperger's disorder. These suggestions are based only on my personal experiences, and are intended to stimulate further discussion. A rough and tentative outline of nosological suggestions for the entire autism spectrum is presented in Figure 1 below, entitled "Nosological suggestions for Autism Spectrum Disorders".

I postulate that Asperger's disorder can be usefully separated, from a clinical and treatment perspective, into three types. This division is based to a large extent on which side of the split in the self is usually predominant, the bully aspect or the victim aspect.

Kernberg (1976) suggests that an internal object relations unit consists of a self-representation linked to an object representation which is

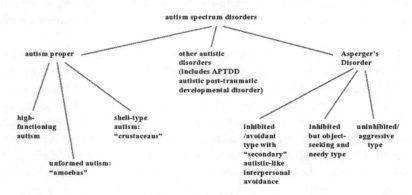

Figure 1. Nosological suggestions for autism spectrum disorders.

coloured by a predominating affect. Splitting of the self complicates this picture to some extent.

In addition to which aspect is the predominant aspect of the split self, the internal object linked with this aspect of the self, and the affective matrix which predominates, one more characteristic is used to distinguish the three types of Asperger's disorder. This characteristic is the predominant form taken by the child's external object relationships. This refers to the degree to which the Asperger's child is actively object-seeking (wishing for and attempting to establish friendships), or object-shunning (generally avoiding contact with others and tending to be a loner), or else object-rejecting (tending to engaging in angry, hostile, and aggressive interactions with others).

Three types of Asperger's

There is at least one other clinician who has attempted to outline types or subtypes of Asperger's disorder. I refer to Rhode (2011b, pp. 289–290). Her experience is that Asperger's children "fall into two broad groups." She distinguishes "two main subtypes" of Asperger's, these being separated "according to whether coping mechanisms are predominantly obsessional or schizoid". It seems likely to me that most if not all Asperger's children have *both* obsessional characteristics *as well as* schizoid ones. The former include the "restricted repetitive interests", the "encompassing preoccupation with one or more stereotyped and restricted patterns of interest" in the old DSM-IV diagnostic criteria (as they appear on p. 77 of the DSM-IV). The latter would include the DSM-IV "qualitative impairment in social interaction." Nevertheless, Rhode's (2011b) emphasis on which aspect is *predominant* is a very helpful suggestion. She elaborates that some Asperger's children "are predominantly withdrawn and make use of obsessional coping mechanisms" (Rhode, 2011b, p. 289), whereas children in her other subtype, the schizoid one, rely "on schizoid mechanisms such as minute fragmentation and projection" (ibid, p. 290).

These are useful distinctions. Rhode's obsessional subtype may overlap to a fair degree with what I refer to as the "inhibited but object-seeking and needy" type, and her schizoid subtype may overlap with what I call the "inhibited/avoidant and object-shunning" type. It is of interest that in our different ways of attempting to find different types of Asperger's children, both of us anchor our distinctions in the predominant means of defence used by the children. Rhode focuses on obsessional defences *vs.* schizoid ones (fragmentation and projection) whereas I focus primarily on splitting of the self and which aspect of this split predominates. Keeping both ways of categorising Asperger's children in mind may be useful. Perhaps the two points of view might be integrated in some way, likely based on the defensive structure used by the child.

(1) The inhibited/avoidant type who are object-shunning

The three types of Asperger's patients my experience suggests are as follows. There is the inhibited/avoidant type. These children tend to be behaviourally shy, reticent, inhibited, and phobic or avoidant of inter-personal relationships. There is sometimes *secondary* and autistic-like interpersonal avoidance. It is the victim aspect of the split self which predominates. At least initially, the transference tends towards ideali-sation of the therapist. Projective identifications toward the therapist tend to be strongly restrained. Their typical anxieties tend to be existen-tial in nature, wondering if they figure at all in the minds of others, or even exist for others in any substantial way. In terms of their external object relations, these are the object-shunning children. These children may sometimes be difficult to diagnostically differentiate from high-functioning autistic children, though after a period of treatment, this is likely to be fairly easy (as in the differences between Sam and Dan I referred to earlier). Of my Asperger's patients you have overheard, Dan is likely the best illustration of inhibited/avoidant object-shunning type of Asperger's.

(2) The inhibited but object-seeking and needy type

The second type is the inhibited but object-seeking and needy type. These children want, need, and strive for interpersonal relationships, often with a high degree of frustrated and painful desperation, and often with strong fears of being rejected. There tend to be oscillations, sometimes quite rapid ones, between the victim and the bully aspects of the split self. Transference tends to involve a mixture of idealisation and more subtle denigrations of the therapist. Their anxieties tend to be a mixture of existential ones (wondering if they even exist for others) and relational ones (could others ever find them valuable as friends?).

Projective identifications toward the therapist tend to be quite restrained earlier in therapy, but may appear when the bully aspect of the spilt self becomes predominant. Of my patients, Matt is a good example of this inhibited but object-seeking and needy type of Asperger's.

(3) The uninhibited and aggressive type who are object-rejecting

The final and in some ways most interesting type I refer to as the uninhibited and aggressive type. These are likely the people whom Hans Asperger himself found to be over-represented in the prison population. They are children in which Asperger "noted sadistic behaviour and frequent acts of malice, about which they showed delight" (Rhode & Klauber, 2004, p. 30). All Asperger's children are capable of such acts when the bully part of their split self is predominant, but they are especially typical of the uninhibited/aggressive type. This is the object-rejecting group in terms of their external object relations, and there is often strong hostility in how they reject others. The bully aspect of the split self predominates for these children. Their typical anxieties are relational with strong paranoid-schizoid aspects, including feelings that others are "out to get them". Denigration of the therapist can be strong, and projective identifications strong.

The volume edited by Rhode and Klauber (2004) characterises this type of Asperger's child quite well. These children prefer being "an active bully rather than a passive victim" (p. 65) and may demonstrate "the classic picture of bullying, locating the discomfort, fear and hatred in another" (p. 66). Such children "can easily begin to behave as if the whole world is cruel and as if they have no choice but to identify with the cruelty … that they believe is there" (p. 66). These children "can sometimes do whatever is the most unpleasant or hurtful in a particular situation," (p. 64) may have "violent and sadistic phantasies" (p. 36) and may need "help in managing their aggressive impulses" (p. 23). There is also a comment about "the association of Asperger's syndrome with an increased risk of violent and criminal behaviour" (p. 35). In their discussion of violence and Asperger's, Mawson, Grounds and Tantum (1985, p. 569) conclude that "this association between Asperger's syndrome and violent behaviour is more common than has been recognised". Of my patients, both Thomas and Anthony seem to belong to the uninhibited and aggressive type who are object-rejecting.

I summarise the central characteristics of the three types of Asperger's in Table 1 below.

Treating the inhibited/avoidant type—Dan

We can now consider these three types of Asperger's children in greater detail and pay some attention to what each type may need from a therapist when in treatment. If there are "burnt-out schizophrenics", then the inhibited/avoidant type may represent something akin to "burnt-out Asperger's" children. Using Dan as an example, he told me about his emotional struggles around whether he would ever be able to live with other people, or would spend his life living alone. My countertransference experience was one of doing a difficult act of precision balancing, so that I felt allied with the part that could think about living with others, while at the same time, in order to treat him effectively, I also had to entertain and contain the possibility (and my sad feelings around the possibility) of Dan living as a lifelong loner.

Dan told me of his hopelessness about having relationships with others; his mistrust, disappointment, sense of rejection, sense of others

Table 1. Characteristics of the Three Types of Asperger's.

Types → Characteristics ↓	Inhibited/avoidant type	Inhibited/object-seeking and needy type	Uninhibited/aggressive type
Predominant aspect of the split self	Victim aspect	Oscillates between victim and bully (sometimes rapidly)	Bully aspect
Attitude to real external objects	Object-shunning (pseudo-autistic)	Object-seeking (but fearfully so)	Object-rejecting (often with hostility)
Transference tendency	Idealization of the therapist	Mixture of idealization and denigration of the therapist	Some idealization but with the risk of severe denigration of the therapist
Typical focal anxiety	Existential ("Do I even exist for others in any significant way?")	Mixture of existential and relational ("Will others value me and do I exist for them?")	Relational and paranoid-schizoid (Why are others out to hurt and belittle me?")
Use of projective identification in respect to the therapist	Projective identifications are initially avoided and rigidly restrained toward the therapist	Projective identifications are usually quite restrained toward therapist, but may appear if the bully aspect of the split predominates	Projective identifications are sometimes restrained toward therapist, but can be central and very powerful

lacking empathy, and his despair. He also let me know of his defensive arrogance, especially in relation to his peers; his sense of his peers as being frivolous, pleasure-seeking, lazy, irresponsible, disrespectful of authority, and full of aggression and hostility.

Again using Dan as an example, I propose that the key object relations structure for those with the inhibited/avoidant type of Asperger's is the following. The predominant aspect of the split in the self is the victim aspect (though the bully aspect makes occasional appearances). This gives rise to the predominant object relations structure—the victim aspect of the split in the self (developmentally rooted in what I have called the overwhelmed and vulnerable self), in relation to an internal object experienced as rejecting, abandoning, uncaring, and completely lacking in attunement, with a focal affective tone involving hopelessness, disappointment, and despair. These are the children who tend to shun connections with external objects and back away from or avoid friendships.

In treatment, as with all three types, a central concern is likely to involve work on reintegration of the split in the self. This is likely to involve some rehabilitation of the bully aspect of the split, so that aggressive fantasies and their motivations are clearer, and so that some sense of superego anxiety and guilt can emerge in place of arrogantly self-righteous hostility and denigration, so there is a closer approximation to the dynamics of the depressive position. As with all types of Asperger's children, the therapist is likely to be called upon to contain and process aspects of their functioning for a fairly long time. With the inhibited/avoidant type, this is especially true of the more self-righteously aggressive (but infrequently appearing) aspects. These are likely to appear as projective identifications into remote objects, such as Dan's projections into King Kong, or the *Star Trek* alien "Q". These projective identifications are likely to have some if not all of the characteristics of what Ogden (1982, p. 152) refers to as "violent" projective identifications, in which "the feelings of the projector are so intense and powerful as to be felt by him to be violently self-destructive", this probably being part of the reason for the use of remote objects as the targets of projective identifications. The therapist may find herself making for long periods of time what Ogden (1982, p. 31) refers to as "silent interpretations" in which the interpretation is "formulated in words in the therapist's mind, but not verbalised to the patient" and which as a result of their being silent "contain much more self-analytic material than one would include in an interpretation offered to the patient".

Dan also kept his therapist very free of any negative attributions and in an idealised position. The therapist may feel a little too content with this comfortable position, and may need to become aware of such distancing idealisations.

Treating the inhibited/object-seeking and needy type—Matt

Now consider the inhibited/object-seeking and needy type of Asperger's child, using Matt as an example of this type. There is a yearning, even a desperate seeking of connection with external objects. Matt was certainly in a state of anguished neediness in his wish for friendships with peers. There may be a sense of others as being in an almost teasing relationship with these children, so that friendships seem to be possible, but just out of reach. Friendships become as frustrating as the teasing torture he endured was for Tantalus.

With the inhibited/object-seeking and needy type, the split in the self seems to be more evenly balanced than for the other two types, with both the bully aspect of the split and the victim aspect making frequent appearances (though at least for Matt, it was the victim aspect that tended to be more his "default position"). It is with this type that the frequent alternation between the bully aspect of the split in the self and the victim aspect is most noticeable, likely to the immense confusion of those such as teachers who must deal with the child, and in all likelihood for the child himself (not to mention the therapist). As noted with Matt, the two sides of the split interact with each other, though they are still split off from one another in terms of the emotional nexus they express, the attitudes to objects and the typical behaviours involved. If Matt is a good example, then this type of Asperger's child may be the most capable of depressive position functioning, this referring mainly to the capacity to experience interpersonal guilt, as well as the capacity for some degree of ambivalence. Matt expressed considerable feelings of guilt, self-blame, and even fear of himself in reference to the bully (tiger) aspect of his split self.

Because both sides of the split are quite familiar with and influence each other, and because they oscillate frequently with each other, it may be easiest to heal the split with this type of Asperger's child. The therapist must still act as a container for long periods of time, of both hostile and especially of needy/dependent affects.

The predominant internal object relations structure with the inhibited/object-seeking type seems to involve an oscillation between the bully and victim sides of the split self, the former connected within the internal object experienced as persecutory in a hostile and rejecting manner, and the latter connected with the internal object having the quality of possessing a teasing potential availability but then being abandoning. There is an accompanying oscillation in the feeling states which tend to be predominant and which involve, using Matt as our guide, desperation for relatedness, feelings of hostility and hurtfully being spurned, and also feeling states involving self-blaming guiltiness and culpability.

There is projective identification into remote objects, but these targets of projective identifications, though remote, seem to be less extreme and more realistic than for inhibited/avoidant children. Dan projects into King Kong and aliens, whereas Matt uses cartoon figures.

Another aspect should be highlighted with the inhibited/object-seeking and needy type (again, if my experiences with Matt can be used as a guideline). My treatment with him terminated earlier than I hoped for because of his experience that I couldn't *do* anything for him in order to help him make the friends he desperately wished for (a situation similar to that I reported on with the high-functioning autistic adolescent Josh in Holloway, 2013). I think that Matt and Josh have a point to make. When Asperger's children become desperate, about being able to make friends or about feeling unjustly treated by the school, then perhaps the therapist needs to adopt a more supportive role with the child and engage in "reclamation" or else refer to someone who does such work. This supportive aspect of psychotherapy might involve observation and supportive intervention with staff in the school setting, the teaching of social skills, and similar interventions. Without these didactic/supportive interventions, the Asperger's child can all too easily experience the therapist as unhelpful, uncaring, and as unwilling to be directly involved with the child.

Treating the uninhibited/aggressive type— Thomas and Anthony

Finally, we turn to the uninhibited/aggressive type of Asperger's child, using Thomas and Anthony as our examples of this type of child. With this type, external object relations tend to be confrontational, blaming, hostile, angry, and often aggressive. Open aggressiveness toward others, not excluding his mother, was characteristic of Thomas. Anthony had been physically aggressive with his younger sister, and seemed always on the verge of physical confrontations with others he felt had demeaned him. These children are usually object-rejecting in their external object relations.

With this type, it is the bully aspect of the split that is clearly predominant. The needy/dependent aspect as manifest in the victim part of the split is seen on occasion, but seldom. In Thomas, it was seen in his need to be caressed by his mother. In Anthony, it was seen mostly in his sexual activity as a "sub" in search of a woman who could be a long-term partner as his "dom".

With the uninhibited/aggressive type, the bully side of the split is certainly predominant. This is likely to be related to an internal object having hurtful, hostilely rejecting qualities. The predominating affects seem to be self-righteous anger coupled with persecutory anxieties. With this type, the therapist is also more likely to experience denigration rather than the "distancing idealisation" more characteristic of the inhibited/avoidant type. There is projective identification into remote objects (for example politicians and political entities for Anthony), but with this type projective identification into the therapist may be more likely. With Thomas, for example, I could not avoid feeling powerless, stupid, worthless, incompetent, and helpless, and could not find any way out of being trapped within this role.

The therapist dealing with uninhibited/aggressive Asperger's children may need to contain these types of feelings states for them, that is, feelings of being powerless, helpless, and worthless. The therapist may also need to hold onto and contain feelings involving neediness for relationships with others. These feelings will eventually be returned to the patient, but in carefully timed and titrated doses that the patient is able to tolerate.

With children such as Thomas, other supportive measures may also be needed. Such interventions might include sensitive and appropriately geared behavioural management within the school setting, to prevent the child from hurting other students, angering and alienating teaching staff, and digging himself into a self-destructive role.

The next chapter builds on this one and provides some more extended suggestions about treatment approaches to Asperger's children.

PART IV

TREATMENT APPROACHES TO ASPERGER'S CHILDREN

CHAPTER FIFTEEN

Thoughts about the treatment of Asperger's children

Forming the background to these comments on the treatment of Asperger's children is the conception of different types of therapeutic intervention developed by Paulina Kernberg and her colleagues (Kernberg, Frankel, Heller, Scholl & Kruger, 1988) in concert with the ideas outlined by Anne Alvarez (2012) on different levels of therapeutic approach to children. In her magnificent book, Alvarez (2012) outlines the three levels of psychoanalytic therapy that are differentially useful in the treatment of disturbed children (and adults). Her broadly based levels of therapy are derived from evaluating the status of the child's ego capacities and the child's internal object relationships. These levels overlap to a considerable degree with the types of psychotherapy outlined by Kernberg and her colleagues. Alvarez establishes her foundation on British object relations theories, Kernberg on American object relations and ego psychology. Alvarez describes a whole range of therapeutic interventions, whereas Kernberg and her colleagues focus exclusively on the types of *verbal* interventions therapists use within each of their four types of psychotherapy. What follows now is a truncated summary of the four types of psychotherapy outlined by Kernberg and her colleagues followed by a similar summary of the three levels of psychoanalytic therapy described by Alvarez.

Before beginning this psychoanalytic outline of types and levels of treatment, however, I provide a brief survey of some of the typical suggestions for treatment of Asperger's children in the non-psychoanalytic literature. This provides a context for considering the suggestions based on psychoanalytic understanding which I then make.

Treatment suggestions from the non-psychoanalytic literature

In the non-analytic literature, structured social skills groups are frequently recommended for Asperger's children. One psychologist suggests that a preferred format includes both "structured skill lessons" as well as time for more natural interactions among members. (*NJ Psychologist Magazine*, 2000, p. 11).

Asperger's children in an educational setting do better in structured situations and worse in unstructured social situations (such as recess) or in novel situations. They perform best in "highly structured and routinized or otherwise academically driven situations" (Klin & Volkmar, 2000, p. 343). The moral of this is that Asperger's children require highly structured school programmes, and support in dealing with unstructured situations, especially social ones. Klin and Volkmar (2000, p. 345) suggest that "a relatively small setting is usually preferable" with "ample opportunity for individual attention, individualized approach, and small work groups." They recommend "opportunities for social interaction and promotion of social relationships" within a structured and supervised context (ibid, p. 346). In fact, "the most important component of the intervention program for individuals with [Asperger's] involves the need to enhance communication and social competence" (ibid, p. 350). Social and communication skills, they say, should be taught explicitly. This would include the use of "social stories", and teaching theory of mind concepts. Social stories are stories written in the first person about a social situation. These stories contain descriptions about what is happening in the situation, why and how people think and feel as they do in the situation, and they contain directive statements about what to do in the situation. These social stories "are read repeatedly to children until they have over-learned them" (*NJ Psychologist Magazine*, 2000, p. 14).

Asperger's children, say Klin and Volkmar, need to develop "awareness of conventional pragmatic or conversational rules" (Klin & Volkmar, 2000, p. 353) and the ability to read social cues, these cues including "the meaning of eye contact, gaze, and various inflections, as well as tone of voice and facial and hand gestures" all of which may require teaching "in a fashion not unlike the teaching of a foreign language" (ibid, p. 354). In addition, making new acquaintances is to be "rehearsed until the individual is made aware of the impact of his or her behaviour on other people's reactions to him or her" (ibid, p. 354). "Self-monitoring in conversation" (ibid, p. 355) also often needs to be taught.

Because Asperger's children have cognitive deficits in the area of "executive functions" (higher level planning and organisational skills and the ability to inhibit irrelevant responses), it is suggested they receive help in organising their activities, completing tasks in an efficient manner, and in avoiding getting stuck in counterproductive routines (ibid, p. 356). At times, anxiety management may be important.

One psychologist uses Stanley Greenspan's "floortime" model of child psychotherapy in which the parents are supported in getting down on the floor, playing with their child, and then supported in understanding what occurred during the play. Her goal is to improve the play and social skills of her Asperger's patient. Communication, she states, best develops "in the context of pleasurable interactions within relationships" (*NJ Psychologist Magazine*, 2000, p. 9).

Klin and Volkmar (2000, p. 361) make a statement which is, because of their authority, often parroted in the literature. They state that: "Although insight-oriented psychotherapy is not usually helpful, it does appear that fairly focused and structured counselling can be useful for individuals with [Asperger's], particularly in the context of alleviating overwhelming experiences of sadness, negativism, or anxiety …". They give no evidence in support of this statement. Their statement unfortunately betrays a lack of familiarity with psychotherapy. Not all psychotherapy is "insight-oriented psychotherapy". Psychoanalytic psychotherapy is conceived as falling along a continuum. "Pure" insight-oriented psychotherapy is at one end of the continuum. At the other end is supportive psychotherapy. In between are mixtures of supportive with insight-oriented psychotherapy. Paulina Kernberg and her colleagues have operationalised these distinctions in terms of exactly what kinds of verbal interventions a therapist makes, and does not make, within each level of psychotherapy.

With an Asperger's patient, the therapist would seldom begin at the "pure" insight-oriented end of the psychotherapy continuum. Instead, one would begin with supportive psychotherapy, perhaps not greatly different from the "focused and structured counselling" suggested by Klin and Volkmar. However, the aim over time is to move away from the supportive mode and more towards the insight-oriented mode, to the extent and at a pace that is useful to and tolerated by the patient. Most importantly, however, instead of prodding the patient to improve social and other skills in a didactic relationship and a rote manner, psychoanalytic psychotherapy would begin with an attempt to *listen empathically* to what the patient had to say, and to respond supportively and empathically to the patient's communications.

On the website of the American Academy of Child and Adolescent Psychiatry, under the heading "Asperger's Disorder" and dated 1999, there is the comment that: "Currently, the most effective treatment [i.e., for Asperger's] involves a combination of psychotherapy, special education, behaviour modification, and support for families". With *this* statement it is possible to agree.

For Asperger's children, there is an ongoing problem in decoding the implicit meanings of other people, their nonverbal and nonliteral forms of communication. The Asperger's child may have the experience that "people say what they do not mean while meaning things they do not say". They lack an "insider's view" into the surrounding social world, which for Asperger's children "makes that world quite inaccessible and sometimes hostile" (Klin, Volkmar & Sparrow, 2000, p. 10). In my experience, the social world *frequently* seems hostile and rejecting to the Asperger's child. It is these difficulties in understanding others and the social world, and in being understood by others, that psychotherapy primarily seek to address.

Let's consider the question of what Asperger's children most need. I suggest that initially at least, what they most need is to be listened to in an empathic and understanding way. They need to first have a sense of *being understood*, and then to build on this in order to themselves understand their social world and other people in it. One of my little Asperger's patients, nine-year-old Peter, has said it best. During one session, he described, in an anguished and agitated manner, being forcibly confined by his teacher in the "quiet room" at school after he'd had some behavioural problems. This was his comment on his experience: "I wish that they would listen to me. They think they're helping me, but they're not. This does not feel like it's helping. They treat me like

I'm just a noise or a nuisance. They don't seem to want to listen to me". I suggest that the first step with an Asperger's child is receptive and empathic listening. This is where psychotherapy comes in.

In psychoanalytic psychotherapy, the main vehicle of treatment is *the transference*. By this is meant the spontaneous relationship that the patient sets up with the therapist. Understanding the kind of relationship the patient sets up is a major goal. Psychotherapy with an Asperger's patient would first try to create an environment in which the Asperger's child would feel *secure* enough to begin to spontaneously relate to the therapist. Once this had happened, one could begin to try, along with the patient, to understand the kind of relationship that was set up, and the unstated expectations, hopes, fears, and wishes embedded in this relationship. Then, or so the theory goes, this would generalise to an understanding of other relationships in the child's life. Along the way, with an Asperger's child, the therapist would also be helping him to understand others in his world, and the reasons for their reactions to the child. Use of the transference in an expressive form of psychotherapy would not be enough, however. I outline below the need to move across different types of psychotherapy, and to use the supportive modality with some frequency.

One example would help. A very bright and verbal Asperger's child began the first few sessions of his therapy with me by playing wordlessly with his back to me for most of the session. Then at the end of the session he would wordlessly take a large ball of wool, make a huge spider web from this wool all over my office, tie my chair and sometimes myself up with the wool, put a toy spider on the web he'd made, and silently leave my office. This was repeated a number of times. I came to understand this behaviour as having two main meanings. First was a fear that I might be nasty to him, just as he had experienced peers and teachers being. The spider web symbolically entrapped and immobilised me, making me his victim, with him in the role of spider/bully/predator. But more importantly, there was also a fear that when he was away from the therapy, there might be changes which he could not tolerate, including the possibility of my leaving him and abandoning him. The spider web symbolically held me safely immobilised until his next session, and, in fantasy, prevented any change from occurring from session to session. We slowly began to be able to talk about how nice it might feel if everything could remain exactly the same between his sessions.

Psychoanalytic views #1: Paulina Kernberg's approach to types of psychotherapy

Kernberg and her colleagues describe their four kinds of psychotherapy based solely on the kinds of verbal interventions the therapist makes (and limits herself to) when dealing with her child patients. This limitation of focus which concentrates solely on the kinds of verbal interventions used by the therapist in order to judge the kind of psychotherapy she is employing is both the main strength and the main weakness of their approach. It is the main strength of their approach because it allows one to clearly and consensually "operationalise" the four different kinds of psychotherapy and to validate which level is being used through inter-rater agreement. In my opinion, it is the main weakness of this approach because it completely glosses over other crucial activities of the therapist—use of the countertransference in order to understand the patient and the patient's transference, and exercising a containing function for the patient—to mention only two crucial *nonverbal* activities of the therapist.

The "Global Verbal Interventions for Children Scale" (GVI-C) is an addendum to their "Therapist Verbal Interventions with Children" (TVI-C) (both Kernberg, Frankel, Heller, Scholl & Kruger, 1988). In the former document, Kernberg and her colleagues outline their conception of psychotherapy as occurring along a spectrum of treatment interventions, beginning with supportive psychotherapy, then supportive-expressive, expressive-supportive and finally expressive psychotherapy which is equivalent to "pure psychoanalysis". Each of these four modalities of psychotherapy is systematically connected to types of statements the therapist will (and will *not*) make. For example, interpretations of unconscious material are mostly confined to the expressive modality of psychotherapy.

In the TVI-C, they outline eight possible kinds of statements a therapist can make to a child patient. These possible kinds of therapeutic statements include:

1. ordinary social verbal behaviour such as conventional expressions of greeting, leave-taking and politeness;
2. statements or questions relating to the treatment which set out the structure of therapy sessions and the boundaries and rules involved;

3. requests for factual information in which the therapist asks the child to provide objective information so as to fill in informational gaps the therapist encounters;
4. supportive statements in which the therapist attempts to allay the child's anxiety and increase his sense of competency, mastery and self-esteem through the use of education, suggestion, encouragement and empathy;
5. facilitative statements in which the therapist enhances the dialogue with the child through invitations to continue ("Can you tell me more?") or which review parts of the therapy;
6. directing the child's attention, including by the use of "see the pattern" statements (usually called clarifications), as well as other "see the pattern" statements such as "Have you noticed that every time we start to talk about me, you change the subject?" (usually called confrontations);
7. interpretations—about defences, about motives, and about past experiences (the latter referred to as genetic interpretations);
8. the final category, which includes other verbal interventions such as when the therapist asks for repetition because the patient could not be understood.

Which of the four *modalities* of psychotherapy is being used is brought into alignment with the *types* of statements the therapist uses. In *supportive* psychotherapy, "the therapist makes educational comments, suggestions, offers encouragement, reassurance and empathy" (Kernberg, Frankel, Heller, Scholl & Kruger, 1988, p. 1). She also facilitates the interaction between child and therapist by conveying ongoing interest in the child elaborating and continuing. The therapist may also have restated and summarised the child's material.

At the second slightly more elaborate and sophisticated level of psychotherapy, called *supportive-expressive* psychotherapy, the therapist engages in all the types of verbal behaviour used in the supportive level, so that she may make educational comments, suggestions, offer encouragement, reassurance and empathy, and invite the child to continue. In addition to these verbal interventions, however, the therapist may *add* comments which direct the child's attention to his own behaviours, affects, and experiences. In the traditional psychoanalytic terminology, the "holy trinity" consists of *clarification, confrontation,* and *interpretation.* Directing the child's attention in this way is equivalent to *clarification.* The therapist may also make interventions which imply the *possibility* of new meanings and connections.

The third and again more sophisticated level of psychotherapy is called *expressive-supportive* psychotherapy. At this level, the therapist does *not* use educational comments or make suggestions, but may as in the previous two levels offer encouragement, reassurance, and empathy. Also, as in the previous level, the therapist may direct the child's attention to his own behaviours, affects, and experiences. The therapist may also propose meanings and make the child aware of patterns of behaviour. This kind of "see the pattern" statements represents the beginning of unconscious territory, and in the traditional terminology would be labelled as *confrontations.* At this level of psychotherapeutic sophistication, the therapist might also propose meanings or links in the child's interaction experiences of which the child is unaware. In other words, some initial interpretations start to be given at this level.

Finally, at the highest level of sophistication, there is *expressive* psychotherapy, which is different minimally if at all from psychoanalysis proper. At this level, the full array of clarification, confrontation, and interpretation is used. At this level, suggestions, educational comments, and reassurance are used hardly at all. Expressions of encouragement, reassurance, and empathy are used only as a background. The therapist points out the child's repetitive behaviour patterns (confrontations) and interprets the child's experience and behaviour by proposing on an ongoing basis meanings and links between the child's behaviours, feelings, and ideas of which the child is aware (which includes clarifications) as well as attitudes, assumptions, and beliefs of which the child is unaware (interpretations). At this level, interpretive links made by the therapist may refer to current defences (defence interpretations) or experiences (interpretations about motives) but also to the child's past wishes and his early experiences of which he is unaware (genetic interpretations).

Psychoanalytic views #2: Alvarez's levels of psychotherapeutic intervention

Alvarez (2012) outlines three levels of psychotherapeutic intervention, at the highest end this being the *explanatory* level, involving the offering of alternative meanings to the patient. I would also call this the *hermeneutical* level, that of interpretive understanding. The next lower level (this hierarchical ordering reflecting the developmental level on which the patient is currently operating), is called the *descriptive* level. It involves ascribing or amplifying meaning. Note that there may be frequents shifts in the level at which the therapist is operating in terms of her interventions. The lowest level, perhaps better called the most basic level, is the *intensified and vitalising* level. It involves the therapist insisting that meaning can be found, and drawing the patient's attention to this possibility, frequently by the therapist using the technique of "reclamation".

The explanatory level is the Freudian level and it involves the patient having the capacity for linking two aspects of the self while holding both in mind at the same time. This demands that the patient be able to grasp a two-part explanatory interpretation and have the ability to think two thoughts or hold two feelings (as well as the link between them) at the same time. The therapist may offer an interpretation which is a hermeneutical intervention (involving interpretive understanding) such as: "You felt sad about missing me last week during my vacation, so today you have to show in how you play how hurt and angry you felt at my leaving". If such an intervention is to be effective, the patient must be able to hold in mind two parts (last week sad and today angry) as well as the sense that these two parts are causally linked and interact in a meaningful way.

The descriptive level is confined to only one track rather than demanding that the patient be able to coordinate two tracks at once, as is the case with the explanatory level. The descriptive level is concerned with naming and describing exactly what the child feels, and the simple lending of meaning to experience, or the amplification of meaning with patients who have ego deficits. Asperger's children certainly have ego deficits. The main one is their lack of capacity for appropriate social interactions as it is anchored in deficits in their internal objects. This is frequently accompanied by a deficit in the capacity to acknowledge, name, and to regulate their emotions. The use of splitting of the self as a central way of experiencing may create a deficit in the capacity to hold onto two different self-states at the same time. Asperger's children, because of the developmentally based split in their self, may require the recognition and identification "of unconscious affects that were never developmentally interactively regulated" (Alvarez, 2012, p. 17). The descriptive level may also involve projective identifications, these being into remote objects for Asperger's children, and may require the therapist to contain these over time and to process and detoxify them before eventually returning them to the patient in a digested and detoxified manner. What is often projected is the bully aspect of the split self, and sometimes the victim aspect, depending on which is more problematic for the child.

The third and most basic level of work is one which is intensified and vitalising. The therapist insists that meaning is there and can be found. This way of working is applicable to children "with defects both in self and internal object" (Alvarez, 2012, p. 21) and thus seems to be applicable to Asperger's children who have both a defect in the self (which is powerfully split) and in the internal object related to each aspect of the split self. What Alvarez has come to call "reclamation" is a common approach at this level. The therapist works by "calling the child into contact with the therapist" and by attempting to spark the child's interest and help the creation of meaning (Alvarez, 2012, p. 13). Alvarez also approvingly quotes a therapist who "has suggested that work with Asperger's patients involves a process of constant mini-reclamations" (Alvarez, 2012, p. 13). Tremelloni (2005, p. 227) describes reclamation as based on a vital countertransference response to a patient's withdrawnness, in which vitality and activity by the therapist are employed in response to the patient's inability to make contact.

My experience suggests that the use of reclamation at this level of work is often needed with Asperger's children, especially with the inhibited/avoidant type, but also with the inhibited/object-seeking type. It becomes necessary when the deficits in the child's self and his internal objects and his resulting painful experiences with external objects have mobilised a state of mind involving a sense of empty isolation, futility, abandonment, rejection, cynicism, and despair (often a despairing cynicism). Such states of mind seem most frequent with "burnt-out Asperger's" children of the inhibited/avoidant type who have already or are on the verge of giving up all hope for gratifying relationships with others, and who are on the verge of withdrawing into a shell of detachment. Their shell is sometimes coloured by feelings of arrogant superiority, and sometimes by resentful, revengeful, aggressive, and self-righteous counter-rejection of others.

My experience with Asperger's children also suggests that the work of reclamation is most often needed in two areas—in the difficulties they encounter in functioning in a school setting and in the difficulties they have with social skills and in making friends. Dan and Matt are cases in point. Dan remained in treatment right up to the time of his tragic and untimely death. Matt, after two years of therapy, decided I couldn't help him anymore and convinced his parents to allow him to terminate. In retrospect, Matt may well have been missing something I should have provided in his treatment. My effort to maintain "therapeutic purity" blinded me to the practical, supportive interventions he so much needed, especially in the school setting.

A constant theme with Dan was whether in the future he would always live completely alone or would instead have some kind of relationships with others. He despaired of having friendships with peers or even understanding what he felt to be their self-indulgent and even sociopathic activities. With a veneer of arrogant superiority, he felt himself to be far ahead of his peers both morally and in his behaviour. However, there were hopeful aspects. When he entered university in the last year of his life, he opted to live in residence, where he was able to form friendships with a number of other students. Previous to this, he took a summer job (based on his deep interest in history) as a tourist guide in a historical "pioneer village". This job required ongoing interactions with strangers. My "reclamation" with Dan took the form of expressing strong interest in these activities, enthusiasm for them on my part, and underlining the benefits he seemed to be getting from them. At the time of his death, we were both feeling optimistic about his future.

In the dialogue Matt and I had which was reported previously, he described a "hissy fit" he had at school, and the difficulties he experienced there. He also described his strong and tearful wish to be able to establish friendships with peers. These difficulties called out for supportive work, for reclamation, which I did not quickly enough realise I needed to provide for him. The reclamation would have taken the form of supportive interventions at his school, and providing social skills training for him. I might have done this myself, or if I preferred to be psychotherapeutically "pure", I could have asked a colleague to do this work. Matt, I believe, was correct in wanting me to "do something" to help him. Most, if not all Asperger's children require "hands-on" supportive work and the activity of reclamation by the therapist, especially in the areas of school functioning and social functioning.

The theories of Kernberg and her colleagues and of Alvarez represent two different but useful lenses through which treatment may be viewed. There is value in attempting to map Alvarez's more inclusive theory onto Kernberg's more restricted theory (confined to only the verbal interpretations of the therapist). Alvarez's intensified and vitalising level including therapeutic reclamation as she describes it would map onto the supportive level of psychotherapy as Paulina Kernberg describes it. Anne's intermediate level, the descriptive level, involving naming and describing what the child feels, amplifying the meaning of experiences, and naming, understanding and contextualising feeling states, would map onto Paulina's supportive-expressive and expressive-supportive types of psychotherapy. Anne's most sophisticated level, the explanatory or hermeneutical level, maps very well onto Paulina's expressive level of psychotherapy. If this way of mapping Anne's levels onto Paulina's types is accurate, then both ways of understanding therapeutic interventions are mutually complimentary and mutually enhancing. Using both lenses to view therapy may help us to view it in a "binocular" way.

The essential point for the treatment of Asperger's children seems clear—the therapist will be required to shift levels of treatment intervention quite frequently and sometimes quite suddenly, likely much more frequently and suddenly than is the case with most children. Using Alvarez's model, the therapist will need to make frequent shifts among the explanatory, descriptive, and intensified, and vitalising levels. Or on the basis of Kernberg's model, there will be frequent shifts along the whole spectrum of types of psychotherapy from supportive to expressive.

Implications for the treatment of Asperger's children, adolescents and adults emerge from the clinical data and the two theoretical outlines of treatment interventions we have just considered. One experience proved very helpful to me in both my cognitive and emotional understanding of autism spectrum disorders. Until his recent and distressingly early death at twenty years of age, I had been privileged to meet with Dan, the Asperger's patient reported on previously, every Thursday for six years. Overlapping this period of time, I met every Wednesday with Sam who was six years younger than Dan. (For a full description of Sam, see Holloway, 2013.) Sam's treatment still continues. Sam had come to me with a psychiatric diagnosis of HFA (high-functioning autism). My experience with Sam along with an accumulating collection of evidence from various psychiatric, psychological, and speech evaluations Sam had undergone strongly supported the correctness of this diagnosis. I was therefore in the privileged position of being able to compare the experience of what it was like to interact therapeutically with an HFA patient "back-to-back" with the experience of interacting with an Asperger's patient. This overlap extended for a period of more than four years. The experiences of being with Sam and being with Dan were very different experiences.

With Dan, as with many child psychotherapy patients, my experience was one of a gradual unfolding and deepening of a number of important themes. In the countertransference, there was also an experience of a slowly deepening relationship with and understanding of Dan, though with my feeling "stuck" in an idealising transference that was not always comfortable for me. This was accompanied by a gradual shift in some of Dan's capacities, especially those relating to forming and maintaining interpersonal relationships. I never felt completely disconnected from Dan, and never partly disconnected for more than very brief periods of time. To be sure, Dan's treatment involved silences, him feeling uncertain how to begin, and sometimes Dan verbally stumbling around in attempting to express himself. His stumbling was especially noticeable when he was attempting to describe his affective responses to other people. These kinds of difficulties could eventually be handled in "standard" analytic fashion, though sometimes needing preliminary supportive interventions. In spite of these impediments, there was no sense of being cut off or disconnected from Dan or from his lively inner life.

Until more recently, when he has begun to emerge from his chronic autistic state, the experience of being with Sam has seemed to me to be qualitatively different. With Sam, my experience has been one of progressing in fits and starts, with frequent regressive backsliding. With Sam, I have frequent experiences of being disconnected from him so that my thoughts start to wander away. I "lose my place" with him, and I have to regroup and push myself to reconnect with him. There follows two brief examples of this kind of experience with Sam—Sam's cartoon booklets and his use of my window as a mirror.

Sam was able to draw excellent (though stereotyped) cartoon characters to which he then added the comments he wanted his cartoon characters to make in speech bubbles. He drew a cartoon booklet on the occasion of "black history month" in which he portrayed every imaginable ethnic group experiencing rejection, refusal, and discrimination. I felt his therapy made a bit of headway when I referred to some of the hurtful rejections and discrimination Sam has experienced because of his autism. But over time, Sam has repeatedly returned to his "Black History" cartoon booklet and in an addictive and perversely sadomasochistic way, he has rehashed the scenes of discrimination he previously drew. This rehashing is mostly left untouched by any attempts on my part to interpret the content. I feel shut out from contact with Sam and his apparently addictive, perverse, and excited pleasure in rehashing the scenes of rejection, humiliation, and discrimination (sadomasochistic scenes) that he had drawn months or even years ago.

Anne Alvarez (1997) has referred to her patient engaging in repeated actions "with a masturbatory and highly sensual pleasure" and to "perverse excitements, the bathing in thrills and frenzies" (Alvarez, 1997, p. 234). Betty Joseph (1989, p. 131) refers to a form of speech she calls "chuntering" which is actually "the complete antithesis of thought" and is instead an enactment of sadomasochistic fantasy. Sam's rehashing of his booklet full of detailed pictures of discrimination falls in the area suggested by Alvarez and Joseph—that of masturbatory and sadomasochistic excitement.

The dynamics of Asperger's children also involve strong sadomasochistic elements. But these very seldom take the form of dead, ritualised sadomasochistic excitements. Instead, they take the form of a split in the self between the sadistic/bullying aspect and the masochistic/victim aspect, a split which seems to cover over and defuse a considerable amount of underlying conflict. Even Anthony, who at age thirty-one participated in openly sadomasochistic sexual activities, taking the role of a "sub" (subordinate) in relation to female "doms" (dominants), found these activities conflictual and disturbing. He also described a clear split between his bully aspect and his victim aspect. The first implication for treatment is that this kind of split in the self needs to be confronted. In particular, the sadistic and bullying aspects (which usually but not always tend to appear later in treatment than the victim aspect) need careful but detailed exploration.

Return to a consideration of another difference between Sam and Dan, the difference in what it felt like to be with them. I would see Sam in the late afternoon. Often during winter afternoons it was dark outside so that my office window functioned as a mirror. I would often catch Sam gazing off at the two of us reflected in my darkened window. It felt to me as if he were immersed in his own private alternative world, represented in the reflected scene, so that for me he was out of contact, unavailable, and disconnected. I would start to feel weary and my thoughts would wander off.

Almost never did this kind of experience of disconnection happen in the treatment with Dan. At times, the experience would be one of both of us working very hard to get on the same track with one another. At other times, there would be a strong connection on a cognitive and intellectualised level, so that I found myself wondering about his affect and how we could connect emotionally. If anything, the experience with Dan was of a mutual connection that he desired and sought after. Sometimes this relational connection required sustained work in order to make it feel solid, stable, and mutually generative. There were no experiences of "disconnect" as there were with Sam.

The implication for treatment is that for some of the time, a more or less "standard" analytic approach is likely to be useful for Asperger's children and adolescents. The beautiful work of Anne Alvarez on the "reclamation" of autistic children makes it clear that this is not the case with autistic children—nor was it the case in my experience with Sam. Autistic children are said to require "more active measures" (Grotstein, 1997, p. 267) including "an active form" of holding environment along with "firm encouragement of the child to play and to cooperate". However, there are also times when a form of reclamation is needed with Asperger's children.

Consider an example from the work with my high-functioning autistic patient, Sam. Several years ago, my work with him was briefly interrupted when I attended a conference. Sam asked that I keep the boarding passes I was given in my airplane flights to the conference and back. I complied with his request. Sam's focal interest was in my seat numbers on the various flights. Sam would latch onto factual and numerical aspects of other people (birth dates, ages, seat numbers) both as a way of maintaining some kind of firm and factual contact with his external objects, and also as a way of creating a barrier between him and his objects by relating only to one dimension of others— their "factual-numerical" aspects—and not to the whole person or the emotional experience of that person. Alvarez (1997, p. 249) refers to a stereotypy in which "an apparently meaningless opposite of an object-related contact" is nevertheless used in "an object-related way". In his use of "factual-numerical" aspects, Sam flipped back and forth between a primitive object-relatedness and a walling off of object-relatedness. When Sam dug out from his box these airplane boarding passes for about the tenth time, when it was over two years after my brief absence to attend the conference, my countertransference took the form that

Alvarez so clearly describes—profound and tormenting boredom, "terrible weariness", and despair. In my despair, I told Sam that instead of airplanes and airplane boarding passes, we needed to also talk about trains. Trains always had to go back and forth along the same track and could never leave their track to go anywhere new. Planes, however, could turn in the air to go around storms and could fly to new places. I said that his interest in boarding passes was like being on a train that always travelled along the same old track. I said that instead of being like a train on the same old track, I hoped that something new could happen between us, like a plane flying to a new place. Maybe instead of just talking about my seat number and how I got to my seat (Sam's habitual concerns), we might talk about something different. We might be able to talk about what it felt like for one person to be on a plane going away from another person. My experience is that this type of more active and confrontational intervention is sometimes needed in response to the masturbatory rituals of high-functioning autistic children. At first, Sam did not make any obvious overt response to my attempt to get him away from his repetitive track. Over time, however, this and similar repetitive activities have faded away, with occasional outbreaks when Sam has been under stress.

Are more active measures also sometimes needed with Asperger's children? Some writers suggest that this is the case. For example, Alvarez (1997, p. 245) quotes Barrows as stating that "the perseveration and non-relational aspects of the play of an Asperger's child demand the therapist actively intervene to draw the child out," and that she structures the play of the child "so as to introduce symbolic or reciprocal content where [the child] would have persisted in ritualistic behaviour". It seems likely that if and when the Asperger's child engages in masturbatory rituals, then more active interventions are likely needed. In many other situations, a standard analytic approach is often likely to be most helpful.

Dan in treatment

Three examples from the treatment of Asperger's children may be illuminating. They are a physical ritual used by Dan and preoccupations displayed by Arturo and by Matt. First consider Dan's ritual. From time to time, Dan would for a sustained period of time twist the fingers of both his hands around each other, weaving his fingers around each other in what seemed to be highly complex and repetitive patterns. I would gently confront him about engaging in this activity, of which he seemed completely unaware. I initially reacted to this physical ritual as a kind of hand-wringing and attempted to relate these episodes to states of anxiety. This was only partly successful. I later understood that I had missed the autosensual and masturbatory nature of these "finger weaving" rituals, what Tustin might refer to as an "autistic shape". This understanding occurred only when I was able in the countertransference to acknowledge to myself a degree of irritation and annoyance in response to the rituals, feeling at one point that I might like to tell him (though I didn't actually do so): "Stop fidgeting, Dan! Don't you know that can be off-putting to others?" A more active and containing response to these rituals was needed.

Arturo in assessment

Like high-functioning autistic children, Asperger's children also have their overwhelming preoccupations and masturbatory-like intellectual rituals and interests. These consuming interests represent the "encompassing preoccupations with one or more stereotyped and restricted patterns of interest", which is one of the DSM-IV diagnostic criteria for Asperger's. As a second example in addition to Sam, I think of twelve-year-old Arturo, whom you did not hear in dialogue with me previously. I was able to undertake a full assessment of Arturo twice, once when he was twelve years old, and once again at age eighteen before he entered university. He vigorously declined my offer of treatment (an offer which was strongly supported by his parents) because of his terror of engaging in any relationships at all outside of his family. Arturo had one and only one interest in his life—armadillos. Incredibly but actually, Arturo at age twelve years was literally a world expert on armadillos. He had managed to acquire stud books for armadillo matings from zoos all over the world. He was consulted by zoos as to which armadillos should or should not be mated with others in order to avoid incestuous couplings. His knowledge of armadillos was amazing. So the question arises: how would a therapist deal with this kind of preoccupation if Arturo had entered treatment? Arturo's preoccupation with armadillos certainly had extremely positive and ego-syntonic features for him. It provided him with well-deserved and narcissistically gratifying attention from adults he felt were important to him, and earned him their genuine and appropriate respect. On the other hand, his all-encompassing preoccupation with armadillos drowned out any other interests he might have shared with his peers, and served in the social area only to isolate him and insulate him from interactions with others, especially his peers. His overwhelming interest was experienced by Arturo (and *their* preoccupying interests are also experienced by other Asperger's children) as enlivening, vitalising, and intensely interesting and appealing, seeming to be in line with Alvarez's intensified and vitalising level of treatment intervention. Any challenge to his interests (or their overwhelming nature) or any questioning of them would have been experienced by Arturo as an assault on a core aspect of his self. So what is to be our therapeutic approach in such cases? Do we support their preoccupying interests, try to analyse them away, alternate between both attitudes, or what?

Matt in treatment

I turn to a third example from my patient Matt (whom you heard in dialogue with me) for help in thinking about this question. The encompassing and overwhelming preoccupation with a stereotyped and restricted pattern of interest was, for Matt, his preoccupation with "transportation" (his word). He had a consuming interest in planes, trucks, boats, cars, and especially trains. He would speak to me at length about his experiences of travelling by train in Europe, including the European train stations he'd visited, how these stations were constructed, the systems of signalling that are used, the different gauges of the track that are used, and how some trains could not run on the same track because they were adapted to different gauges of track. In how our interactions developed, there was a typical progression in how I responded to what Matt told me. This progression was usually from the most basic of Alvarez's three treatment modalities to the most sophisticated. (My treatment of Matt took place before Alvarez's 2012 book, and derived from my own fumbling interactions with him). This could also be seen as a progression through Kernberg and her colleagues' four levels of psychotherapy, from a supportive to an expressive stance. Using Alvarez's (2012) model to describe my interaction with Matt, I would typically begin my response to his preoccupations at the intensified and vitalising level. I would make supportive comments to Matt involving approval and admiration, such as: "Matt, you have so much wonderful knowledge about trains". This would be Kernberg and colleagues' supportive modality. It would usually soon be possible to move to Alvarez's descriptive level (and Kernberg's supportive-expressive mode) with comments such as: "How frustrating if your train couldn't go to where you wanted because it was the wrong gauge of track for it" and "It sounds like sometimes *you* find it hard to be 'on track' with the other kids". I then tried to use and exploit Matt's preoccupations in order to talk about "making connections" with other people, how people "send social signals" to each other, and how people get and stay "on the same track" with each other. Finally, after some time working at the descriptive level, a move to Alvarez's explanatory level would become possible. I might make a more complicated two-part comment, an interpretation such as: "Matt, it sounds like one part of you wants to be 'on track' with the other kids and share in their interests, but another part of you feels like that would be 'off track' for you and not part of your own interests". I think that this sort of experience for the therapist of moving "up the levels" as I did with Matt (whether these are Alvarez's or Kernberg's levels) may not be an unusual progression with many Asperger's children. I offer this experience as a preliminary suggestion in answer to the question of how to deal with their preoccupations.

To take up another theme that arose in my work with Matt—Matt also brought with him to most sessions a small toy clenched in his palm, usually a small toy train, boat, car or other vehicle in line with his preoccupation around transportation. These objects seemed to be "hybrid objects" located on the continuum between a transitional object and Tustin's "autistic object". These objects, as Alvarez (1980, p. 71) has commented, are sometimes "used less as a transitional object in Winnicott's sense and more as an autistic object in Tustin's sense". These objects as Matt used them seemed to represent both some wish for connectedness (which could be addressed interpretively), but also to be a source of auto-stimulation of a more autistic nature. Interpretive comments did not greatly reduce Matt's tendency to carry these objects around. As a result, I used caution about giving Matt interpretations about the toys he carried, trying to register in my countertransference which kind of use he was making of these objects.

With Asperger's children, a more active and supportive kind of intervention seems likely to be needed, especially in three areas. These three areas include: stereotypical rituals, including the ritualised use of autistic-like objects; the experiencing, expressing, and decoding of the affects of other people and the understanding and expression of their own internal affects; and the appropriate understanding of the behaviours of other people, including the registering and using of social cues (what might be called "interpersonal reality testing").

Asperger's children may need support in naming the affect they or other people are actually experiencing, so that the therapist may need to suggest a specific name for the affect under consideration. Almost invariably, for Asperger's children, adolescents, and adults, the behaviour of other people is also poorly understood. The therapist may need to call to the patient's attention other possible ways of interpreting how others are acting. This may slow down the patient from quickly defaulting to the almost automatic perception of being ridiculed and rejected by others that many Asperger's children and adolescents are predisposed to experience. To give a single example—Michael, age nineteen, described his mother as being always "on my case" and as making demands, criticising him for playing computer games instead of studying, and generally treating him in what he felt to be an angry and denigrating way. I had been able to meet with his mother, and had formed the impression of her that she was competent and caring, though perhaps overprotective of Michael. I explored with Michael how he interacted with his mother and eventually suggested it might be possible that his mother was "on his case" because she was anxious about him, not angry with him. We talked about how she could be anxious that his actions might negatively affect his future. Michael considered this possibility, and after a while agreed that it was likely so.

The supportive and vitalising aspects with Asperger's children

Asperger's children can also complain that they are *talking* with the therapist a lot about peer relationships (especially when these are desperately wanted) but that the therapist is really *doing* nothing to be helpful. There are times when this is an appropriate complaint. It may signal to the therapist the need to move, at least temporarily, into what Kernberg and colleagues (1988) call supportive psychotherapy and what Alvarez (2012) might view as the intensified and vitalising level, perhaps requiring the therapist to engage in "reclamation". This may involve becoming didactic and teaching the child about aspects of social interaction. Several excellent books are now available to help therapists actually teach Asperger's children about social exchanges. For adolescents, a referral for a group experience in social skills training may have value. The aim is to move from the supportive closer to the expressive end of the psychotherapy continuum. It may be that a supportive-expressive or even an expressive-supportive stance might be of value, in which a more expressive exploration of the patient's understanding of others and of the patient's reality testing is combined with a more supportive and didactic training in aspects of social interaction, recognising social cues, and thinking about and appropriately responding to others.

There is one feature of the psychodynamic functioning of the Asperger's child which should be given careful attention. This is the sadomasochistic aspect which seems to be regularly present. As a regular though not invariant feature, the masochistic aspect is likely to appear first. There may be a history of the child being bullied, feeling unfairly treated by the world, and generally being victimised. However, the clinician needs to be alert for the sadistic aspect which is likely to appear later. The clinician also needs to be prepared to deal with the connections between the sadistic and the masochistic aspects, and how these two aspects may serve to evoke each other.

I suggest the possibility of an additional refinement in how Asperger's children might receive treatment. Recall the original work of Hans Asperger. He found that a higher proportion than expected of the children he tried to understand were involved in aggressive interactions with others and a higher than average proportion of these children had had experiences of being imprisoned. I have suggested that the evidence points to there being three types of Asperger's children. The delineation of these three types is linked to the child's typical ways of behaving, but also has strong links to the sadomasochistic psychodynamic aspects. I have called the three types the inhibited/ avoidant type, the inhibited/object-seeking type, and the uninhibited/ aggressive type. Of the children described here, Dan might be the best representative of the inhibited/avoidant type, Thanos or Matt of the inhibited/object-seeking type, and Anthony of the uninhibited/aggressive type. Matt presented as desperately wanting to make friends but as extremely preoccupied with how others might see him, worried about how he would be received by others and generally as feeling reluctantly standoffish and left out. Thanos did not display the level of anxiety that Matt did. He too wanted friends, but phobic avoidance was not at the forefront for him. Instead, he was able to form a few close friendships and hovered on the periphery of the main group while expressing concerns about their aggressive humour, use of drugs and so on.

Anthony could easily have ended up in jail. He told chilling stories of feeling so harassed and rejected at high school that he took a knife to school planning revenge on the first person who put him down. Thankfully, he didn't use his knife. He also spoke of overhearing two peers in the locker room malevolently joking about a geeky kid who reminded Anthony of himself. He became enraged and "accidentally" bumped into one of these two peers, preparing himself for a physical altercation. Again, this thankfully did not occur. Anthony still embroils himself in significant verbal disagreements with others, gets kicked off websites for his provocative opinions, and he is invited to "go outside" by others who feel antagonised by him. Anthony has not yet been arrested, but he is at risk for this.

Treatment approaches to the different types of Asperger's

It is likely the case that if these three types are accurate characterisations, they may benefit from some differences in treatment approach. The inhibited/avoidant type may be the one which would most benefit from a supportive and didactic approach including the teaching of social skills and support in the accurate perception of social cues. The inhibited/object-seeking and needy type may be most amenable to treatment with standard techniques of psychoanalytic psychotherapy. These children may benefit from detailed exploration of how they interact or fail to interact with their peers and with some support in forming judgments about the behaviour of these peers (that is, support in reality testing). The uninhibited/aggressive type may be the most difficult to treat. They may tend to experience their aggressive episodes as at least achieving some positive and ego-syntonic result for them in that these episodes can gain them a degree of "respect" from their peers. When Thomas felt so destructively put down by some of his peers that he lashed out at them and beat them up in the hallway at school, he felt a degree of control over the situation and an increase in his self-respect, along with experiencing more respectful treatment from his peers. This respect from peers had been lacking for him until he displayed his aggressiveness. At least initially, his aggressiveness was highly ego-syntonic. Children exhibiting this type of Asperger's may become more treatable when their aggressive behaviours get them into significant trouble, so that aggressiveness is no longer experienced as ego-syntonic and treatment may offer a better alternative to repeated punishments.

CHAPTER SIXTEEN

Treatment of Asperger's children—the Toronto experiment

Jack, his family, and three therapists cooperating

"Put your money where your mouth is!" This old adage means, of course, that a person should have the courage to practice in the real world those principles they espouse in their words. In this chapter, I attempt to put my money where my mouth is. Or more accurately, because three psychoanalytically trained therapists have been cooperating in treating a young Asperger's adolescent we can call Jack, and his family, we will together outline how we are attempting to put our money where our mouths are in the form of our ongoing experiment in the treatment of Jack.

The principles we espouse with our mouths were described in the previous chapter. These are the general principles which we have found to be most useful in treatment approaches to Asperger's children. We single out the principle of flexibility in the treatment of Asperger's. By flexibility, we mean the ability to move with the patient and the patient's needs along the spectrum outlined by Paulina Kernberg from supportive forms of therapy, through supportive-expressive and expressive-supportive modes, up to a purely expressive mode (that is "pure psychoanalysis"), to the extent that this latter modality can be tolerated by the Asperger's patient. At the same time, there will be flexibility in the types of interventions the therapist is most likely to use which, based on Anne Alvarez's work, will range from the vitalising level including reclamation of aspects of functioning which are stunted in Asperger's children such as social skills, and including supportive measures such as dealing with the stresses of attending school and interacting there with other students. Interventions will range through Anne's descriptive level, including naming and contextualising of emotional states. Finally, interventions will also at times reach the explanatory level involving the kinds of psychoanalytic interpretations that are familiar to psychoanalytically trained therapists. Recalling the mapping of Anne's levels of intervention onto Paulina's types of psychotherapy suggested earlier, we could say that psychotherapy with Asperger's children often demands that the therapist be prepared to shift quickly among vitalising interventions undertaken within a supportive mode of psychotherapy, interventions at a descriptive level made within a supportive-expressive or expressive-supportive mode of psychotherapy, or interventions at an explanatory (interpretive) level made within an expressive mode of psychotherapy.

Now, there are likely some psychotherapists who are both skilled and nimble enough to be quickly flexible with their Asperger's patients in the manner just outlined. I admit that this degree of psychotherapeutic agility and nimbleness is likely to stretch my capacities severely. I suspect this kind of limitation may extend to other therapists as well. So the question then arises—is there a way to provide Asperger's children and adolescents with a very flexible treatment approach, including quite basic and probably didactic supportive measures, along with uncovering and interpretive interventions when these are possible and likely to be helpful, while not stretching the therapist's abilities too severely? My own answer to this question was easy—two therapists working together might be able to do this. This answer was easy for me, because I had a particular colleague in mind whom I was sure I could work with. My colleague is a young woman trained as a psychoanalytic psychotherapist who also has years of experience providing social skills training to children and adolescents who are "on the spectrum" along with a background of working for years in a school setting specialising in these children. This is the origin of what I have called "The Toronto experiment".

I call what we are attempting "The Toronto experiment" for several reasons. An experiment it certainly is—with positive results so far, but still very much a "work in progress" which continues as this is being written. The three psychoanalytic therapists (more about why there are three of us below) involved in treating Jack and his family know each other well and are all graduates of the psychoanalytic training institute based in Toronto called CICAPP (the Canadian Institute for Child and Adolescent Psychoanalytic Psychotherapy, earlier called the Toronto Child Psychoanalytic Program). In addition to being graduates of CICAPP, the three of us are also members of the association for graduate psychoanalytic psychotherapists called CAPCT (Canadian Association of Psychoanalytic Child Therapists). All three of us work in private practice in Toronto (two of us at The Willow Centre) and we must charge a fee for service. As things now stand in Canada, the publicly funded system provides only rudimentary services, mainly in group formats, such as "psychoeducational support groups" for parents of children on the autism spectrum. As a result, being able to afford sufficient services is an ongoing issue for Jack's family.

Much of the remainder of this chapter derives from the clinical presentation of Jack and his family that all three cooperating therapists made to the CAPCT (Canadian Association of Psychoanalytic Child Therapists) in April 2014. The three therapists are Ms. Robyn Weddepohl, Dr. Rex Collins, and I. I will refer to the three of us as Robyn, Rex, and Robin, with the similarity in names hopefully not being confusing for the reader. Note that one of the conditions for therapy agreed to by Jack, his younger sister and his parents was that the three therapists should have complete freedom to engage in an ongoing exchange of information. This has proven immensely valuable, supportive, and containing for all of us. I emphasise that it also means each of us takes up ideas suggested by the other(s), reworks these ideas, recycles them to the other two therapists, and the other two therapists may then build on the ideas further. The end result is that it is sometimes impossible to distinguish which ideas or information "belong" to which therapist. In addition to this, there was a lively and vitalising discussion when the three of us presented an outline of our experiment to CAPCT in April 2014, including many stimulating suggestions from our psychoanalytic colleagues. These suggestions have also seeped into the exposition that follows. I have attempted to acknowledge the contributions made by my colleagues Robyn and Rex whenever this has been possible. Whatever gold there may be in what follows, it may well derive from Robyn, Rex, and my other colleagues in the CAPCT. For whatever is dross and tailings, I accept responsibility.

Referral and assessment of Jack and his family

I first heard about Jack when a referral from his family doctor landed on my desk in May 2013. This referral was quite brief, mentioning "Jack Jeffries, thirteen-year-old with Asperger's, has high anxiety and suicidal thoughts, along with some suicidal gestures". Because of the mention of suicidal thoughts and gestures, I quickly contacted his parents. They asked to meet with me on the following day, which I was able to do.

I met with Jack and both of his parents, Wally and Cheryl. Not at this first meeting was the other member of the family, Jack's younger sister Emily, age eleven years.

It was quickly apparent that the mother, Cheryl, had a significant physical disability requiring her to walk with leg braces and crutches. This turned out to be a degenerative neurophysiological disorder which is likely to have a negative impact on her lifespan. This is a black shadow which continues to hang over the whole family, and which all family members find it exceedingly difficult to discuss.

With hesitation and reluctance, Jack told me his main concern was that everyone at his school (he was in grade eight) treated him "like crap", and he despised them all and hoped the new school he would go to in September to begin high school would be better than his present school. He grudgingly admitted to thinking about suicide. When I asked whether he had ever done anything to himself, he seemed to perk up, smiled in what I experienced as a supercilious and perhaps triumphant manner, and said "Well, I cut myself". He reported he had done this twice. When I asked if he might do it again, he seemed to perk up once again and said "Well ... I might".

When I met with Jack's parents, they described their concerns about Jack's high level of anxiety, suicidal thinking and self-cutting, episodes of selective mutism in which he refused to speak, and especially concerns about his difficulties regulating his emotions, particularly his anger. They described "meltdowns" in which Jack had raged around their house yelling, screaming, smashing things, and threatening to "kill all of you". He terrified his younger sister Emily, so that all three ended up spending one night barricaded together inside the parental bedroom, while Jack raged on outside the bedroom. At times, the parents have felt the need to call the police in order to have some control over Jack and ensure the physical safety of his younger sister Emily. The physical disability of his mother Cheryl has been mentioned, and his father Wally is a slight man shorter than Jack, so the parents feel unable to control him during his rages. It was not difficult for me to assess Jack as best fitting the "uninhibited/aggressive" type of Asperger's. Note that describing him in this way is a broad and general categorisation which is not intended to apply to all aspects of his behaviour. For example, when it came to openly expressing his interest in a female peer, whose name was Valerie, Jack was *strongly* inhibited, and was shy, restrained, and reluctant rather than being aggressive. The aggressive part came after he felt rejected by her, and this aggression was expressed in fantasies of how he would like to see her punished for her "betrayal" of him.

The parents also told me about their desperate attempts to find adequate services for Jack within the publicly funded system. They reported having obtained services from many public agencies, including his school board, public hospital child psychiatry departments, youth crisis centres, and centres to support families with a child on the autism spectrum. While they felt each agency had been helpful "in some way," they also felt they had exhausted all available free services, and that what they got "was never enough, never long enough, never for everything Jack is struggling with." The parents therefore came to me with a sense of desperation, willing to pay "whatever it takes to help Jack," even though this might not be easy for them.

At the end of my initial meeting with them in mid-May 2013, I recommended that the best approach would be for me to undertake a full therapeutic/collaborative psychological assessment (more about this below) with Jack to get a fuller view of the difficulties he was facing and to decide on the best treatment approach. The parents eagerly agreed to my suggestion, and asked me to start as soon as I could. The therapeutic/collaborative assessment took place in May and June 2013, with the results to be described shortly. For details about therapeutic assessment, see for example the wonderful book by my esteemed colleague Stephen Finn. His 2007 book is entitled *In our Client's Shoes: Theory and Techniques of Therapeutic Assessment*. Stephen has published numerous other books and papers.

Close to the end of the therapeutic/collaborative assessment in June 2013, I had a consultation with my colleague Robyn outlining the results of the assessment, and suggesting that if Jack's parents were agreeable, we could attempt the experiment of treating Jack collabora-tively, with me focussing on a more traditional therapeutic approach. Robyn, because of her skills in these areas, would focus on social skills and interpersonal communication training, and support in peer interac-tions. She would also deal with the school environment and interacting with teachers, and support in making the transition (difficult enough for any young person) between elementary school (grade eight) which Jack was just completing (at the end of June) and high school (grade nine) which he would begin in September. Robyn and I discussed the details of our proposed treatment experiment. She was agreeable to proceeding.

As a result, the four of us (Robyn, Robin, and both parents) met in late June 2013 to discuss treatment planning for Jack. We evolved a treatment plan including biweekly visits with Robin to start after school had begun in September, along with weekly visits with Robyn to start in the summer. These meetings were to include support for Jack around the transition to high school, along with social communication skills training. These arrangements went according to plan.

After Robyn and Robin had both begun their work with Jack, in the fall of 2013, the parents spoke to me about their concerns around his sis-ter Emily. They were concerned about her difficulties handling school. The parents requested a psychoeducational assessment for Emily, won-dering about a possible nonverbal learning disability. This is where the third therapist, Rex, came in. I referred Emily to Rex for psychoeduca-tional assessment. He completed this assessment but without a learning disability being identified. Rex empathised with Emily's experience in the family, where her troubled brother takes up so much psychic space in the family, so much of the parents' time, their physical and emotional energy, that Emily often feels marginalised, forgotten in the ongoing chaos. Emily is a carrier of the disease her mother suffers from, and is aware that she is. When she met with Rex, Emily's own concerns related to her status with her peers and whether or not she was liked by them; her safety in the face of her brother's aggressive, sometimes violent behaviour; and her worries about her mother dying and/or her parents getting a divorce. Rex became concerned with Emily's social/emotional functioning, Emily impressing him as a very anxious, depressed, and distressed youngster. In her testing, she endorsed test items indicating suicidal thinking. She reported that she had made an effort to cut herself with a knife (as her brother Jack had done). Emily was a girl who did not feel safe in the family. During the course of the interviews with her and her parents, it emerged that she had been witness to an incident where Jack had badly cut himself, following which the police were called and he was hospitalised. Rex concluded that Emily needs long-term treatment. He offered to provide psychotherapy for Emily, but the parents postponed this because of strains on their finances.

We now jump ahead to the spring of 2014. Emily's school reported her to the local child protection agency because of concerns she might be "suicidal". She has reported to her teacher that she has twice attempted to drown herself, this being in the bathtub at home.

As a result of this, Emily once more met with Rex. One of Emily's concerns was worries about her mother's serious physical disability. Rex was able to refer her for some treatment to a publicly funded agency. He has offered to see Emily individually if this is needed after the publicly funded treatment ends. He has also offered to see the parents for ongoing parent support, and to see the mother Cheryl individually in order to help her come to terms emotionally with her physical problem. The parents are eager to use these services if they can get into a position so that they can afford them. (Charitable funding support for the family and its treatment needs has now been obtained). We now go back to June 2013 when Jack's assessment was undertaken by Robin.

Jack's therapeutic assessment

An approach to assessment which has been called either "collaborative assessment" or "therapeutic assessment" has come to the fore over the last decade or two (for example, see Finn, 2007). It has been called collaborative assessment because it views the person being assessed and the person undertaking the assessment as needing to collaborate together as co-equals in order to fully tease out the meaning of the assessment results as they are applied to the person being assessed. It has been called therapeutic assessment because the process itself is seen as having an inherent therapeutic potential. The briefest possible summary of this process is that psychological tests are used to derive some initial information about the person and then the assessor and the person assessed go over this information and process it so that it contributes maximally to understanding the person in a way the person being assessed can accept. Three different levels of information are typically produced as a result of a therapeutic assessment. These three levels are: first, results which the person being assessed quickly recognises as being part of their functioning so that they can say something like "oh yeah, that's just like me". Second, there are results which the person does not initially recognise as being like them, but after some discussion is able to accept and say something like "it seems that when we think about it carefully, that does seem to be how I am". Finally, the third level produces results which the person does not recognise as being part of how they function, and which requires a lot of work for the person to understand and to be able to accept. If we call these three levels respectively, conscious, preconscious, and unconscious, perhaps this would not be too far off the mark.

In the therapeutic assessment I undertook with Jack, I used two tests—the Rorschach and the MACI (Millon Adolescent Clinical Inventory). The results of both were extremely helpful, and the two tests were mutually informative and elaborated on each other. Without going into all the details, the "personality patterns" section of the MACI suggested the possibility of a schizoid kind of withdrawal, depressive personality aspects, along with both angry and rebellious as well as self-critical aspects. The presence of depressive feelings stood out as well as insecurity with peers, self-devaluation, and identity confusion. Most concerning, a scale measuring suicidal tendency was highly elevated. The Rorschach confirmed and elaborated on most of these findings. The results of the Rorschach pointed to depression, low self-esteem, and significant difficulty with other people including peers. The difficulties included a definite lack in social skills, and a deficit in reality testing as this applied to understanding other people. The elevation on the MACI scale measuring "impulsive propensity" was supported by a Rorschach finding suggesting very fragile emotional controls. Anxiety was also strong as measured by the Rorschach. As a result of this, I discussed a treatment plan with Jack and then with his parents. I wrote a brief summary of the results which I sent to the referring family doctor and also to Robyn.

A typical procedure in undertaking a therapeutic assessment with a child or an adolescent is to write at the end of the process a summary of some of the things we discovered in the assessment. This was what happened with Jack. I give a very brief and summarised rendition of how I arrived at the story I wrote for Jack—a story I called "A Dragon Called DD".

One of Jack's responses to the Rorschach cards was as follows: "I see a dragon shooting something out of its mouth". Part of the process used in a therapeutic assessment is to undertake what is called an "extended inquiry" of some of the person's responses to the Rorschach. The evaluator chooses what seem to be some of the most salient Rorschach responses and asks the person to imagine that they actually *are* what the person saw in the Rorschach. I chose five Rorschach responses from Jack's protocol for extended inquiry. One of these was his response of a dragon shooting something out of its mouth. Here is part of the extended inquiry. I ask Jack to imagine he was the dragon and what he could be shooting out of his mouth. "It could be some sort of projectile it has, like fire or something like that." Then I asked what the target of the dragon might be. "It's shooting everywhere—and at everyone—with the exception of a few." Finally I asked what the dragon might be feeling. Jack replied: "Anger. It's angry at the world. It doesn't succeed in doing what it wants".

This is an extremely shortened version of the process of therapeutic assessment. However, I hope it will give you some inkling of how the assessor goes from the test results to the final written communication. The story I wrote for Jack—"A Dragon Called DD"—was intended to both summarise some of the results of testing and to set the stage for the therapeutic intervention Robyn and I were to collaborate on together.

Treating Asperger's adolescents collaboratively—start of the Toronto experiment

I was aware of the work Robyn was doing in supporting children and adolescents who are "on the spectrum" both within their school settings as well as her individual and group work in the area of social skills training. I began to think about modifying my treatment approach to Asperger's adolescents as a result of my work with an Asperger's preadolescent, twelve-year-old Matt who was then in grade seven (see Chapter Three for Matt—some of the material in this chapter is summarised here). At the beginning of one session, Matt wanted to tell me about what he called "a hideous disaster" which had happened in his school classroom. A shortened version of what Matt told me is as follows: one day his class unexpectedly had a supply teacher because the regular teacher was away sick. (Notice that Asperger's kids regularly have trouble with any changes, especially unexpected ones, in their usual routine or schedule, so this already set Matt up for potential difficulties). This supply teacher allowed the class free time to draw anything they wanted on the chalkboard. Instead of starting to draw right away, Matt self-righteously decided he needed to finish his work first. He did so, and then went up to the chalkboard for his—as he felt it, now appropriate and allowable—turn at drawing on the board. But by now, there was no chalk left. So, in his self-appointed role as a considerate and helpful student, he went to the chalk supply and returned with a full box so everyone could have some. He took out a piece of chalk and just as he was about to have his well-deserved turn, the supply teacher said that time was up and the drawing time was finished. As Matt was trying to absorb and process what he felt was a horrendously unfair and unempathic personal wounding of himself by the supply teacher, he received another hideous and unempathic wound from a girl who was a fellow student. She pointed to her drawing on the chalkboard of a distorted and weird-looking figure and whispered in Matt's ear "Matt, that's *you*".

Matt could not tolerate these two deeply wounding events which occurred in quick succession. He had what he called a meltdown. He ripped off his glasses, threw them down and smashed them to pieces with his feet. He began to yell and scream and then throw desks and chairs everywhere. He ended up curled in a little ball crying loudly behind one of the overturned desks with the rest of the students around him in a circle and taunting him, the supply teacher having fled the room to get help from the principal's office.

In describing this scenario, I think Matt was giving me a strong hint that I needed to intervene on his behalf in a concrete and practical way. I think I should have gone to the school, observed Matt in his classroom, and spoken to his school staff in a supportive way in order to try to help them cope with Matt's difficulties. I didn't do this. I treated what Matt told me in a purely psychotherapeutic manner, trying to understand the details of what had happened and what made him react as he did. This was helpful, but only to a limited extent. In retrospect, I feel that direct, supportive, and concrete interventions with Asperger's children are almost always needed, accompanied by the psychotherapeutic interventions we have spent so much time learning. My feeling is that Asperger's children typically need "hands-on" and concrete supportive interventions in two main areas—dealing with the school and their difficulties functioning within the school system, and dealing with their peers and their difficulties in understanding and appropriately interacting with other kids in their age group, including reality testing in social situations.

One way of looking at this that I have found helpful in my own thinking is to invoke the old distinction between a conflict psychology and a deficit psychology. To say it briefly—Asperger's children have both conflicts and deficits. To some extent, both their conflicts and their deficits can be handled within the traditional psychotherapeutic environment. But I think more is also needed. Consider the example of the significant deficit in social skills which is the lot of all Asperger's sufferers. This is a deficit in both receiving and sending social signals—a deficit in reading social cues and in understanding the nonverbal aspects of behaviour, facial expressions and language. We now understand that even though Asperger's children often have very strong and even superior verbal skills, they also tend to take language very literally and are unable to process aspects such as irony or sarcasm. There is a corresponding deficit in their capacity for socially responding to others and in calibrating their responses so as to be suitable for both their interlocutors (adult authority figures such as vice-principals *vs.* excitedly gossiping peers) and for the immediate context (being sent to the principal's office *vs.* attending a party with peers).

My initial theory was that these kinds of deficits could be handled within the context of understanding developments in the transference/countertransference dialectic. In other words, if we were able to understand what was happening in the interplay of transference and countertransference and work on issues in *this* context, then the results would generalise and also help the child understand and work on issues in other environments, including with peers. I still think there is a great deal of value in working in this way. But I now think that by itself it is not enough and that frequently it may not work fast enough. If the therapy is to last long enough so that work with the transference/countertransference dialectic is to become useful, then you also have to move in very early on in the treatment with specific supportive measures that allow the treatment to last—most importantly, supportive intervention in the school setting and specific training in social sensibilities and social skills. It may be possible for a single therapist to accomplish all this. In the specific case of my intervention with Jack, I knew someone who had much more experience than I did in implementing these kinds of specific supportive measures—Robyn. The result was our collaboration and the present ongoing experiment in the treatment of Jack. My impression is that so far our collaboration has worked very well and has resulted in some important shifts in how Jack is able to function. It is nevertheless still "a work in progress."

I now bring together two lenses or ways of looking at treating Asperger's children in general, and Jack in particular, and try to amalgamate these to some extent. The first lens through which to look at things is the "conflict *vs.* deficit" lens. The second lens is one provided by Anne Alvarez, in her magnificent book *The Thinking Heart*, and the three levels of therapeutic intervention she describes there. Let's first consider Jack through the lens of conflict *vs.* deficit in terms of how he relates to his peers. Based on material from his psychotherapy sessions, it is as if he were saying something like: "I want to kill all my classmates who seem to denigrate and laugh at me, but I also know that wouldn't help me and it would prevent them from accepting me in the way I want them to". This is an internal conflict of a kind we are quite used to in conducting psychotherapy. But he also says something like: "I *lack* the social skills to interact with my classmates, to deal with their occasional teasing of me in an appropriate and perhaps humorous way, and to make strong relationships with them". This is a deficit. The conflict aspect can be dealt with mostly or even entirely by means of individual psychotherapy. The deficit, I am suggesting, can be dealt with only partially through individual psychotherapy and often requires more direct supportive intervention.

I give a very brief summary of the material described in the previous chapter—the three levels of clinical intervention outlined by Anne Alvarez. She refers to these as the *explanatory* level, the *descriptive* level, and the intensified and *vitalising* level. When using the first or explanatory level, which I refer to as the *explanatory/hermeneutical* level, hermeneutics referring to the interpretive understanding of texts, we offer *alternative meanings* to the patient. This is the level of typical psychoanalytic interpretation. There is a behaviour or a feeling or thought at the overt and surface level, a different underlying alternative at a depth level, and a link is made between the two. We offer the patient explanations such as: "You did *x* because unconsciously it reminded you of *y* and it made you feel *z*". A typical interpretation at the explanatory/hermeneutical level might go something like: "You felt sad about missing me last week when I went away on vacation. As a result, in how you are playing today you seem to need to show me how hurt and angry you felt at my leaving and going away".

The *descriptive* level involves naming and describing what the child feels, amplifying the meaning of experiences, mirroring, and the naming, understanding, and contextualising of feeling states. It may also involve the normalising of intense feeling states such as murderous rage. Jack specifically expressed the feeling of wanting to burn his classmates at the stake so that they could truly understand, and would themselves suffer, the intensity of the emotional pain they created for him. The normalising (*not* expressing openly or acting on, but normalising) of such a feeling, in the context in which it is experienced, is part of the work with Asperger's children. These children are notorious for difficulties in understanding and naming the emotions experienced by both themselves and others so that describing and naming emotions is also important.

The intensified and *vitalising* level underlines the idea that meaning can be found in all situations. It involves what Anne Alvarez refers to as "reclamation", meaning the reclaiming of meaning, liveliness, and vitality for children who seem to lack these aspects. It is as if the therapist were saying to the patient: "you can and do have feelings and it is appropriate to have them". It also involves sparking interest in the child and helping the child to feel alive and in contact with others. I think it is also at this level that the therapist provides *support* for deficits in functioning, reclaims capacities that have been stunted or have never actually developed, and has a vitalising effect on the child as a result of these efforts. In brief, I suggest that the Asperger's adolescent has deficits in functioning and therefore a deficit psychology, that their deficit psychology requires concrete and hands-on supportive measures, and that supportive interventions occur at Anne's intensified and *vitalising* level of therapeutic intervention.

Some extracts from Jack's therapy

I provide some extracts from Jack's psychotherapy with me and I view these extracts through the lens provided by Anne Alvarez which has just been described. You will hear a bit about four different sessions— one each from January, February, March, and April of 2014. In the session from January—we had been talking about how Jack views and evaluates other people. We were able to speak about the "internal pictures" (my way of describing it to Jack) that he has of others, what in psychoanalytic language we might call internal object representations or internal objects. Jack quickly referred to these as his "structures" or his "profiles" of other people. He said that his "profiles" contained different "towers" and that the towers were composed of a number of floors. Note the architectural metaphor. Jack is intensely preoccupied with architecture. He gave names to four of the "towers" included in his "profiles" of other people. One of these towers represented trust, and another represented friendliness. Jack told me that a person could add floors to each tower in their profile and make it higher by doing positive things, but floors could also be removed from towers on the basis of negative things they did. He indicated that the height of different towers in a person's profile could change quite quickly—even for the towers in the profile of his best friend. He seemed to be talking about intense sensitivity and intense emotional reactivity. I wondered aloud to him whether his "profiles" being consistent over time would give a person a sense of stability and continuity in the world. If his profiles changed quickly, wouldn't this mean that the world would seem changeable and not very stable? He then said that his profiles of others did tend to be stable and did not tend to change that much.

I then took what I felt might be a risk and brought our discussion to the transference. I said that I probably had a "profile" in his mind and I wondered what my profile and the towers in it might be like. He said that I had a pretty good profile and that the tower representing trust was fairly high and that the more times we met, it might get even higher. I went on to talk about possible times when I could make a mistake with him and lose some floors from the trust tower in my profile. I tried to describe one difference between what we did and how people usually interacted. This difference was that he could tell me clearly and directly if I said something he didn't like or didn't agree with or that struck him as being negative. We might then be able to correct my mistakes and perhaps he could even use some of what we learned from this and apply it to how he dealt with other people as well.

I suggest that in this part of the session, I was working with Jack mainly on Anne's levels one and two, especially level two. We were mainly describing and clarifying how Jack experiences other people. Level one creeps in when I tried to link his way of experiencing things with a sense of stability and continuity, but this doesn't get very far. Level three also seems to creep in when I tell him in a sort of educative manner that he can correct my mistakes and I also tried to suggest that our experiences of each other can be enlivened in this way.

In the February session, Jack and I spoke about what he referred to as his "barriers", which I understood as referring to an autistic or autistic-like shell. We were talking about a girl in his class whom he wanted to get to know but whom he also felt had shunned him. (He brought up the same situation with Robyn in his work with her—more appears below about how she dealt with what for Jack was a crucial issue). He said he has a barrier that protects him and it's very strong and nobody can get through, though sometimes people might sneak through when he was under stress, such as happened with the girl. He said in reference to this girl, Valerie, that when he had spoken to her, his barrier had become "paper thin". He spoke of his barrier as usually being extremely strong, like carbon fibres, like some of the strongest material going. I wondered about him letting people in and he said that this takes a considerable amount of time. I then took another risk in terms of the transference. I said that his barrier or wall was operating between him and me in the room right now as we spoke. Could he describe what was happening with his barrier right now? He didn't answer my question directly, but he said it would take me a long time to get all the way through his barrier. Again in this part of the session, it seems to me like we were operating mostly on Anne's level two, developing a detailed description of how things were working inside of him.

In the April session, Jack made an aggressive, disparaging, and denigrating comment about some of his peers. This kind of comment is very familiar to me from Asperger's children. They make morally self-righteous and denigrating statements about flaws in others, and view themselves as being morally superior and lacking the faults they are so quick to see in others. To put it directly—there is a lot of projective identification going on into what I call remote objects, other people they have no intense relationship with. Jack made a specific comment as follows: "I really want to *eliminate* all the twelve-year-olds who talk so much about sex and drugs, that's what they deserve". He told me that among his peers, sex and drugs were all they talked and thought about; all the jokes they told were about sex. He then whipped out his mobile phone and, seized with morally superior indignation, showed me something on his phone about parents who teach their children to "twerk". This recently coined word refers to a recent form of sexually very suggestive dancing. In other words, he was likely suggesting that adults have a sexually corrupting influence on adolescents. I sucked in my breath and wondered if it would be appropriate to try and talk about sexuality or if he would just see me as another corrupted and corrupting adult. I took a chance and said that it seemed to me that when they reach a certain age, everyone has sexual feelings of some kind. He surprised me. He quickly agreed and said that he had sexual feelings as well. I was tremendously surprised by his ability to make this confession. So I continued. I wondered if he had any impressions about what was the most common sexual feeling for twelve year-olds and young adolescents. He looked at me quizzically, paused and shook his head. I said the strongest sexual emotion was probably anxiety—fear. He nodded. I then went on. I said that for humans, sexual stuff wasn't built in but had to be learned. People did this in different ways. Some people tried to suppress or ignore sexual feelings and make themselves into a sort of celibate Catholic priest. Some people tried to deal with these feelings in private by using masturbation. Some people tried to push their anxieties away by jumping right into bed (that is, counterphobically). Some people found a partner with whom they could experiment with sexual feelings over time, beginning with stuff like holding hands, hugging, and kissing. People have different choices. He nodded, and then he changed the subject.

I think that in this part of the April session, Jack and I were operating mainly on Anne's level two with a peek into level one and some implications for level three interventions. We were again mainly describing things, but with a foray into a level one interpretation in my suggestion that anxiety and fear are likely to be primary sexual emotions in early adolescence—something I think is true in general but also likely very applicable to feelings that Jack has. Note that there are also very strong implications for level three in terms of direct supportive intervention. In fact, this has actually happened, thanks to Robyn. Recall the girl in his class (Valerie) that Jack desperately wanted to talk to. He didn't know how to break the ice and accomplish this. He spoke to Robyn about it, and they developed a specific plan which Jack had the confidence to actually put into action. Even though the final result was not what Jack would have ideally wanted, he still seemed to benefit very much from Robyn's support and from actually making an attempt to meet this girl. Here is where our collaborative work with Jack is likely to bear fruit. Jack and I can talk in a psychotherapeutic context about this girl breaking through his autistic-like emotional barrier, and about trying to deal with the extremely frightening sexual feelings she arouses in him. At the same time, Jack and Robyn can work together to come up with specific and practical as well as socially acceptable ways in which he might be able to get to know the girl. In my level two intervention, I can suggest to Jack that there are slower, less scary, and more modulated ways of dealing with sexual feelings and impulses than either becoming a morally superior celibate or diving into bed with someone. At the same time, Jack can work with Robyn to come up with specific ways of putting into action the optimal way of dealing with sexual feelings I was trying to suggest. Put slightly differently—I try to deal with the *conflict* (you must be either celibate or sexually hyperactive) while at the same time Robyn tries to deal with the *deficit* (how the heck do you go about even talking with a girl anyway?).

Finally, let's consider some parts of the session from March, specifically 25 March. Jack arrives fifteen minutes late, panting and out of breath. He apologises for being late. I tell him to sit down and get his breath and that I am glad he has been able to make it. He tells me that the problem is his mobile phone. In my usual manner, I repeat his statement back to him as a question—"your mobile phone?" He says that his mobile phone is still on standard time rather than daylight savings, so it was set an hour earlier than the actual time. He said he noticed this but if he hadn't noticed he would've come here at the end of his appointment instead of at the beginning. Well, today is 25 March and the change to daylight savings occurred on 8 March, seventeen days ago. Do I confront him with this? Is this a conflict about coming to see me and the daylight savings issue is just a red herring? Or is this more of a deficit and he has actually forgotten to readjust his phone for a full seventeen days? I don't know the answer to this. So I keep quiet and wait.

He surprises me and says it's nice to be here. He says he can see through my office window the new building that is being constructed next door. He reminds me of his interest in architecture and becoming an architect and he says this is still what he wants in the future and he imagines many different architectural designs. I think this might be an opportunity so I ask him if he wants to draw some of his designs for me. He agrees, and eventually sketches out twelve different designs. I'm genuinely impressed by what he draws. I try to comment on his drawings as he does them in what seems to me later as being at the level three or the vitalising and enlivening level. I comment on the interesting curves of some of his designs, how they seem to thrust and aspire upwards, how they seem to be alive and even growing so that one impresses me as having an almost botanical feel to it, like a shoot of asparagus growing upwards. He responds to this and says he has a mobile phone app which shows all the new buildings going up in Toronto. He invites me to look at it. I roll my chair over right next to him and feel very comfortable being this close to him—it's as physically close as I've ever been to him. He shows me all the new buildings going up in Toronto and makes comments about them and the features of the different buildings. I start to feel this is the closest and the most intimate I've ever been with him and I experience that it feels very good. We start to talk about the soaring buildings and his own "soaring aspirations" as well as aspirations *vs.* reality. He spoke a little bit about "perfecting things" and I was able to say it would feel good to perfect things but it sounded like it also involved a heck of a lot of work.

In this session, it felt like I was doing a lot of mirroring. I was able to link up with his enthusiasms and his aspirations and it was as if what I was saying was something like "I think this is how you're feeling and I get it". We are able to come physically closer together based on his interests and his feelings and my receptivity toward both of these. As I mentioned, this work of mirroring seemed to occur at Anne's level three or the vitalising and enlivening level. Later in the session, this seemed to allow him to go on with other topics such as feeling that the school is not taking him seriously.

In working with Asperger's children and adolescents, we move a lot among Anne's three levels of therapeutic intervention; more moving around among the levels than with most adolescents. With Jack, in my part of the work with him, there seems to be a lot happening at level two, with something happening at level one and at level three as well. The hope is that as the psychotherapy progresses, the number of interventions will shift towards level one over time. But with the Asperger's patient, level three cannot be ignored. If the concrete support at the vitalising and enlivening level of intervention is too much for a single clinician, then perhaps two clinicians can do the job. This is the reason behind the collaborative endeavour, the experiment, in which Robyn and I are engaged.

Excerpts from Jack's work with Robyn

Robyn and I communicate constantly using email, and with her consent I have used her communications (including the presentation all three therapists made to the Canadian Association of Psychoanalytic Child Psychotherapists) to provide a brief sketch of some facets of how she works with Jack.

In his first meeting with Robyn (June 2013), Jack was selectively mute. Robyn became quite anxious, wondering how she could teach him social skills if he wasn't speaking (was this projective identification into Robyn of his own anxiety and his own sense of incompetence with social skills?). However, when she handed him a pen, Jack began to write in response to Robyn's questions, and this allowed her to speak to Jack about aspects of nonverbal communication and how these aspects relate to social skills (Anne Alvarez's level three).

The issue of how you ask for your needs to be met, specifically with teachers, arose in Robyn's session with Jack in September 2013. My own experience with Asperger's adolescents is that they are regularly extremely reluctant to ask for any help from teachers, as if this would be both a narcissistic injury and would also involve the risk of the victim aspect of their split self being rejected by the teacher and feeling victimised once again. Even if they are willing to request help, they are reluctant to do so because their deficit in social communication skills makes them completely uncertain as to how to ask for help in an appropriate manner which is acceptable to the teacher.

Jack began his communication with Robyn in a way very typical of Asperger's children—"nobody really cares about me, including the school and my teachers". Her response to this was to ask Jack what, if the school were to care, would he *want* them to care about? He responded that he didn't want the school to change his schedule as they were proposing to do because he needed this routine. Also, he said he needed help from the teachers with his work in English. Robyn supported him in making these two requests to the school. The end result was that he got what he wanted. This kind of supportive work with Jack is on Anne's level three.

Robyn arranged for Jack to participate in a small social skills training group which involved two other Asperger's adolescents. From his initial attitude of sitting with his head down, ignoring the other two participants and focusing on a popular iPhone game (which the other two adolescents were also taking turns playing), Jack ended up, with Robyn's support, actively involved with the other two participants and offering to share with them duplicates he had of some of the characters in the game. This kind of supportive/structured/didactic intervention would be part of Anne's level three.

A common source of terror and tribulations for many thirteen-year-olds is making connections with peers of the opposite sex. If the adolescent has Asperger's, the terror and tribulations are multiplied by three. I wrote previously about Jack's interest in a female peer in one of his classes, Valerie, and how my level two interventions with him were geared toward lessening Jack's conflicts about approaching her. I wrote that Jack had also brought this issue to Robyn as well. It seemed in the end helpful to him to get a male point of view from me, and a female point of view from Robyn. I now report on Robyn's interventions with Jack in dealing with his feelings and actions toward Valerie.

In an October 2013 session with Robyn, Jack spoke to her about a girl in his class whom he feels looks at him "sheepishly". He feels that this girl, Valerie, may be like him in ways, because she's often alone in class. Jack tried saying "hi" to her. She didn't respond, so Jack is not sure she heard him. Robyn got Jack to role-play his manner of saying "hi" to Valerie—this being with his head hung low, no smile or expression of affect, and reticent in his manner towards her rather than confident. As a result of this role-play, Jack is able to understand that Valerie may not have heard him say "hi" because he was so subdued and quiet, and even if she did hear him, she might have had trouble responding because of how he presented himself.

Robyn wonders how Jack might approach Valerie, drawing a map of the hallway at school. Jack laughed and made it clear he would not risk the potential for humiliation in approaching her while in a group—it would have to be while she was alone. But what could he talk about, Robyn wonders—could he perhaps think of a compliment to make about her? They then together evolve a plan that Jack could "accidentally" drop a pen near Valerie in the hope she would pick it up and allow Jack to say it was his and start talking to her. Jack tells Robyn that this is a brilliant idea, and he's going to collect pens that aren't working because he wouldn't want to drop a good pen! All of these supportive interventions seem to be on Anne's enlivening and supportive level three.

Jack was also able to express to Robyn how he experiences both of us and the differences between us. He tells her: "I think you both find me interesting and you like seeing me. Robin is a wise man, but he doesn't need white hair [which I have] to be wise. You are more of an advisor, more kid-like and playful and you give me useful tips and strategies". While I am more sceptical than Jack about how wise I am, this seems overall like a pretty accurate summary of how Robyn and I tried to share our collaborative work with Jack.

Bumps in the road

No therapy proceeds completely smoothly and without difficulty, complications, and struggles. This is certainly true of our work with Jack and his family. I briefly outline two "bumps in the road" we have had to navigate—a meltdown of rage by Jack at his home, and a therapist enactment by Robin.

One evening, Jack lost the expensive public transit monthly card which he used in order to travel to school. He "knew" it was somewhere in his home. After being unable to find it for some time, he started screaming, yelling, and tearing his room to pieces, wildly searching for it everywhere. When he was unable to locate the card in the debris of his bedroom, he started to scream that his younger sister Emily had taken it and must have hidden it in her room. She shut her bedroom door, cowering in fear, while Jack hammered on her door and wrenched the door handle, trying to get in to search for his card. Their parents had to stand in front of Emily's bedroom to prevent Jack from smashing through it. Because of his diminutive stature, his father was unable to restrain Jack from assaulting the door. His mother's physical limitations prevented her from restraining him. Neither parent was able to calm Jack down using verbal means. Eventually, fearing for Emily's safety, the parents called the police, though they later disagreed strongly as to whether they should have done so. As soon as the police arrived, Jack calmed down.

In reviewing this situation with Robyn, she was able to add more to the available information around this incident because of her contact with Jack's school. Shortly before his tantrum, Jack had received a very low grade in mathematics; something he had previously felt was a definite strength for him. This seemed to be a significant narcissistic wound for Jack, and was also something he had neglected to tell his parents about. We therefore felt it was possible that part of Jack's tantrum may have involved displacement of his resulting narcissistic rage.

Both Robyn and I responded to this incident, in different ways. Robyn discussed with Jack how he could handle the situation better if he again felt himself becoming enraged. With the parents, she discussed how they could together formulate a "safety plan" that everyone would know about in advance, so that everyone would be safe if this kind of uncontrolled tantrum were to occur again. Her interventions were mainly at Anne's level three supportive interventions. My interventions tended to be more at Anne's level two—what were you feeling when all this was happening? When I asked him about this, Jack gave me a minimal answer in which his anger was rationalised. We were also able to talk about his anger at his math grade (which Robyn and I had surmised may have been displaced into the tantruming incident). He was able to say that his low math mark really bothered him but he minimised his difficulty, saying it was only one section of the math book and now they had gone past it to stuff he understood. I experienced anxiety that he would minimise his difficulty with this one section, avoid dealing with this material, and then the material could become a problem in the future. As a result of this, Jack and I had the following exchange:

ROBIN: Do you mind if I ask what the section was that was, I mean the, ah, nasty one for you?

JACK: Radicals.

ROBIN: As in roots, square roots, and that sort of stuff?

JACK: Yeah, like how you get them from triangles.

ROBIN: (Confused) Get them from triangles? But ... (then a light goes on in my head) oh, you mean like the Pythagorean theorem—square on the hypotenuse equals the sum of the squares on the other two sides?

JACK: Uh, yeah (reluctantly) that's the one.

ROBIN: (Fighting off a brief impulse to speak of triangles in an Oedipal sense) So ... just so I can understand the problem ... let me grab a piece of paper ... if we have a right angled triangle like this one I've just drawn and the shortest side is 2 units, the next side is 3 units, then we want to find the length of this line, the hypotenuse?

JACK: That's the one, alright.

ROBIN: So can I do it now and we'll see what the problem is?

JACK: Go right ahead (now apparently interested in what I'm doing).

ROBIN: Okay, so we make the hypotenuse x^2 because it's the *square* on the hypotenuse, right? And the other sides are 2^2 which is ...?

JACK: Four.

ROBIN: Yeah, and 3^2 which is ...?

JACK: Uh, nine.

ROBIN: Sure, nine. So the two sides are 9 and 4, giving us a total of 13 when we add them, right?

JACK: Right.

ROBIN: Now we're left with the old hypotenuse, which you remember was the length x^2?

JACK: (Excitedly) So *that's* what ... *yeah*, oh yeah!

ROBIN: Yeah. So x^2 is 13, meaning that the length of the hypotenuse, x, is the square root of 13.

JACK: Oh, shit, so *that's* how they got the radical! (Excitedly) The stupid teacher didn't show me *that*!

ROBIN: Stupid teacher? You mean he ... no, *she*, right?

JACK: She—Ms. Kofax.

ROBIN: So, Ms. Kofax wasn't very helpful with this section?

JACK: No, not in any way.

ROBIN: And you decided not to ask her to clarify it for you?

JACK: No, not after the rotten mark the bitch ... the mark she gave me.

In this vignette, I have been operating very much at Anne's level three—supporting Jack in understanding the math problem, and, I think, enlivening him a little when he discovered he *did* understand what was going on in the math problem. The aim would then be to see how far it might be possible to proceed to Anne's level two in understanding his feelings (anger in particular) and to make forays into her level one (explanation and interpretation). Perhaps Jack would allow some exploration of his inner world at level one. For example, the *teacher* is stupid, not him, so is there projective identification at work? What do people do when they start to feel stupid? It might be possible as well to try to explore the "rotten mark" (the teacher only gives me her rotten and decayed breast) or "bitch" (the teacher only feeds her "litter" of students scantily and uncaringly).

When the two therapists responded to this tantrum incident, Robyn tended to intervene at level three, with Robin also going to level three after a start at Anne's level two. After this tantrum, Jack's behaviour at home has been stable.

Now we consider an enactment by Robin, and how this played out in our therapeutic endeavour, hopefully for the good. Recall that initially, our interventions had been scheduled on a biweekly basis for Robin, and a weekly basis for Robyn. As Jack's therapy proceeded, I started to chafe under this arrangement, feeling we could make quicker progress if I were able to see him on a *weekly* basis just as Robyn was doing. I raised with Jack the issue of changing our meetings to weekly ones on a number of occasions. He always put me off with what I experienced as flimsy excuses, such as "We meet on Tuesdays and I can't meet you every Tuesday because that's cheap movie night and I want to go to movies I can afford with my friends". My therapeutic ambition had raised its head and this blinded me to the possibility that Jack might not yet be ready for the heightened intensity and closeness that would be part of increasing our meetings to weekly frequency. This ended in Robin blurting out a verbal enactment after Jack had once more refused to increase our sessions to a weekly frequency.

"Well you know", I said, deliberately giving my words a humorous expression so that what I said could be heard as irony, "maybe I could feel a little jealous that you and Robyn meet every week". What flashed through my mind in the way of justifying such an enactment was that if Jack saw that there could be emotional tensions between Robyn and myself and that we could work these out, this could be of therapeutic benefit to him. My self-deception in this enactment was strong enough to make me repress the knowledge I had had for years—that Asperger's children often fail to understand humorous implications and irony, so that giving a humorous expression to my words was likely to have very little impact on Jack processing them as anything but quite serious in intent. This is of course what happened.

I reported my intervention to Robyn, along with my now increasing scepticism that saying what I did had been a good idea. For her part, Robyn was extremely tactful in agreeing that I had likely blundered. She reported back to me that Jack had commented to her, just after my enactment, that "the two of you should grow up and stop fighting over me".

In the next session with me, Jack opened the door for me to talk about the comment I had made. He began this session based on his interest in architecture and urban planning, saying that Toronto was one of the fastest growing cities in the world and speaking of how the amalgamation of the separate and independently governed boroughs that had not long ago made up the city had contributed to the city's growth.

After a while, I said that something which his talking about growth reminded me of was the comment he had made to Robyn about what I had said to him—that the two of us should grow up and stop fighting over him. He looked at me and silently nodded. I said in many ways I agreed with his comment; that *growth* was very important in the work the three of us were doing—especially *his* growth. As to fighting over him, I said that our aim was not to fight *over* him, but together to fight *for* him.

This intervention seemed to allow Jack to become much more comfortable, and he even started to joke. In a joking tone of voice, he said yes, it was like he was "the last slice of pizza" we were fighting over.

I paused and then told him I felt his comment about feeling like "the last slice of pizza" we were fighting over was very helpful. It sounded in a way like he could be talking about greed and selfishness for that last slice of pizza—my own greed and selfishness in wanting a slice of him equal to that Robyn got in seeing him every week.

In spite of controversy about the degree of self-disclosure the therapist should allow himself, I continued with the comments that now follow. I felt Jack was correct in his implication, and I felt it was essential to support his reality testing in this regard, rather than fail to communicate my own feelings. So I told Jack that I likely did have some greed and selfishness as part of the comment I had made—that I was probably greedy for things to go more quickly with him and show what a good therapist I was—and maybe that was why I had been pushing him for weekly sessions. So maybe I should back off and just see what happened with our biweekly sessions.

We continued to talk. He reminded me that after I made my comment about maybe being jealous of his weekly meetings with Robyn, he'd told me that the work with her was difficult. I said I remembered that. I also said I remembered what I replied to him—that the work he and I did together was difficult as well.

I went on to tell him that I was probably being defensive. I now thought that how I responded to him was an error. Instead of defensively saying how difficult our work was, I should have picked up on what *he* felt about how difficult for *him* the sessions with Robyn were.

I pointed to some books about the autism spectrum in my bookcase Robyn had suggested to me. I said that I agreed the work he and Robyn did together was difficult. I didn't think I could do that kind of work. That's why I had wanted both of us to work together with him. I added that when two therapists worked together, some kind of tensions always arose. The important thing, however, was whether mutual respect and attachment, mutual admiration, and caring were stronger than the greed, selfishness, and jealousy we had been talking about.

Jack then picked up again on his theme of the amalgamation of the various boroughs with separate governments as they had been amalgamated into the so-called "megacity" of Toronto, and how other cities within the so-called "GTA" (Greater Toronto Area) might also amalgamate. But he also spoke of the loyalty people felt to the boroughs they lived in, and even the greed and selfishness of people living in some of the surrounding areas not wanting to amalgamate because they were doing well and didn't want to share local benefits with others. He also spoke of different levels of government financing important projects such as expansion of subway lines, and whether these levels of government could work together cooperatively.

I said to Jack that I wondered whether I might also be hearing in what he was saying some echoes of other important issues. He looked at me quizzically. I said well, your two therapists, Robyn and me. Can we amalgamate our work so as to help him, or would our greed and selfishness around our local and personal interests get in the way? And the different levels of government that have to work cooperatively to expand the subway system—can Robyn and I work cooperatively to expand the ways in which he can succeed?

Jack looked at me quite seriously, and said his concern was that if his two therapists didn't cooperate, he would "fall through the cracks and be lost in outer space". His way of expressing this anxiety surprised me. It sounded as if we were here touching on some quite primitive underlying fears that included existential anxieties functioning on the autistic level. Was Jack's experience that if his therapists could not cooperate and therefore emotionally abandoned him, might he then start to experience the "separateness anxiety" described previously, and start to feel he was lost in some kind of black and infinite void or hole?

Several months after my enactment, Jack has expressed no more fears that his therapists will be unable to work together, or that he might fall through the cracks and be lost in outer space. Nor has there been another tantrum either at home or at school. My impression is that over the longer term, how these "bumps in the road" have been handled has in fact had some beneficial and stabilising results for Jack.

"The Toronto experiment"—current status

At the time of writing (early 2015) the Toronto experiment continues. We have obtained some additional funding so that a third therapist, Rex, can move in and provide additional support to both parents and to the functioning of Jack's family. He will also offer support to Jack's mother and the family in trying to come to terms with her serious physical illness and present physical limitations.

This experiment of course represents an idealised intervention. There are likely to be severe limitations on how many families can afford ongoing interventions by two or by *three* psychoanalytically trained therapists! The funding source we mobilised is very limited in extent. And how many therapists are there who possess both training in psychoanalytic psychotherapy along with extensive skills in supportive work in schools and social skills communication training? Our hope is that if we can make this admittedly idealised model work, then different "scaled-down" versions of it might also prove effective. We may be able to extract from our experiment an understanding of those aspects which are most essential for Asperger's children. Perhaps a team approach involving just one therapist trained in psychoanalytic child psychotherapy could be useful. Our experiences, as well as the literature, both suggest that interventions by more than one therapist in a team modality could always be helpful for Asperger's children.

Up to this point, our experiment seems to have worked fairly well. There have been no more suicidal gestures or self-cutting by Jack. Though Jack has expressed fantasies of burning his peers at the stake and eagerly plays games (sometimes at the beginning of our sessions together) involving the destruction of humanity by deadly plagues, there has been no suicidal talk on Jack's part.

Jack has tolerated the transition to a new school and to high school reasonably well. He gradually learns how to negotiate with school staff. Instead of wanting to start what he refers to as "shoving riots" when peers bump into him in the crowded school halls, he takes the bumping by his peers in stride and as an everyday and expectable occurrence.

Jack has had one huge tantrum at home as has been described above. He has had no tantrums at school. We certainly expect more "bumps in the road" as our experiment continues. At this point, the therapists three who are cooperating, Jack's parents, his teachers, and I believe Jack himself, are all pleased with how our experiment has gone so far.

CHAPTER SEVENTEEN

Packing up, moving out, and bidding farewell

I have sketched out an initial and rudimentary theory which tries to account for the psychodynamic functioning of Asperger's sufferers. This was done on the basis of how my Asperger's patients have presented themselves to me over the years when they were in therapy. I have presented, though in a very selective and limited way, some of the evidence my patients have presented to me. It is this kind of evidence which has prompted me to develop the notions I have presented here. Perhaps some of you also started to develop similar notions as you read through the selections presented here of some of my interactions with these patients. The unavoidable and crucial core of any psychoanalytic presentation of this kind of clinical evidence is the *transference-countertransference dialectic* which unfolds during treatment. Here, this crucial dialectic has been hinted at and outlined in a very summary form. In future case presentations, I plan to outline in more detail some of the patients whom you have overheard here.

I selected the evidence I presented—in the form of transcriptions of segments of the interactions between my Asperger's patients and myself—on the basis of the ability of this evidence to highlight what I referred to as numerous "dichotomies" in how my Asperger's patients presented themselves in their therapies. Although I believe these patients experiencing "dichotomies" is an accurate description when their experiences are observed from outside their own subjectivities, this description is likely oversimplified. For example, Alan, as his therapy progressed, described himself as struggling with an internal "trichotomy" (consisting of dead kid, living kid with potential for growth, and veteran). Thanos described an even more complex set of internal splits involving the Greek, Turkish, Bulgarian, and Macedonian parts of his self. Nevertheless, in all of my patients there seemed to appear (in those who spent enough time in an ongoing therapeutic relationship with me) a basic dichotomy. This dichotomy assumed a number of guises for each person. However, the different guises in their clinical forms boiled down, in every single instance, to a dichotomy between victim and bully aspects of the self.

I then took what seemed to me to be the next meaningful step. I started to view the regular appearance of this central dichotomy in every one of my Asperger's patients as strong evidence for a split in the self between a victim part of the split and a bully part of the split. I attempted to highlight some of the noteworthy qualities of this splitting. These qualities included the fact that different parts of the split were regularly fully aware of each other. In other words, they were not split apart in terms of consciousness. They were not dissociated from each other as may often be seen in patients with histories of severe abuse ("dissociative identity disorder" in the DSM). Additionally, the two (or more) aspects of the split frequently interact with each other and even wrestle with each other in a hostile and mutually derogating way. The clearest example of this was given to us by Matt, so that the antelope part of his split self engaged in "self-punishment" for the actions that this part experienced as the unacceptable social transgressions perpetrated by the tiger part of his split self.

The split in the self is manifest in different self-states which have very different cognitive/emotional/behavioural structures. The thinking which is usually characteristic of one aspect of the split, the predominating emotions of this aspect and the typical patterns of behaviour are radically different from those of the other aspect of the split, and they have little or no capacity to change each other. In the therapeutic setting, the Asperger's child can to some extent function "equidistantly" from the two aspects of the split and can describe both aspects from a position that is apparently "outside" both aspects, that is, he can describe both aspects from the viewpoint of an observing ego. Recall that Dan experienced this as needing to have a "neutral" presentation when interacting with others. On closer inspection, however, one aspect of the split regularly seems to predominate, even within the transference-countertransference dynamic. For Dan, this was the victim aspect of the split. For Thomas it was the bully aspect, and for Matt there was more of an oscillation between the two aspects.

In addition to a regularly observed and typical split in the self involving a victim and a bully aspect, there is also projective identification into remote objects. The use of such remote objects is again a very regular phenomenon observed in all of the Asperger's patients I have been privileged to treat. The "remote" quality involved projective identifications into mythological figures, animals, countries, cartoon figures, historical figures, and famous people. This projective identification into remote objects functions for Asperger's children as handmaiden and adjunct to splitting. The splitting of the self in Asperger's sufferers is regularly between the strong, powerful, dominant bully aspect (for Matt, for example, this being his tiger part) and the weak, threatened, harried, and overwhelmed victim aspect (for Matt, this being his antelope aspect). There is a strong additional suggestion contained in Matt's tiger/antelope split of predator/prey aspects as well. Projective identification of self aspects into these two distinct and unalterably opposed objects (which are also quite remote in being animals) supports, strengthens, and contributes to the maintenance of the split in the self. For Matt, the two work hand in glove.

In addition, I outlined how those affected by the Asperger's typically nurse a sense of victimisation and rancour (in the victim part of the split self) along with a self-righteous striving for retaliation and vengeance, at least in fantasy, in the bully part.

I tried to suggest how this unremitting search for vengeance and payback likely distorts the experience of time for Asperger's children. Time becomes compacted into a punctilinear emotional experience of nodal points along a line. The nodal points are real or phantasised moments of brutal victimisation or merciless revenge (as with Jack wanting to burn his peers alive) or even of both experiences superimposed. There is no sense of the past with depth or a future with potential and hope, only a series of points, of stab wounds, involving being victimised and stabbed by others, or of getting revenge by stabbing them.

Much of the available literature, including the Psychodynamic Diagnostic Manual (PDM Task Force, 2006) characterises all autism spectrum disorders, including Asperger's Disorder, as a neurological disorder. The PDM, for example, places Asperger's disorder under the rubric of "neurodevelopmental disorders of relating and communicating" (PDM Task Force, 2006, p. 357). This suggestion is not problematic, at least as far as it goes. But the psychoanalytic clinician who is seriously interested in treating Asperger's patients will want to go considerably further. A neurological deficit or limitation in infancy is likely to have consequences in the area of internal (and external) object relations. The pathology and the psychodynamics of Asperger's need to be viewed in an *interactional* light. That is, there will be some sort of *interaction* between the neurological deficit or limitation and the structure of internal object relations which develop over time. This structure of internal object relations is anchored in the infantile period. There are also relational difficulties with external objects that are rooted in the neurological limitations, primarily relational struggles and anxieties between the Asperger's infant and his mother. The structure of internal object relations develops and unfolds within the context of the neurological problems infant is born with. The psychoanalytic clinician does well to take into account *both* neurological limitations in the child and the structure of internal object relations which develops in tandem with and under the influence of these limitations. The psychoanalytic clinician will thus be alert to the unfolding interactions between the child's neurology and his psychology. The psychoanalytic clinician will also be alert to any possible traumatic elements, including cumulative trauma, in the child's development.

I have sketched out some preliminary ideas about this interaction between neurology and psychology. I suggested that the infant destined to function as an Asperger's child is born with a neurologically-based sensory vulnerability. This involves having a thin sensory skin and results in a tendency to feel deluged and overwhelmed by sensations, along with hyperacute sensory receptivity, so that a small squeak may be experienced as a big bang. The infant's thin sensory skin can make the infant feel overstimulated and in need of protection. The infant also suffers from a deficit in the normal capacity to send to his mother and to receive from her the typical infantile nonverbal communications that are so crucial.

The mother typically strives to her utmost both to establish a nonverbal connection with her infant as well as to protect him from feeling overwhelmed by a deluge of sensory stimulation. She is able to succeed at times, but also fails frequently as well. Over time, this contributes to a developmental split in the infantile proto-self accompanied by a split in how he experiences his mother. I have labelled these two aspects the protected self which is linked to the connected mother, in contrast to the overwhelmed and vulnerable self which is linked to the disconnected mother. These two developmentally split aspects of the self form the foundation for the later and defensive split between bully and victim aspects of the self.

I went on to apply ideas about the bully/victim split and projective identification into remote objects to the diagnosis of types of Asperger's and to the treatment of Asperger's. This was based mostly on which aspect of the split self tended to predominate. I outlined three types of Asperger's—the inhibited/avoidant type, with the victim part of the split self at the forefront, the inhibited/object-seeking type, with rapid oscillations between the victim and bully parts of the split self, and finally the uninhibited/aggressive type in which the bully part of the split is clearly the strongest. This last type may often be correctly but confusingly diagnosed with a conduct disorder rather than as suffering from Asperger's.

As to treatment, I used two different models types of treatment intervention on which to base some suggestions—that proposed by Kernberg and her colleagues (1988) and that proposed by Alvarez (2012). I suggested that the therapist will need to provide treatment in a very flexible manner, so that she is more likely than with most children to be called on to provide a range of types of psychotherapy, from very supportive interventions to more typical expressive interventions involving interpretations. There are likely to be, following Alvarez, variations in the level of intervention used by the therapist. Interpretations will be offered at the explanatory/hermeneutical level. But the therapist will also need to operate at the descriptive level, and at the intensified and vitalising level, using supportive interventions and reclamations. This will likely require the therapist (or a suitable colleague) to provide "hands-on" supportive interventions within the school system, and specific training to support the development of adequate social skills.

My association to the challenges involved in writing a volume such as this is that this task resembles what is involved in writing a love letter! Writing a love letter involves huge challenges and attendant terrors. The writer is forced to ask many nagging questions about the love letter being written. Have I expressed myself accurately so that the recipient will understand? Have I communicated clearly enough to be understood? How will the letter be received and responded to? Will the letter be welcomed or will it be tossed aside with a shrug of indifference? Have I expressed myself fully enough to get across what I hope to get across, or have I done the opposite and exposed my inner self too much, so that I risk taking on heavy load of chagrin and humiliation? And most important, will the letter have the outcome that I yearn for?

In this case, the yearned for outcome would be some increase, however small, in our knowledge of Asperger's children and our ways of responding to them in our attempts at psychoanalytic treatment. If this can be the outcome, then the risk of chagrin becomes tolerable. Bion (1977) expresses the situation beautifully when he comments about psychoanalytic writing that "it should stimulate in the reader the emotional experience that the writer intends ... and that the emotional experience thus stimulated should be an accurate representation of the psychoanalytic experience ... that stimulated the writer in the first place" (Bion, 1977, p. 32). So then, the question becomes: has this emotional experience come through, or has it been lost in the clutter of windblown debris scattered around by my own defensive intellectualisations? Hopefully, some flowers have sprung up through the debris.

Perhaps, though, I have a respectable path along which I can escape from the terrors of having penned this love letter to my readers. In the "Acknowledgments" which began the writing, didn't I say that my experience was that this present volume was actually written by a large community of people? Very well then! I assume the role of a conduit for the ideas of many, the role of recording secretary for a large committee. *We* send *our* love letter to you. Our hope is that you have received it in the spirit it was intended—to lightly tincture our way of understanding Asperger's children and perhaps our way of approaching them in the therapy we provide to them.

REFERENCES

Adamo, S. (2012). The aesthetic experience in the process of recovery from autistic states. *Journal of Child Psychotherapy, 38*: 61–77.

Allured, E. (2006). Developing the intersubjective playground in the treatment of childhood Asperger's Syndrome. *Journal of Infant, Child and Adolescent Psychotherapy, 5*: 397–419.

Alvarez, A. (1980). Two regenerative situations in autism: Reclamation and becoming vertebrate. *Journal of Child Psychotherapy, 6*: 69–80.

Alvarez, A. (1992). *Live Company: Psychoanalytic Psychotherapy with Autistic, Borderline, Deprived and Abused Children*. London: Routledge.

Alvarez, A. (1997). Verbal rituals in autism: The concept of the autistic object and the countertransference. In: T. Mitrani & J. Mitrani (Eds.), *Encounters with Autistic States: A Memorial Tribute to Frances Tustin* (pp. 231–256). Northvale, NJ: Jason Aronson.

Alvarez, A. (2005). Autism and psychosis. In: D. Houzel & M. Rhode (Eds.), *Invisible Boundaries: Psychosis and Autism in Children and Adolescents* (pp. 1–24). London: Karnac.

Alvarez, A. (2012). *The Thinking Heart: Three Levels of Psychoanalytic Therapy with Disturbed Children*. London: Routledge.

American Academy of Child and Adolescent Psychiatry. (1999). Asperger's disorder. Retrieved from www.aacap.org last accessed 6 July 2015.

American Psychiatric Association. (1994). *Diagnostic and Statistical Manual of Mental Disorders, Fourth Edition*. Washington: American Psychiatric Association.

American Psychiatric Association. (2000). *Diagnostic and Statistical Manual of Mental Disorders, Fourth Edition, Text Revision*. Washington: American Psychiatric Association.

American Psychiatric Association. (2013). *Diagnostic and Statistical Manual of Mental Disorders, Fifth Edition*. Arlington: American Psychiatric Association.

Attwood, T. (undated). Asperger syndrome: Motor clumsiness. Asperger syndrome coalition of the U.S. Retrieved from www.aspergersyndrome. org last accessed 6 July 2015.

Bion, W. (1965). *Transformations*. New York, NY: Jason Aronson.

Bion, W. (1967). *Second Thoughts: Selected Papers on Psycho-Analysis*. New York, NY: Jason Aronson.

Bokanowski, T., & Lewkowicz, S. (Eds.) (2009). *On Freud's "Splitting of the Ego in the Process of Defence"*. London: Karnac.

Bromberg, P. (1998). *Standing in the Spaces: Essays on Clinical Process, Trauma, and Dissociation*. Hillsdale: The Analytic Press.

Bromberg, P. (2006). *Awakening the Dreamer: Clinical Journeys*. Hillsdale: The Analytic Press.

Bromberg, P. (2011). *The Shadow of the Tsunami and the Growth of the Relational Mind*. New York, NY: Routledge.

Cecchi, V. (1990). Analysis of a little girl with an autistic syndrome. *International Journal of Psychoanalysis*, 71: 403–410.

Cuaron, A. (2013). *Gravity*. Warner Bros. Pictures.

Durban, J. (2014). Despair and hope: On some varieties of countertransference and enactment in the psychoanalysis of ASD (autism spectrum disorder) children. *Journal of Child Psychotherapy*, 40: 187–200.

Erikson, E. (1968). *Identity, Youth and Crisis*. London: Norton.

Fargione, K. (2013). Climbing a waterfall: Understanding an adolescent boy in autistic retreat. *Journal of Child Psychotherapy*, 34: 171–188.

Finn, S. (2007). *In Our Clients' Shoes: Theory and Techniques of Therapeutic Assessment*. Mahwah: Lawrence Erlbaum.

Folstein, S., & Santangelo, S. (2000). Does asperger syndrome aggregate in families? In: A. Klin, F. Volkmar & S. Sparrow (Eds.), *Asperger Syndrome*. (pp. 159–171). New York, NY: Guilford Press.

Freud, S. (1940a). An outline of psychoanalysis. *S. E.*, 23: 141–207. London: Hogarth.

Freud, S. (1940e). Splitting of the ego in the process of defence. *S. E.*, 23: 273–278. London: Hogarth.

Gabbard, Glen O. (2005). *Psychodynamic Psychiatry in Clinical Practice, Fourth edition*. Washington: American Psychiatric Publishing.

Ghaziuddin, M., & Gerstein, L. (1996). Pedantic speaking style differentiates Asperger syndrome from high-functioning autism. *Journal of Autism and Developmental Disorders, 26*: 585–595.

Gillberg, C. (1992). Autism and autistic-like conditions: Subclasses among disorders of empathy. *Journal of Child Psychology and Psychiatry and Allied Disciplines, 33*: 813–842.

Gillberg, C., & Gillberg, O. (1989). Asperger syndrome—some epidemiological considerations: A research note. *Journal of Child Psychology and Psychiatry, 30*: 631–638.

Grinberg, L. (1962). On a specific aspect of countertransference due to the patient's projective identification. *International Journal of Psychoanalysis, 43*: 436–440.

Grinberg, L. (1979). Countertransference and projective counteridentification. *Contemporary Psychoanalysis, 15*: 226–247.

Grinberg, L., Sor, D., & Tabak de Bianchedi, E. (1977). *Introduction to the Work of Bion*. New York, NY: Jason Aronson.

Grotstein, J. (1981). *Splitting and Projective Identification*. Northvale, NJ: Jason Aronson.

Grotstein, J. (1997). One pilgrim's progress: Notes on Frances Tustin's contributions to the psychoanalytic conception of autism. In: T. Mitrani & J. Mitrani (Eds.), *Encounters with Autistic States: A Memorial Tribute to Frances Tustin* (pp. 257–290). Northvale, NJ: Jason Aronson.

Haag, G. (1997). Encounter with Frances Tustin. In: T. Mitrani & J. Mitrani (Eds.), *Encounters with Autistic States: A Memorial Tribute to Frances Tustin* (pp. 355–396). Northvale, NJ: Jason Aronson.

Holloway, R. (2013). On emerging from autism and into the terror of relationships. *Journal of Child Psychotherapy, 39*: 39–58.

Houzel, D. (1995). Precipitation anxiety. *Journal of Child Psychotherapy, 21*: 65–78.

Joseph, B. (1989). *Psychic Equilibrium and Psychic Change*. London: Tavistock/Routledge.

Kancyper, L. (2009). Splitting and trauma: Their relationship with après-coup and historicization. In: T. Bokanowski & S. Lewkowicz (Eds.), *On Freud's "Splitting of the Ego in the Process of Defence"* (pp. 111–133). London: Karnac.

Kernberg, O. (1976). *Object Relations Theory and Clinical Psychoanalysis*. New York, NY: Jason Aronson.

Kernberg, P., Frankel, A., Heller, R., Scholl, H., & Kruger, R. (1988). Therapist verbal interventions with children (TVI-C). Unpublished manuscript.

Khan, M. (1963). The concept of cumulative trauma. *Psychoanalytic Study of the Child, 18*: 286–306.

Khan, M. (1964). Ego distortion, cumulative trauma, and the role of reconstruction in the analytic situation. *International Journal of Psychoanalysis, 45*: 272–279.

Klin, A., & Volkmar, F. (1995). Asperger's syndrome: Guidelines for assessment and diagnosis. Retrieved from www.childstudycenter.yale.edu. last accessed 6 July 2015.

Klin, A., & Volkmar, F. (2000). Treatment and intervention guidelines for individuals with Asperger syndrome. In: A. Klin, F. Volkmar & S. Sparrow (Eds.), *Asperger Syndrome* (pp. 340–366). New York, NY: Guilford Press.

Klin, A., & Volkmar, F. (2003). Asperger syndrome: diagnosis and external validity. *Child and Adolescent Psychiatry Clinics of North America, 12*: 1–13.

Kiln, A., Sparrow, S., Marans, W., Carter, A., & Volkmar, F. (2000). Assessment issues in children and adolescents with asperger syndrome. In: A. Klin, F. Volkmar & S. Sparrow (Eds.), *Asperger Syndrome* (pp. 309–339). New York, NY: Guilford Press.

Klin, A., Volkmar, F., & Sparrow, S. (Eds.) (2000). *Asperger Syndrome*. New York, NY: Guilford Press.

Lesinskiene, S. (2002). Children with Asperger's syndrome: Specific aspects of their drawings. *Journal of Circumpolar Health, 61*: 90–96.

Levine, H., & Brown, L. (Eds.) (2013). *Growth and Turbulence in the Container/ Contained: Bion's Continuing Legacy*. New York, NY: Routledge.

Levy, A. (2011). Psychoanalytic psychotherapy for children with asperger's syndrome: Therapeutic engagement through play. *Psychoanalytic Perspectives, 8*: 72–91.

Mawson, D., Grounds, A., & Tantum, D. (1985). Violence and asperger's syndrome: A case study. *British Journal of Psychiatry, 147*: 566–569.

Mayes, S., Calhoun, S., & Crites, D. (2001). Does DSM-IV Asperger's Disorder exist? *Journal of Abnormal Child Psychology, 29*: 263–271.

McDevitt, S., & Carey, W. (1978). *Toddler Temperament Scale*. Mimeographed document.

Mitrani, J. (1996). *A Framework for the Imaginary: Clinical Explorations in Primitive States of Being*. Northvale, NJ: Jason Aronson.

Mitrani, J. (2010). Minding the gap between neuroscientific and psychoanalytic understanding of autism. *Journal of Child Psychotherapy, 36*: 240–258.

Mitrani, J. (2014). Working with autistic protections in adult patients. Paper presented at the 7th annual conference on the work of Frances Tustin, Boston, MA, July 24, 2014.

Mitrani, J. (2015). Trying to enter the long black branches: Some technical extensions for the analysis of autistic states in adults. In: J. Mitrani & T. Mitrani (Eds.), *Frances Tustin Today* (pp. 174–193). London: Routledge.

Mitrani, T., & Mitrani, J. (Eds.) (1997). *Encounters with Autistic States: A Memorial Tribute to Frances Tustin.* Northvale, NJ: Jason Aronson.

Mitrani, J., & Mitrani, T. (Eds.) (2015). *Frances Tustin Today.* London: Routledge.

NJ [New Jersey] Psychologist Magazine. (2000). Retrieved from www.aspennj. org/psych.html last accessed 21 July 2015.

Ogden, T. (1982). *Projective Identification and Psychotherapeutic Technique.* New York, NY: Jason Aronson.

Ogden, T. (1994). *Subjects of Analysis.* London: Karnac.

Ogden, T. (1997). Some theoretical comments on personal isolation. In: T. Mitrani & J. Mitrani (Eds.), *Encounters with Autistic States: A Memorial Tribute to Frances Tustin* (pp. 179–193). Northvale, NJ: Jason Aronson.

Ogden, T. (2008). Working analytically with autistic-contiguous aspects of experience. In: K. Barrows (Ed.), *Autism in Childhood and Autistic Features in Adults: A Psychoanalytic Perspective* (pp. 223–242). London: Karnac.

Ozonoff, S., & Griffith, E. (2000). Neuropsychological function and the external validity of Asperger syndrome. In: A. Klin, F. Volkmar & S. Sparrow (Eds.), *Asperger Syndrome* (pp. 72–96) New York, NY: Guilford Press.

Parada, N. (1996). Transference and countertransference in the analysis of a child with autistic nuclei. *International Journal of Psychoanalysis, 77*: 773–786.

Parada Franch, N. (2008). "Peter Pan sails with Captain Hook"—Comments on the work of Dr. Robin Holloway—Toronto. Presented at the International Psychoanalytic Association Third International Inter-Regional Conference on Clinical Infant, Child, and Adolescent Psychoanalysis in our changing world. Toronto: November 2008.

PDM Task Force. (2006). *Psychodynamic Diagnostic Manual.* Silver Spring: Alliance of Psychoanalytic Organizations.

Pozzi, M. (2003). The use of observation in the psychoanalytic treatment of a 12-year-old boy with Asperger's syndrome. *International Journal of Psychoanalysis, 84*: 1333–1344.

Racker, H. (1974). *Transference and Countertransference.* London: Hogarth.

Reid, S. (1999). Autism and trauma: Autistic post-traumatic developmental disorder. In: A. Alvarez & S. Reid (Eds.), *Autism and Personality: Findings from the Tavistock Autism Workshop* (pp. 93–109). London: Routledge.

Rhode, M. (2011a). The "autistic" level of the Oedipus complex. *Psychoanalytic Psychotherapy, 25*: 262–276.

Rhode, M. (2011b). Asperger's syndrome: A mixed picture. *Psychoanalytic Inquiry, 31*: 288–302.

Rhode, M., & Klauber, T. (2004). *The Many Faces of Asperger's Syndrome.* London: Karnac.

Schultz, R., Romanski, L., & Tsatsanis, K. (2000). Neurofunctional models of autistic disorder and Asperger syndrome: Clues from neuroimaging. In: A. Klin, F. Volkmar & S. Sparrow (Eds.), *Asperger Syndrome* (pp. 172–209). New York, NY: Guilford Press.

Shuttleworth, J. (1999). The suffering of Asperger children and the challenge they present to psychoanalytic thinking. *Journal of Child Psychotherapy*, 25: 239–265.

Smith, I. (2000). Motor functioning in asperger syndrome. In: A. Klin, F. Volkmar & S. Sparrow (Eds.), *Asperger Syndrome* (pp. 97–124). New York, NY: Guilford Press.

Spoladore, A. (2013). A young boy grows away from autism. *Journal of Child Psychotherapy*, 39: 22–38.

Szatmari, P. (2000). Perspectives on the classification of asperger syndrome. In: A. Klin, F. Volkmar & S. Sparrow (Eds.), *Asperger Syndrome* (pp. 403–417). New York, NY: Guilford Press.

Szatmari, P., Bryson, S., Streiner, D., Wilson, F., Archer, L., & Ryerse, C. (2000). Two-year outcome of preschool children with autism or Asperger's syndrome. *American Journal of Psychiatry*, 157: 1980–1987.

Tantum, D. (2000). Adolescence and adulthood of individuals with asperger syndrome. In: A. Klin, F. Volkmar & S. Sparrow (Eds.), *Asperger Syndrome* (pp. 367–399) New York, NY: Guilford Press.

Tremelloni, L. (2005). *Arctic Spring: Potential for Growth in Adults with Psychosis and Autism*. London: Karnac.

Tustin, F. (1972). *Autism and Childhood Psychosis*. London: Hogarth.

Tustin, F. (1986). *Autistic Barriers in Neurotic Patients*. New Haven: Yale University Press.

Tustin, F. (1990). *The Protective Shell in Children and Adolescents*. London: Karnac.

Tustin, F. (1992). *Autistic States in Children—Revised Edition*. London: Tavistock/Routledge.

Volkmar, F., & Klin, A. (2000). Diagnostic issues in asperger syndrome. In: A. Klin, F. Volkmar & S. Sparrow (Eds.), *Asperger Syndrome* (pp. 25–71). New York, NY: Guilford Press.

Wing, L. (2000). Past and future research on asperger syndrome. In: A. Klin, F. Volkmar & S. Sparrow (Eds.), *Asperger Syndrome* (pp. 418–432). New York, NY: Guilford Press.

Winnicott, D. (1975). Transitional objects and transitional phenomena [1951]. In: *Through Paediatrics to Psycho-Analysis* (pp. 229–242). London: Hogarth.

Wolff, S. (2000). Schizoid personality in childhood and asperger syndrome. In: A. Klin, F. Volkmar & S. Sparrow (Eds.), *Asperger Syndrome* (pp. 278–305). New York, NY: Guilford Press.

INDEX